RELIGION AND SPIRITUALITY

MEDITATION

PRACTICES, TECHNIQUES AND HEALTH BENEFITS

RELIGION AND SPIRITUALITY

Additional books in this series can be found on Nova's website under the Series tab.

Additional e-books in this series can be found on Nova's website under the eBooks tab.

RELIGION AND SPIRITUALITY

MEDITATION

PRACTICES, TECHNIQUES AND HEALTH BENEFITS

LUCIA BREWER
EDITOR

Copyright © 2018 by Nova Science Publishers, Inc.

All rights reserved. No part of this book may be reproduced, stored in a retrieval system or transmitted in any form or by any means: electronic, electrostatic, magnetic, tape, mechanical photocopying, recording or otherwise without the written permission of the Publisher.

We have partnered with Copyright Clearance Center to make it easy for you to obtain permissions to reuse content from this publication. Simply navigate to this publication's page on Nova's website and locate the "Get Permission" button below the title description. This button is linked directly to the title's permission page on copyright.com. Alternatively, you can visit copyright.com and search by title, ISBN, or ISSN.

For further questions about using the service on copyright.com, please contact:
Copyright Clearance Center
Phone: +1-(978) 750-8400   Fax: +1-(978) 750-4470   E-mail: info@copyright.com.

NOTICE TO THE READER

The Publisher has taken reasonable care in the preparation of this book, but makes no expressed or implied warranty of any kind and assumes no responsibility for any errors or omissions. No liability is assumed for incidental or consequential damages in connection with or arising out of information contained in this book. The Publisher shall not be liable for any special, consequential, or exemplary damages resulting, in whole or in part, from the readers' use of, or reliance upon, this material. Any parts of this book based on government reports are so indicated and copyright is claimed for those parts to the extent applicable to compilations of such works.

Independent verification should be sought for any data, advice or recommendations contained in this book. In addition, no responsibility is assumed by the publisher for any injury and/or damage to persons or property arising from any methods, products, instructions, ideas or otherwise contained in this publication.

This publication is designed to provide accurate and authoritative information with regard to the subject matter covered herein. It is sold with the clear understanding that the Publisher is not engaged in rendering legal or any other professional services. If legal or any other expert assistance is required, the services of a competent person should be sought. FROM A DECLARATION OF PARTICIPANTS JOINTLY ADOPTED BY A COMMITTEE OF THE AMERICAN BAR ASSOCIATION AND A COMMITTEE OF PUBLISHERS.

Additional color graphics may be available in the e-book version of this book.

Library of Congress Cataloging-in-Publication Data

ISBN: 978-1-53613-223-6

Published by Nova Science Publishers, Inc. † New York

CONTENTS

Preface		**vii**
Chapter 1	Benefits of Prenatal Meditation on Maternal Health, Fetal Health and Infant Health *Ka Po Chan*	**1**
Chapter 2	The Degeneration of Contemporary Mindfulness: Re-Asserting the Ethical and Educational Foundations of Practice in Mindfulness-Based Interventions *Terry Hyland*	**43**
Chapter 3	The Business of Meditation and the Expectation of "Results": Kundalini Rising in a Culture of Instant Gratification *Melanie Saraswati Takahashi*	**79**
Chapter 4	A Comparison of Mindfulness Meditation and Tai Chi/Qi Gong in the Moderation of Cancer Pain in Adults *Carol A. Rizer*	**109**

Chapter 5	Concentrative Meditation as a First Step of Mindfulness: The Effects on Worry, Dispositional Mindfulness, Decentering, and Attention *Keisuke Tanaka and Yoshinori Sugiura*	**135**
Chapter 6	Cognitive Decentering and Eating Disorder Symptoms: The Mediating Role of Thinking Errors *Tomoko Sugiura and Yoshinori Sugiura*	**161**
Chapter 7	Exploring the Relative Contributions of Self and Mindfulness Differentiation for Predicting Burnout *Thomas V. Frederick, Scott Dunbar, Susan Purrington, Sarah Y. Fisher and Richard Ardito*	**185**
Index		**205**

PREFACE

The Many Benefits of Meditation addresses prenatal meditation and its positive effects on maternal health, fetal health and infant health. The authors evaluate a Prenatal Eastern Based Meditative Intervention (EBMI) program developed for pregnant Chinese women in Hong Kong in order to evaluate the effects of meditation on pregnancy. The conceptual framework was based on the postulation of positive relationships between meditation and pregnancy health which is important for fetal health and child health. The following chapter discusses how the exponential growth of mindfulness-based interventions (MBIs) in recent years has resulted in a marketisation and commodification of practice (popularly labeled 'McMindfulness') which divorces mindfulness from its ethical origins in Buddhist traditions. Another article is included which examines the elusive primordial energy that the ancient yogis referred to as Kundalini. This energy is said to ascend through each of the seven chakras from the base of the spine to the crown of the head. When the Kundalini reaches the crown chakra, cosmic consciousness, a restructuring of the psyche, and paranormal abilities have been reported. The authors use a multi-disciplinary approach to explore how Kundalini is typically expressed and safely managed, and the importance for recognition by health care professionals. Next, a review is presented with the objective of determining whether evidence exists that directly compares the utility of tai chi/qi gong and mindfulness meditation in the treatment of cancer pain in adults. Several articles described the benefits of tai chi/qi gong on the pain experience of adult cancer patients, and multiple articles discussed the positive effects of mindfulness practices on pain. A paper is presented which examines the effects of Concentrative Meditation on worry, attention, dispositional mindfulness, and decentering. The results suggest that short-term uses of concentrative meditation are likely to be effective for worry, which may be associated with enhanced selective attention and decentering. Later, the effects of cognitive decentering and thinking errors on eating disorder symptoms among women's college students are examined. A structural equation model of questionnaire data (N = 173) revealed that cognitive decentering reduced eating disorder tendency by ameliorating thinking errors. The last study combines three distinct literatures. Burnout is a huge concern as workers and employers experience losses and challenges due to its effects, and DoS and mindfulness have been identified as important psychological traits for coping with burnout. The results of this study suggest that both DoS and Mindfulness are negatively correlated with burnout, indicating that these traits are important buffers against and resources for coping with emotional exhaustion.

Chapter 1 - Prenatal meditation has positive effects on maternal health, fetal health and infant health. A Prenatal Eastern Based Meditative Intervention (EBMI) program was developed for pregnant Chinese women in Hong Kong in order to evaluate the effects of meditation on pregnancy. The conceptual framework was based on the postulation of positive relationships between meditation and pregnancy health which is important for fetal health and child health. The EBMI developed was based on the positive effect of psychoeducation, cognitive intervention, mindfulness practice, Four Immeasurables Meditation and Mind Body Exercises on health. The benefits of EBMI were evaluated through both quantitative and qualitative studies. Scientific evidence showed that prenatal meditation can enhance positive appraisal, reduce antenatal stress and decrease postnatal physical distress for pregnant women. Raised cord blood cortisol levels in intervention groups indicate beneficial effects on fetal health. The positive effects of prenatal meditation on infant behaviors are that they have better temperament. Details on how to practice EBMI will be discussed. The Prenatal Meditation Program should be incorporated into present antenatal care systems as routine.

Chapter 2 - The exponential growth of mindfulness-based interventions (MBIs) in recent years has resulted in a marketisation and commodification of practice – popularly labeled 'McMindfulness' – which divorces mindfulness from its ethical origins in Buddhist traditions. Using examples from education, the workplace and popular culture, this chapter critiques such commodification by utilising ideas and insights drawn from work in educational philosophy and policy analysis. The 'McDonaldization' process is applied to the emerging populist versions of mindfulness, and analysed in some detail, alongside the capitalization and marketisation of MBIs on the 'McMindfulness' model. The central argument is that the crucial educational function of MBIs needs to be informed by the moral virtues which are at the heart of Buddhist mindfulness. Without such an ethical and educational foundation – actively connected with engaged Buddhist foundations aimed at individual and social transformation - mindfulness becomes just another fashionable self-help gimmick or popular psychological technique that is unlikely to be of any lasting benefit or value to practitioners or society.

Chapter 3 - This article examines the elusive primordial energy that the ancient yogis referred to as Kundalini. This energy when aroused, is said to ascend through each of the seven chakras from the base of the spine to the crown of the head. When the Kundalini reaches the crown chakra, cosmic consciousness, a restructuring of the psyche, and paranormal abilities have been reported. Many regard Kundalini as the next stage in the evolution of human consciousness and a necessary constituent in reaching one's highest potential. Kundalini is most often wakened from meditation and the yoga teachings pertaining to it, were traditionally veiled in secrecy, only being revealed orally from guru to discipline. In 1969, many of these techniques were revealed by Yogi Bhajan who introduced, developed, and popularized Kundalini yoga in the West. If an aspirant is mentally and physically unprepared for the awakening, the Kundalini encounters blocks during its ascension, as expressed by physical and emotional disturbances that psychologists refer to as a "spiritual emergency." It is argued that due to the unsupervised and unstructured appropriation of Eastern modalities in a Western context, the growing curiosity of Eastern expressions of spirituality, the commodification of these practices that promise extraordinary results, and a distracted technologically savvy population that expects them, spontaneous Kundalini awakenings are on the rise. Moreover, with Kundalini becoming the holy grail of New Age spirituality, many seekers are purposefully attempting to waken this energy unmediated by a teacher. Using a multidisciplinary approach and informed by my own personal experience with Kundalini, this paper will explore these issues in depth. How Kundalini is typically expressed and safely managed, and the importance among health care professionals to recognize the fine line between transcendence and spiritual emergency will also be reviewed.

Chapter 4 - Background: Pain is a ubiquitous and often debilitating symptom that can seriously affect the quality of life and daily functioning of adults with cancer. Tai chi, qi gong, and mindfulness practices have been shown to improve the pain experience associated with multiple etiologies. In March 2016, the Department of Health and Human Services released a National Pain Strategy encouraging recognition of the different types of pain, accelerating efforts to collect quality data, and encouraging patients' self-management of pain. Objective: The objective for this review was to determine whether evidence existed that directly compared the utility of tai chi/qi gong and mindfulness meditation in the treatment of cancer pain in adults. Methods: A literature search was conducted using CINAHL, Medline, UpToDate, and the Cochrane database, as well as the reference lists of retrieved articles. The search included articles in English published 2003-2016. Findings: Several articles described the benefits of tai chi/qi gong on the pain experience of adult cancer patients, and multiple articles discussed the positive effects of mindfulness practices on pain. However, no articles were found that directly compared the utility of tai chi/qi gong and mindfulness meditation in the treatment of cancer pain.

Chapter 5 - Concentrative Meditation (CM), which focuses exclusively on focused attention, is often employed as an introductory practice for mindfulness meditation. This paper examined the effects of CM on worry, attention, dispositional mindfulness, and decentering. Twenty-six university students (Mean age = 19.7 years, *SD* = 1.73) were alternately assigned to two groups (CM or controls) according to self-reported worry scores. The CM group (*n* = 13) participated in a two-week CM program consisting of five sessions every two or three days, and daily homework; the authors compared them with non-intervention controls (*n* = 13). Both groups completed self-report questionnaires (worry, mindfulness, and decentering) and the Attention Network Test (a performance-based task measuring attentional functions) before and after the intervention. Results showed that the CM group indicated reduced worry, and improved nonjudging and describing facets of dispositional mindfulness than the control group. Furthermore, the CM group indicated a trend for improvement in decentering and orienting (selective attention) than the control group. Correlations between change-scores in the CM group showed that the more selective attention improved, the more decentering increased. These results suggest that short-term uses of concentrative meditation are likely to be effective for worry, which may be associated with enhanced selective attention and decentering.

Chapter 6 - The effect of cognitive decentering, skills to be distanced from distressing thinking, on eating disorders symptoms was examined. The authors focused on the mediating role of thinking errors. Cognitive decentering captures voluntary use of cognitive behavioral therapy- or mindfulness-like techniques in daily life, while thinking errors are the supposed vulnerability to eating disorder. A structural equation model of questionnaire data from women's college students (*N* = 173) revealed that cognitive decentering reduced eating disorder tendency by ameliorating thinking errors. This result is consistent with the recent evidence showing the effectiveness of cognitive behavioral therapy or mindfulness-based intervention on eating disorder. In addition, logical analysis of problems enhanced cognitive decentering in structural equation modeling. This is consistent with the findings that standard cognitive-behavioral therapy also enhances decentering. Prospects for future studies are discussed to suggest that, to enhance the effects of cognitive decentering on eating disorder, it would be essential to include educational interventions that convey physiological knowledge of the human body's functions.

Chapter 7 - This study seeks to combine three distinct, yet important literatures. First, burnout is a huge concern as workers and employers experience losses and challenges due to its effects. DoS and mindfulness have been identified as important psychological traits for coping with burnout. The results of the present study suggest that both DoS and Mindfulness are negatively correlated with burnout indicating that these traits are important buffers against and resources for coping with emotional exhaustion. However, mindfulness is a better predictor of burnout than DoS in the current study. Implications for future research are provided.

In: Meditation
Editor: Lucia Brewer

ISBN: 978-1-53613-223-6
© 2018 Nova Science Publishers, Inc.

Chapter 1

BENEFITS OF PRENATAL MEDITATION ON MATERNAL HEALTH, FETAL HEALTH AND INFANT HEALTH

Ka Po Chan[*], PhD
Centre of Buddhist Studies,
University of Hong Kong, Hong Kong, People's Republic of China

ABSTRACT

Prenatal meditation has positive effects on maternal health, fetal health and infant health. A Prenatal Eastern Based Meditative Intervention (EBMI) program was developed for pregnant Chinese women in Hong Kong in order to evaluate the effects of meditation on pregnancy. The conceptual framework was based on the postulation of positive relationships between meditation and pregnancy health which is important for fetal health and child health. The EBMI developed was based on the positive effect of psychoeducation, cognitive intervention, mindfulness practice, Four Immeasurables Meditation and Mind Body

---

[*] Corresponding Author Email: drchankapo@gmail.com.

Exercises on health. The benefits of EBMI were evaluated through both quantitative and qualitative studies. Scientific evidence showed that prenatal meditation can enhance positive appraisal, reduce antenatal stress and decrease postnatal physical distress for pregnant women. Raised cord blood cortisol levels in intervention groups indicate beneficial effects on fetal health. The positive effects of prenatal meditation on infant behaviors are that they have better temperament. Details on how to practice EBMI will be discussed. The Prenatal Meditation Program should be incorporated into present antenatal care systems as routine.

Keywords: prenatal, mindfulness, meditation, maternal health, fetal health, child health

1. INTRODUCTION

"Every pregnant woman is preparing for two births: her baby's and her own rebirth [1]."

This statement demonstrates that pregnancy is one of the most central and life-transforming events during a woman's reproductive life cycle. Although it is only about 40 weeks, there are many physical, physiological and psychological changes that take place across this period. It has the distinction of being an event that is culturally, socially, and physically transformative. Pregnancy is not a static period of time. Rather, there is a dynamic continuity to pregnancy in which pregnancy factors, such as prior pregnancy outcomes, personality, emotional and spiritual health, and health behaviors, influence the pregnancy and subsequently have an impact on post-pregnancy outcomes. To effectively deal with pregnancy, women must engage in a complex reorganization at biological, physical, cognitive, and emotional levels. Pregnancy is best fitted into the holistic model of health care. A holistic approach to improving the bio-psycho-socio-spiritual health outcomes of mother and infant is appropriate. Scientific evidence shows that bio behavioral adaptation of the infant can be initiated in utero and is influenced by interactions with the maternal world and social world. Meditative intervention is the best choice as it leads to the empowerment of the health of pregnant women and the growing fetus at all levels, including physical, psychological, sociological and spiritual.

Stress in pregnant women has proved to be associated with poorer maternal well-being, including depression. The impact of the psychological health status in pregnancy on clinical outcomes such as preterm labor, pre-eclampsia, epidural use, caesarean section, instrumental deliveries and asymmetric growth retardation are well documented. Scientific research show that psychosocial stress in pregnancy will lead to an adverse environment in utero that alter fetal growth and development and with a potential lifelong impact on health and disease. The negative impact of perinatal psychological distress on the mothers' health, their infants' development and the quality of parent-child relationships is well documented [2]. Meditation is proven to be an excellent adjunctive treatment for many diseases and an essential element in maintaining holistic health [3]. According to the Holistic Intervention Model, fetal and infant health can be improved through empowerment of the body and mind of the pregnant women by prenatal meditation. Interventions during the perinatal period may have a beneficial effect on maternal fetal attachment, maternal expectations, maternal self-efficacy, maternal role competence and fetal programming.

Pregnant women are the most obedient patients as they will accept all productive changes that benefit our next generation. They are eager to take part in any kind of intervention which can improve their pregnancy health, fetal health and future child health. Prenatal meditation can be incorporated into the present prenatal care system to improve the health of our pregnant women and future generations.

2. PRENATAL MEDITATION PROGRAM

The author developed a prenatal meditation program named Eastern Based Meditative Intervention (EBMI) for pregnant Chinese women in Hong Kong in 2007 [4]. The conceptual framework was based on the postulation of positive relationships between meditation and pregnancy health which is important for fetal health and child health. The theoretical background of EBMI is based on the integration of cognitive therapies, psychoeducation, mindfulness practice, mind-body exercise, and the Four Immeasurables Meditation. EBMI includes three aspects of practice, 'Daily Interventions to empower Positive Emotion', 'Meditative Exercise' and 'Four Immeasurables Meditation.' Three Minute Breathing Practice is the essence of EBMI. Contents of EBMI are listed in Table 1.

Table 1. Contents of EBMI

Daily practice of 'self-help, helping others': self-affirmation increases self-compassion and pro-social behaviours
Crisis intervention: wisdom can turn crisis into opportunities
Daily practice of 'Bliss'
Let go
Mindful eating
Walking meditation
Prenatal and Postnatal meditative exercise
Body scan: a mindfulness exercise simply to notice and be aware of your body
Mindful Breathing
Standing Breathing Meditation
Listening Meditation
Sleep Meditation
Four Immeasurables Meditation: generate Loving-kindness, compassion, empathetic joy and equanimity towards an immeasurable number of sentient beings
Three minute Breathing practice

The characteristic of EBMI is that through 'self' meditative practice; pregnant women can have the right awareness, change their mental process, train and transform their mind from negativity to gratitude. EBMI has the capacity to increase awareness of negative thought, bringing mental processes under greater voluntary control and directing them in beneficial ways that give people a greater sense of control. EBMI improves the abilities for recognizing and solving problems. It included strategies that are aimed at increasing awareness of the effect of stress, coping with stressful situations, increase positive thinking and pleasant activities, improving self-esteem, increasing self-care and learning skills to increase social support, and identifying and exploring unrealistic expectations about pregnancy and motherhood. EBMI focuses on training participants in restructuring skills and techniques for identifying and modifying irrational thoughts that may affect their mental health in the perinatal period. Participants were asked to focus on the cultivation of positive emotion and awareness of their strengths to overcome negative thoughts through meditative practice. The program emphasizes on self-discipline and self-directed coping. The acceptability of EBMI is based on the chance to practice on daily basis and become incorporated into the daily activities of the participants. EBMI is trans-cultural and suitable for individuals of diverse faiths.

The elements of 'Daily Interventions to empower Positive Emotion' in EBMI include 'Daily Practice of Self-help, Helping others', 'Cultivation of Power for Crisis Intervention', 'Daily Practice of Bliss' and the practice of 'Let Go.' The characteristics of this intervention is utilized in your daily activities to practice meditation and empower your positive emotions. 'Daily Practice of Self-help, Helping others' aims at cultivation of loving kindness through daily activities. Through this practice, mothers will become aware of the importance of forgiveness, the way to tackle anger and the analogy of self-help, helping-others. 'Cultivation of Power for Crisis Intervention' is important training for helping mothers tackle problems and complications that arise during pregnancy through moment to moment compassion meditation. The practice has training to teach pregnant women how to add the elements of compassion meditation into daily activities which is aimed at problem solving. The idea of turning a curse into a blessing, the coping strategy and their applications in daily life will be elaborated. The practice of 'Bliss' is to help a mother trade bad habits for consistent happiness with the Bliss Habit. This meditation of empathetic joy in daily life and the sharing of others' happiness especially after giving birth is the means to cultivate positive energy. The practice of

"Let Go" or "put it down" in daily life is the working out of equanimity meditation. 'Let go' is to stop holding bad ideas, halt lingering on unpleasant memories, and break thinking about or being angry about the past or something that happened in the past.

Meditative exercises in EBMI include Mindful Eating, Walking Meditation, Mindful Breathing, Body Scan, Mindful Prenatal and Postnatal Exercises, Standing Breathing Meditation, Listening Meditation and Sleep Meditation. The characteristics of meditative exercises in EBMI include elements of mindfulness and mind-body exercises. Mindfulness meditation is found to be beneficial in the management of various physical and mental health conditions. Mindfulness-based intervention is incorporated into a treatment regime in clinical conditions like hypertension, menopause, and oncology. Mindfulness elements were included in EBMI to empower maternal health and fetal health [5, 6, 7]. Meditative exercises in EBMI have added elements of mind-body exercise that can activate the body's muscles, tendons, and the mind are nourished through bodily movements. Mind-body exercises have a long history, the best examples of which are Yoga, Tai Chi, and Baduanjin Qigong [8]. The principle of mind-body exercise is 'relax' your waist and hip to initiate your body movement. Your hip and waist are the axle and your body is the wheel, everything will be pulled together, will unify and become one. The benefits of these bodily motions through 'Vortex motion' work through your whole form which will activate your muscles and joints, strengthen one's physical fitness, promote the internal circulation of energy and improve the quality of life. Mind-body exercises can improve body functions and health since the nervous system affects the endocrine system and immune system while performing these mind-body (MB) exercises. Meditative exercises are important for pregnant women to provide the best in utero environment for the fetus.

The practice of the Four Immeasurables is fully known in both Theravada and Mahayana Buddhism. Four Immeasurables Meditation [9] has a complete model of practice which is easily modified to fit into the pregnancy bio-psycho-socio-spiritual model. This intervention means cultivation of the four immeasurable minds, loving kindness, compassion, empathetic joy and equanimity for all sentient beings, herself, her fetus, relatives and friends, unrelated persons and those disliked. Sending your blessings to others is an important practice of Immeasurables Meditation as to remind yourself that all sentient beings including those you love and hate are always in your mind and affecting you anytime, anywhere. The Four Immeasurables are found in one brief and beautiful prayer:

> May all sentient beings have happiness and its causes,
> May all sentient beings be free of suffering and its causes,
> May all sentient beings never be separated from bliss without suffering,
> May all sentient beings be in equanimity, free of bias, attachment and anger.

The benefits of the Four Immeasurables Meditation were stated as what Tminuthe Buddha taught to his son Rahula:

> "Rahula, practice loving kindness to overcome anger. Loving kindness has the capacity to bring happiness to others without demanding anything in return.
> Practice compassion to overcome cruelty. Compassion has the capacity to remove the suffering of others without expecting anything in return.
> Practice empathetic joy to overcome hatred. Empathetic joy arises when one rejoices over the happiness of others and wishes others well-being and success.
> Practice non-attachment (equanimity) to overcome prejudice. Non-attachment is the way of looking at all things openly and equally. This is because that is. I and others are not separate. Do not reject one thing only to chase after another.
> I call these the Four Immeasurables. Practice them and you will become a refreshing source of vitality and happiness for others. "

Practicing the Four Immeasurables means cultivating Bodhicitta (Mind of Awakening); this is the heart of Mahayana Buddhism. Bodhicitta means the wisdom-mind or wisdom heart. Bodhicitta is a mind (including thought, feeling and speech) totally dedicated to others and to achieve full enlightenment in order to benefit all sentient beings as fully as possible. Bodhicitta is often called the 'Wish Fulfilling Jewel', because like a magic jewel, it brings true happiness. Bodhicitta is not a single attribute. It is the combination of many positive attributes such as the application of compassion, kindness, right view and wisdom. Development of these is, thus, the development of Bodhicitta and all these positive actions that lead a person towards enlightenment. One of the methods to practice Bodhicitta is "treat others as you." If we can "think" ourselves into other people's situations we can understand each other better. When we are good to others, we are happy and satisfied. When we benefit others, we also benefit ourselves. A pregnant woman is particularly suitable in cultivating Bodhicitta because of her relationship with her fetus (maternal-fetal relationships). Every pregnant woman is preparing two births: her baby's and her own rebirth.

Pregnancy is always the beginning of another phase of a woman's spiritual journey and is the best timing to experience the four immeasurable minds. A pregnant woman can easily feel the joy of her life, the new life of her fetus, the active life of her relatives, friends, unrelated people and other nasty people. Cultivation of these Four Immeasurables Minds are the essential keys in promoting maternal health and provide the best in utero conditions for fetal development through the psycho-neuro-endocrinology pathway. Cultivation of the Four Immeasurables have a positive effect on maternal expectations and maternal self-efficacy which play an important role in infant development and parenting. Practice of the Four Immeasurables can improve the social well-being of pregnant women, supporting oneself and others through inner sense. Meditating on all sentient beings including herself, her fetus, her family & friends, other people and even enemies will help pregnant mothers improve the relationship with others. EBMI can enhance the comprehensibility, manageability and meaningfulness of life of pregnant women. Through meditative practices, there are improvements in all aspects of maternal health, physical, mental, social and spiritual. Mothers are more energetic with decreased physical discomfort and their moods are more cheerful.

They are more powerful in solving problems and make it easier to live in harmony with family, friends, colleagues and the social community. Empowerment of maternal health results in a better in utero environment for the development of the fetus in all aspects and expands the learning capacities of the growing fetus. EBMI have positive effect on ratings of Maternal-fetal attachment (MFA). EBMI leads to spiritual empowerment, right maternal expectations and help the pregnant mothers to have the right view of their self-efficacy in performing parenting. Benefits of EBMI for pregnant women were described in Figure 1.

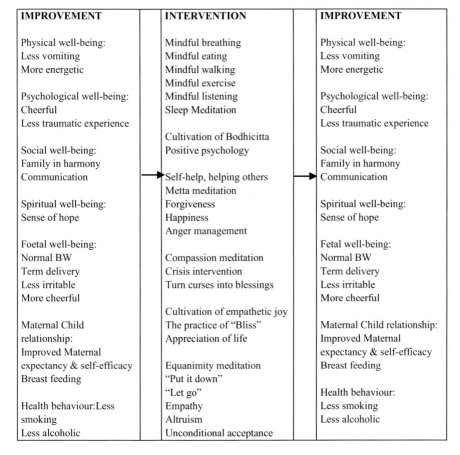

Figure 1. Benefits of EBMI for pregnant women.

3. SCIENTIFIC EVIDENCE OF BENEFITS OF PRENATAL MEDITATION ON MATERNAL HEALTH, FETAL HEALTH AND INFANT HEALTH

The prenatal meditation program named Eastern Based Meditative Intervention (EBMI) [4, 10, 11, 12] was introduced by the author in 2007 in Hong Kong. Seven psychoeducational classes have been conducted from September 2007 to January 2009. A randomized control quantitative and qualitative study was carried out from September 2007 till September 2009 at the Obstetric Unit, Queen Elizabeth Hospital, Hong Kong. The research settings were the perinatal meditation program (Eastern Based Meditative Intervention, EBMI) for pregnant Chinese women in Hong Kong who were attending the hospital clinic for routine perinatal care. The objectives of the research were to assess the effects of Perinatal Meditation on pregnancy health, infant health and explored the perceptions and experiences of pregnant Chinese women in Hong Kong on prenatal meditation.

The quantitative research was a prospective longitudinal randomized control quantitative study. 64 pregnant Chinese women were recruited for intervention and 59 were for control in quantitative study. 36 cases were classified as Frequent Practice (FP) in the intervention group. Data were collected using the Prenatal Distress Questionnaire, Prenatal Coping Inventory, Edinburgh Postnatal Depression Scale, Body-Mind-Spirit Well-Being Inventory (BMSWBI), salivary cortisol of mother and infant, cord blood cortisol and Carey Infant Temperament Questionnaire. Data were collected during first visit, 36th week of pregnancy, 5th week and 5th month after delivery. Quantitative results showed a statistically significant increase in positive appraisal ($p < 0.05$) at 36 weeks, difference in evening salivary cortisol ($p < 0.05$) and decrease in physical distress ($p < 0.05$) at 5th week postpartum in the Frequent Practice (FP) group which suggest positive effects of EBMI on maternal health. The cord blood cortisol level of babies was higher in the frequent practice group ($p < 0.01$) and intervention group ($p < 0.05$), which indicates a positive health status of the newborns and verifies the hypothesis that maternal health can influence fetal health and the importance of prenatal meditation. The Carey Infant Temperament Questionnaire showed that the infants of the intervention group have better temperament ($p<0.05$) at sixth months which reflects the importance of pregnancy health in relation to child health and the positive effects of prenatal meditation. Another important finding is that the frequency of practice of meditation is directly related to its effects.

43 pregnant Chinese women in the intervention group were recruited for qualitative research. Six themes were developed during the 1st interview when the participants first attended the course, which include (1) self-introduction, (2) changes during pregnancy and how to solve problems, (3) self-reported differences in mental and social conditions before and after pregnancy, (4) acceptance of complications that arise during pregnancy, (5) beliefs about bio-psycho-socio-spiritual interaction in relation to pregnancy health and child health and (6) reasons why they participated in the intervention. Three themes emerged from the data collected during the 2nd interview at 36 weeks, including (1) participants' opinion in practicing EBMI, (2) effects of EBMI on bio-psycho-socio-spiritual aspects and (3) suggestions on improvement of EBMI. Qualitative results add to the overall body of knowledge that prenatal meditation is important to help pregnant women in coping with physical distress, be better equipped in crisis management, strengthen social relationships and result in spiritual empowerment. They reported perceived benefits from all aspects of health after EBMI.

This research concluded the positive effects of prenatal meditation on maternal health, fetal health and child health. Cord blood cortisol level, pioneered by this research, is a new indicator for fetal health. Present research illustrates the importance of positive health indicators and recommends more research in this area. Findings of positive fetal health and better temperament of infants in the intervention group broke new ground as scientific bases for fetal education (*Taijiao*). Present study recommends that pregnancy care providers should provide spiritual care and psychoeducation to pregnant women. EBMI, developed by the present study, should be included in the prenatal care system.

4. How to Practice Prenatal Meditation

EBMI included three aspects of practice, 'Daily Interventions to Empower Positive Emotion', 'Meditative Exercise' and 'Four Immeasurables Meditation.' Three Minute Breathing Practice is the essence of EBMI. The essence of the practice is the integration of meditation in daily life activities. The positive energy generated and the benefits of prenatal meditation can only be achieved by frequent practice.

"Daily Interventions to Empower Positive Emotion" is the use of daily behavior training, transforming bad habits to good mode and increasing their positive energy.

"Meditative exercises" in EBMI include Mindful Eating, Walking Meditation, Listening Meditation, Mindful Breathing, Body Scan, Mindful Prenatal and Postnatal Exercises, Standing Breathing Meditation and Sleep Meditation. Meditative Exercise has two elements, mindfulness practice and mind-body exercise. Mindfulness is the basic human ability to be fully present, aware of where we are, what's happening and what we're doing, and not be overly reactive or overwhelmed by what's going on around us. Mindfulness practice has no barriers. It doesn't matter how old you are, what your physical ability is, if you're religious or not. An operational working definition of mindfulness as an intervention is: "the awareness that emerges through paying attention on purpose, in the present moment, and being nonjudgmental to the unfolding of experiences moment by moment." Why we have to practice mindfulness is because our mind takes flight, we lose touch with our body and we are engrossed in obsessive thoughts which are meaningless, about something that just happened or worrying about the future. The principle of mind-body exercise, meditation in motion, is 'relax' your waist and hip to initiate your body movement in whole form. Your hip and waist are the axle and your body the wheel, everything will unify and become one. The benefits of these bodily motions are through 'Vortex motion', using the waist and hip as center, work through your whole form and activate your muscles and joints, strengthen your physical fitness, reduce the physical discomfort during pregnancy, promote the internal circulation of energy and improve the quality of life for you and your fetus.

"Four Immeasurables Meditation" is the practice of meditation after ten to fifteen minutes of mindful breathing exercise. This intervention can transform the negative emotions into positive power. Cultivation of the Four Immeasurables to all sentient beings including herself, her fetus, relatives and friends, those unrelated and those disliked will strengthen maternal-fetal relationships and improve interpersonal relations.

The first thing you do is to relax yourself before practicing prenatal meditation. Relaxation is a state where you feel calm and can manage your stress or anxiety. Relaxation is a process that decreases the effects of pressure on your mind and body. Relaxing is an instinct and is a feeling that you can have anytime and anywhere. If you feel bad or tired and do not have energy to practice, remember to relax and you will have the power to go on.

4.1. Daily Interventions to Empower Positive Emotion

The elements of 'Daily Interventions to Empower Positive Emotion' in EBMI include 'Daily practice of Self-help, Helping others', 'Cultivation of Power for Crisis Intervention', 'Daily practice of Bliss' and the practice of 'Let Go'. "Daily Interventions" mean we utilize our daily activities for behavior training in order to alter our bad habits and generate positive drive. Use of positive languages is a kind of psychotherapy that leads to positive energy. Positive language has a beneficial impact not only on how you feel, but on how others see you and respond to you. Verbal positive language has the power to lead you to a better life. At times when you feel less confident or secure, it's common to slip into using two types of language; qualifiers or weakening statements. Examples of qualifiers and weakening statements are "I could be wrong", "You probably already know this", "It's just a small thing" and "I'm only telling you this." Using this type of language sends a message and gives your audience a negative impression of your ability. This increases your lack of confidence or nervousness, making you more uncertain of yourself. By choosing more positive language like 'faking it till you make it', you actively fight against this happening and will usually feel more confident. Making a few adjustments to your vocabulary can have a large impact on the impression you create and how you feel. What you speak is what you think, this is the reason why positive language is so important because positive language works in your mind. Always thinking with positive language in your mind is a kind of meditation that creates positive emotions and leads to positive action. *Repeating the positive language in your mind and being aware of it moment in moment is a kind of Mantras Meditation.* The positive language to help you to nurture "loving kindness" is "Self-help, Helping others". Thinking of "Wisdom can turn Crisis into Opportunities" can generate "compassion". "Bliss Habit" is the positive language for generation of "empathetic joy." The positive language to cultivate "equanimity" is "Let Go" or "Put It Down." Meditating on positive language can cultivate positive energy and have benefits on maternal health and fetal health.

4.1.1. Daily Practice of Self-Help, Helping Others

Helping others is self-serving and is easy to understand by a pregnant mother. Helping the self and helping others [13] leads to self-affirmation and increases self-compassion and pro-social behavior. Before you assist others, always put your oxygen mask on first. Helping yourself will relieve others' responsibility and helping others can teach you to help yourself. "Self-help, Helping others", is best illustrated in pregnant women because everything that benefits the mother will be good for the fetus. This positive language is the key for pregnant women to cultivate loving-kindness to herself, her fetus, relatives and friends, unrelated persons and even those disliked. The daily practice of Loving-kindness meditation is to plan to do something kind for yourself, your fetus or other people tomorrow before you fall asleep. For example, plan to get up earlier than usual, then the day's working schedule will be less tight and your mood will be more cheerful. You can extend the idea to your fetus, then your relatives, friends, strangers, and finally some people that you dislike.

Self-Help, Helping Others,
Helping Others, Self-Help.

4.1.2. Cultivation of Power for Crisis Intervention

The aim of compassion meditation in daily life in pregnant women is to prepare the mother psychologically to accept the suffering; physical, mental, social and spiritual that arise during pregnancy, and offer psychological preparation for any complications that happen. "Wisdom can turn crisis into opportunities" is the positive language for the cultivation of compassion to solve problems encountered by pregnant women. Crises occur during pregnancy, no matter how we may try to avoid them and in spite of advances in medical technology. They are troubling, unwanted experiences or events that take us way out of our comfort zone. Typically, crises result in some type of loss. The way to deal with crisis is not to think about what you have lost, but to cherish what you have, discover what you have gained. This reverse thinking will lead you to the path to solve the problems. Reverse thinking means turning the problem upside-down, look at the crisis as a blessing in disguise, albeit an unwanted one. The best way to solve a problem is to look at it in a new mode, in an unusual way. Reverse thinking can force you to think about the matter completely differently and come up with a broad range of new ideas that might help to solve it. When you encounter problems, do not complain, don't follow your negative emotion. Ask for help. A logic or decision tree can help you tackle a problem by breaking down possible solutions into parts, and following those parts down new paths. Always accept that unwanted change happens, look beyond it and embrace the discomfort. When you decide to go that way, don't go back. Remember that time can solve all problems; the difficulties will become past tense anyway.

When troubles happen use these four steps to deal with them. The first is "To face it"; the second "To accept it; the third "To deal with it"; and the fourth is to "Put it down". Any problem occurs when we feel that escape is useless, so it is best to face it. When you face it, you have accepted it. Remind yourself that you must accept the things you cannot change. When you accept it, it is tantamount to dealing with it. You may be upset by the problem, and the problem may not have an easy solution. After something happens, you put it down after you deal with it.

Pregnant women will face difficulties and will be afraid of discomfort and pain. Remember the best way to solve these pains and distress is: face it, accept it, deal with it, and put it down. Embrace the suffering with maternal love and replace it with the joy of the arrival of the new life. Whenever you encounter difficulties, think of the positive language, helping you to go through the difficult path. For example, you will be upset when your fetus was found to have some minor abnormalities during a structural scan. You may be in emotional crisis if you think in negative ways. Try positive thinking because minor abnormalities do no harm to the fetus. Enjoy your pregnancy, but at the same time you must have psychological preparation to deal with unfortunate events. Complications of pregnancy do happen in modern dates and in serious cases, may have maternal and fetal morbidity and mortality. Parents expect to have a perfect baby, but need psychological preparation to accept the imperfect life, to cultivate their adversity intelligent quotient and to face the problems in a positive way when the hardships appear.

> With wisdom, turn crises into opportunities.
> Start reverse thinking, create a better tomorrow.

4.1.3. Daily Practice of Bliss

To cultivate empathetic joy in daily life is a kind of meditation because pregnant women are taught to practice "Bliss", make bliss a habit. Pregnant women always experience empathetic joy as they enjoy their own forty-week pregnancy and share in other pregnant women's happiness.

'Bliss' is an ideal moment that seemingly defies time and space. A moment so perfect that your mind sings with gratitude for the chance to experience it. Experiencing a moment of Bliss is timeless and almost always affects us deeply. In those moments we see ourselves most clearly. Within Bliss, the moment of NOW is pure magic and we are amazed and inspired by what it is to be human. The generation of bliss can be kept going all the time. It is possible to experience and re-experience joy and feelings of serene and tranquil bliss. The deeper and more intense the preceding bliss, the deeper and more intense the apprehension of empathetic joy will be.

The practice of empathetic joy meditation may lead to more appreciation of life and is a great antidote to antenatal and postnatal depression. This is particularly effective in pregnant women as a new life will be born in few months' time. 'Bliss' is an unselfish, very positive mental attitude which is beneficial for oneself and others. By rejoicing in others' progress on the spiritual path, one can actually share in their positive action. It refers specifically to rejoicing in the giving birth to the next generation. In long term practice, 'Bliss' may have an anesthetic effect over physical suffering during pregnancy and labor pain.

"Bliss action" is to let bliss be your habit. The practice is simple, every day when you wake up, give bliss to yourself and your fetus. When you brush your teeth, give bliss to your mirror self. When you go out, send bliss to the bus driver and everybody. Bliss is a language without borders, you can relax the thousands of face muscles, remove the inner infinite trouble, while allowing others to share their joy. Bliss can resolve others' hostility and trouble, with a bliss to ask for forgiveness and to create a harmonious atmosphere and relationship. "Bliss" is a good example of using body language to nurture positive emotions. No need to learn how to 'bliss', the difficulty is how to make 'bliss' becomes a habit. Let our mothers have bliss to celebrate the beginning of the day, and have bliss before they fall asleep.

> Make Bliss as a habit,
> Bliss in moment to moment.

4.1.4. Let Go

'Let Go' is the positive language of cultivation of equanimity in daily life. Let Go means to stop thinking about, being obsessive or angry about the past or something that happened in the past. To let go does not mean to get rid of. To let go means to let it be. When we let it be with an equanimity mind, things come and go on their own. Holding on to pain and unpleasant emotions doesn't fix anything. Replaying the past over and over again doesn't change it. Let go of whatever it is that's holding you back from experiencing yourself. Learning to let go is one of the keys to happiness.

"Do everything with a mind that lets go. Do not expect any praise or reward. If you let go a little, you will have a little peace. If you let go a lot, you will have a lot of peace. If you let go completely, you will know complete peace and freedom. Your struggles with the world will have come to an end."

– Achaan Cha, *A Still Forest Pool*

Try not to holding firmly onto something – your story, your fears, losses, expectations, relationships, possessions, negative emotions – all these will cause you and your fetus pain and suffering. Let Go meditation can be an act of release and healing. Do not compare, will feel the joy of relief. Pregnant women always like to compare with others, why they will have a belly and why their babies have so little hair. The negative emotions will hurt them and the fetus, so learn to accept, be inclusive, and practice Let Go Meditation.

When your hands feel tired, you will put down the things that you hold,
When your mind is exhausted, Let it Go.

4.2. Meditative Exercise

Meditative exercises include Mindful Eating, Walking Meditation, Listening Meditation, Mindful Breathing, Body Scan, Prenatal and Postnatal Meditative Exercises and Sleep Meditation. Meditative exercise contains two elements, mindfulness practice and mind-body exercise. Mindful practice can enhance the pregnant women's self-awareness, wellness and resilience. Their relationships with their fetus, relatives and friends, unrelated people and those disliked will improve. The benefits of mind-body exercises are these kinds of meditation in motion using your waist and hip as the center (Vortex motion) can activate your muscles and joints, strengthen one's physical fitness, reduce the physical discomfort during pregnancy, promote the internal circulation of energy and improve the quality of life. Mind-body exercises can improve the physical and mental conditions of pregnant women and provide a better environment for the growing fetus.

4.2.1. Mindful Eating

Mindfulness around eating food can be helpful in many ways, including decreasing compulsive eating that's more about stuffing feelings, increasing awareness of food choices, increasing enjoyment of food, providing an opportunity to strengthen the muscles of presence and training your mind. Being mindful about eating can change the way you think and react to negative thoughts without obeying them. This training can reduce the gastrointestinal symptoms of pregnancy like vomiting, stomach discomfort, and bowels symptoms. By chewing slowly, pregnant women will reduce the volume of air swallowed and reduce stomach gas collection. Food will be easier to digest after mindful chewing. Scientific research has found that mindful eating [14, 15] reduces overeating and binge eating and reduces your body mass index (BMI) which has many benefits for pregnant women, especially those who suffered from gestational diabetes mellitus. First, try a mindful eating exercise with a raisin for 3 to 4 minutes, whenever you feel comfortable. You can practice during your breakfast, lunch and dinner, anytime, anywhere.

4.2.1.1. Meditation Guidelines

It requires the use of raisins; other types of foods can be substituted such as other fruit, popcorn, or peanuts.

1. Find a comfortable seated position. Come into the present moment by taking a few breaths, relax.

2. Place one raisin in your hand. Notice the impulse you might have to pop it in your mouth right away.

3. Take a good look: Look at the raisin, let your eyes explore every part of it, examining the highlights where the light shines, the darker hollows, the folds and ridges, and any asymmetries or unique features.

4. Explore how it feels in your hand: The texture, shape and weight. Notice the color of the raisin and if it has any unique features.

5. Smell the raisin: Slowly bring the raisin to your nose to see what it smells like. With each inhalation, drink in any smell, aroma, or fragrance that may arise, noticing as you do this anything interesting that may be happening in your mouth or stomach.

6. Place the raisin in your mouth: Without biting into it, noticing how the body has to move to get it into the mouth. Explore what it feels like in your mouth, notice what your tongue is doing. Keep it in your mouth without chewing for at least 10 seconds. Notice what it's like to take this time before eating the raisin.

7. Tasting: When you are ready, prepare to chew the raisin, noticing how and where it needs to be for chewing. Then, very consciously, take one or two bites into it and notice what happens, experiencing any waves of taste that come from it as you continue chewing. Without swallowing, notice the sensations of taste and texture in the mouth and how these may change over time, moment by moment, as well as any changes in the object itself.

8. Swallow the raisin: Focus on your sensation. How do you feel physically and emotionally? Is there a lingering taste? Take a little while to consider the experience. When you are ready, swallow the raisin.

9. Sit quietly and notice what you are feeling.

4.2.2. Walking Meditation

Walking provides long-term health benefits for everyone. A regular walking routine lowers your blood pressure, prevents cardiovascular disease and helps you maintain weight loss after dieting. Walking meditation [16, 17] is particularly suitable for pregnant women as the practice can strengthen the physical body and empower the mind. Walking meditation is a meditative exercise with added elements of mindfulness and mind-body exercise during walking. As much of the time we are caught up in our mental worlds, thinking of the past or future, planning and imagining...paying attention to the body as you walk will help you to enjoy simply being alive. Walking at a slow rate of speed is a great workout for your muscles, joints and cardiovascular system. Slow motion is the classical training for mind-body exercises in the East, the practice of "meditation in motion." The essence of mind-body exercise in walking meditation is to '*relax*' your waist and hip to initiate the walking movement and putting weight on your sole *alternatively*. When you practice in time, you can integrate walking meditation into your daily life.

4.2.2.1. Meditation Guidelines

Walking meditation is an outdoor activity. Schedule at least 20 minutes for your walking meditation every day, and try not to combine it with anything else. Let this be a walk just for meditation so that you can enjoy your undivided attention.

First, relax before starting to walk. Spend a little time standing still and bring your awareness to your body, noticing how your body feels as you are standing, and become aware of all the sensations going on in your body. Pay attention to the sensations in your body as you walk. It is natural to find your attention drawn to the sights around you as you walk, but keep bringing your attention to what is going on internally. The idea is to have your attention on the physical experience of walking. If the mind starts getting caught up in thoughts, easily bring your attention back to the experience of walking. '*Relax*' your waist and hip to initiate the walking movement and notice in great detail how the body feels as you walk. The entire body is involved in the act of walking -- from alternation of the left and right foot to the swinging of your arms and hips. When you are moving your left leg, your center of gravity is on your right leg. When you are moving your right leg, your center of gravity is on your left leg. Notice how the soles of your feet feel and put your weight alternatively on your sole. Keep your attention on the rhythm of the walking -- the alternation of left and right foot. Simply notice the experience of the left-right-left-right motion and the *change* of weight bearing of your soles.

4.2.3. Prenatal and Postnatal Meditative Exercise

As the pregnancy progresses, the body begins to undergo a host of physical changes as a way to accommodate the growing baby. More specifically, as the uterus grows, a woman's center of gravity begins to shift. Further, the pelvic floor takes on additional stress as the baby's weight increases, and joints begin to loosen in response to hormones. Poor posture during pregnancy can weaken the muscles of the back and torso, causing back pain and discomfort during pregnancy. In addition to providing cardiovascular benefits, prenatal exercise strengthens the abdominal muscles, which are needed to support the torso and maintain digestion. Postnatal exercises, which are aimed at strength training, flexibility training, and cardiovascular training, are focused on improving physical and mental well-being while still caring for healing the postnatal bodies. Prenatal and postnatal exercises increase your chances of having a healthier pregnancy and an easier labor and delivery. You will have more benefits if you add the elements of mindfulness and mind-body exercise when doing prenatal and postnatal exercises. Be mindful of your body movements and accept the limitations without judgement when you are doing exercises. 'Relax' your body and joints as much as you can and admit to your limits.

4.2.4. Body Scan

The body scan [18] has proven to be an extremely powerful and healing form of meditation. This meditative practice is particularly suitable for pregnant women as it can help them to work with physical discomfort and pain during the perinatal period and empower their mind to accept pregnancy changes. The body scan meditation can help you to find links between emotions and physical sensations and shows you how to use physical sensations as a key to your emotional state. The body scan can be performed while lying down, sitting, or in other postures and you can adjust your position at different stages of pregnancy. It involves systematically sweeping through the body with the mind, bringing an affectionate, openhearted, interested attention to its various regions, in particular the womb and fetus inside the womb. It is not uncommon while practicing the body scan, for the sensations in the body to be felt more acutely, even for there to be more pain, a greater intensity of sensation in certain regions. Just let them go and the intensity of sensations will subside in time. This is the way the practice helps you to deal with sensations. It's important to recognize that the body scan is not a relaxation exercise. The prime intention of a body scan is to incline the mind into sensory experience—to experience how it is to "be a body."

4.2.4.1. Meditation Guidelines

- Take off your glasses and belongings.
- Choose the best position for yourself, lying down or sitting.
- RELAX.
- Close your eyes if that's comfortable for you.
- When you feel ready, gently shift the focus to the breath and be aware of breathing. Breathe normally and naturally and focus on the tip of the nose or the abdomen. Breathing in and knowing you're breathing in, and breathing out and knowing you're breathing out. And now gently withdraw awareness from mindful breathing as you shift to the body scan.
- Notice your body seated wherever you're seated, feeling the weight of your body on the chair or on the floor.
- Notice your left foot on the floor, notice the sensations of your feet touching the floor, the weight and pressure, vibration and heat. Start scanning from the toes of the left foot and then move through the entirety of the foot – to the sole, the heel, the top of the foot – then up the left leg, including in turn the ankle, the shin and the calf, the knee and the kneecap, the thigh in its entirety, on the surface and deep inside, the groin and the left hip, then over to the toes of the right foot, the other regions of the foot, then up the right

leg in the same manner as the left. From there, the focus moves into, successively and slowly, the entirety of the pelvic region, including the hips again, the buttocks and the genitals, the waist, the lower back, the abdomen, the womb and the fetus inside the womb, the fetal movement and then the upper torso – the upper back, the chest and the ribs, the breasts, the heart and lungs and great vessels housed within the rib cage, the shoulder blades floating on the rib cage in back, all the way up to the collarbone and shoulders. From the shoulders, we move to the arms, often doing them together, starting from the tips of the fingers and moving successively through the fingers, the palms, and backs of the hands, the wrists, forearms, elbows, upper arms, armpits, and shoulders again. Then we move in to the neck and throat, and finally, the head and face. Relax your facial muscles and give yourself a bliss.

- Feel fresh air from the nostrils into every part of your body, particularly your growing fetus. Feel dirty air exhaled through the nose.
- Feel the body as a whole organism, with its various physical sensations, thoughts, and emotions. Being present.
- Repeat the practice again and again. For beginners, each section can be ten to fifteen minutes.
- As you come to the end of the body scan, breathing in, feel the whole body rising and expanding on inhalation and falling and contracting on exhalation. You can now open your eyes, stretching and gently getting up. Congratulate yourself for taking this time to be present and doing the practice with your fetus.

Precautions: Body scans should be practiced indoors, at a place with good ventilation but not windy and with appropriate room temperature. Use a towel to cover your knees, maybe also your shoulders and back. The outside environment should not be noisy and don't let any electronics affect you. Don't practice when you are hungry or with a full stomach. Go to the toilet if you want to at any time.

4.2.5. Mindful Breathing

> Breathing in, I know I am breathing in.
> Breathing out, I know I am breathing out.

Breathing is life, it is a bridge between body and mind. We can focus on our breathing, anytime and anywhere. Mindful breathing [19] during pregnancy can protect the health and well-being of mothers and their babies. Pregnant women practicing mindful breathing report reductions in anxiety and negative feelings like distress, hostility and shame. They experience stronger and frequent positive feelings such as enjoyment, gratitude, and hope about pregnancy. The benefits of mindfulness practice during pregnancy may not end with the mother, or with the birth, but extend into childhood and perhaps even beyond. The most basic way to do mindful breathing is simply to focus your attention on your breath, inhaling and exhaling. You can do this while standing, but ideally, you'll be sitting or even lying in a comfortable position. Another method of practice is to count your breathe in or breathe out. The best is to set aside a scheduled time for this exercise, and then you can practice it when you're feeling particularly stressed or anxious.

4.2.5.1. Meditation Guidelines

- Find a comfortable and stable posture either sitting or lying on your back. Allow your back to be straight but not rigid. Let your arms and hands rest in a relaxed position. Tongue on the roof of your mouth or wherever it's comfortable.
- RELAX.
- Notice and relax your body. Try to notice the shape of your body, and its weight. Let yourself relax and become curious about your body seated here—the sensations it experiences, the touch, the connection with the floor or the chair. Relax any areas of tightness or tension.

- Your eyes may be open or closed, but you may find it easier to maintain your focus if you close your eyes.
- Bring your attention to your breathing from three vantage points:
  1. Notice the sensation of your breath going in/out of your nostrils or mouth.
  2. Pay attention to the rise/fall of your chest.
  3. Notice the rise/fall of your belly as you breathe.
- Pick the vantage point that seems to be the easiest for you to focus on. Follow the breath for its full duration, from start to finish. Notice that the breath happens on its own, without any conscious effort. Some breaths may be slow, some fast, some shallow or deep. You don't need to control the breath, you just need to notice it.
- When the mind wanders, you can make a mental note of it. Your mind may wander hundreds of times or more during this five minute practice (or longer if you'd like) – that's ok and quite natural! Your "job" is to catch yourself when you've wandered and to gently bring your focus back to the breath every time, without judging yourself for how "well" or "bad" you're doing the exercise.
- You can count your breath instead of bringing your attention to the vantage point. Remember only count breathe in or breathe out, from 1 to 10 and repeat again and again. If your counting is interrupted, start to count from 1 again.
- As you come to the end of your practice, once again notice your body, your whole body, seated here. Let yourself relax even more deeply and then offer yourself some appreciation for doing this practice with your baby today.

Precautions: Body scans should be practiced indoors, at a place with good ventilation but not windy and with appropriate room temperature. Use a towel to cover your knees, maybe also your shoulders and back. The outside environment should not be noisy and don't let any electronics affect you. Don't practice when you are hungry or with a full stomach. Go to the toilet if you want to at any time.

4.2.6. Listening Meditation

Mindful listening is a kind of meditation that can be incorporated into our daily life. It is a suitable tool for a pregnant lady to use for communication between herself and her fetus. Listening is a function of the entire brain and goes well beyond stimulating the auditory system. Individuals listen and direct attention to sounds in the atmosphere with the whole body. An important characteristic of a pregnant women is her environment including the growing fetus inside her womb. To really listen to others, we must first learn to listen to ourselves. This is how meditation works to helps us become peaceful, still and bright and anchors our awareness through the whole fabric of our life. Listening to the growing fetus is crucial in promoting maternal and fetal health.

Listening meditation works in a different way than other meditative intervention. We do focus inwardly and outwardly in a wide-open manner. We do not create nor imagine sounds. We wait for them to come to us. Any sounds will do -- the roar of a car, the barking of a dog, the twittering of a bird, the sounds of our bowels, the fetal heart beats. We listen attentively to any sounds that might occur with a non-grasping attitude. We open up to the music of the world and of life. We do not name, conjecture or identify the sounds. We just listen as widely and openly as we can to the sounds themselves. If there are no sounds we just listen to silence and its special hum. In listening meditation, we cultivate an open and spacious attitude which waits quietly for the unknown without fears or expectations. When you become acquainted with the practice, you can work it out anytime and anywhere.

4.2.6.1. Meditation Guidelines

- Take off your belongings like your glasses.
- Choose the best position for yourself, lying down or sitting.
- RELAX.

- Close your eyes if that's comfortable for you.
- Listen to the external noise, intensely and totally, with no judgment that it is good or bad.
- Listen to the internal noise, intensely and totally, with no judgment that it is good or bad.
- As you come to the end of your practice, once again notice your body, your whole body, seated here. Relax and offer yourself some appreciations for doing this practice with your baby today.

Listen to your fetus's appeal
Accept different kind of noises

4.2.7. Standing Breathing Meditation

Standing Breathing Meditation is an intervention that combines a breathing exercise with standing meditation. The pregnant woman practices breathing standing still. The essence of the breathing technique in Standing Breathing Meditation is to hold your breath as long as you can. This intervention has the benefit of increasing the oxygenation of your body tissue and the utero-placental circulation. Having an increase in oxygen in blood flow to your body helps promote cell growth and organ function which particularly benefits the growing fetus. Good oxygenation improves brain functions and helps keep your mind sharp and focused and more equipped to handle stressful situations happening in pregnancy. Standing still is one of the most efficient forms of exercise that benefits your mind and body. Standing still can let you become aware of the body and how it stabilizes itself. This is particularly important for pregnant women because their center of gravity changes day to day. Standing meditation teaches the body to use muscles in a 'postural' way (to hold a posture), rather than a 'phasic' way (when a muscle is used for movement). Pregnant women holding a standing posture can cultivate mental and physical relaxation, tranquility, awareness and power and can promote maternal and fetal health.

4.2.7.1. Meditation Guidelines

- Stand still with all your joints open. Drop your shoulders. Relax your waist and hip. Flex your knees slightly. You can use your hands to hold your tummy in late stages of pregnancy. The main point is to put your weight on one leg.
- RELAX.
- Withdraw your jaw and contract your abdominal muscles, breathe in as deep as you can.
- Hold your breath as long as possible. The aim is to try to hold your breath at least for one minute. When you first practice, you can try thirty seconds first and then increase to one minute.
- Exhale.
- Put your weight on one leg during each breathing cycle, feel the weight bearing sensation on your sole. Change your weight bearing leg during the next breathing cycle and continue doing this, alternating legs.
- Repeat the maneuver at least ten times.
- As you come to the end of your practice, once again notice your whole body, relax and offer yourself some appreciation for doing this practice with your baby today.

Precautions: Do not practice under direct sunlight and in a windy place. You may feel muscle pain and joint pain when you first practice standing breathing meditation. All discomfort will disappear when you persist doing this exercise. If you find difficulties in practicing the breathing exercise simultaneously with standing meditation, try them separately. Try to practice the breathing exercise when you are sitting or standing without flexing your knees, ten times and then practice standing meditation with your knees flexed for ten minutes. When you know how to breathe properly, combine the exercises.

4.2.8. Sleep Meditation

Sleep Meditation can help pregnant women fall asleep easily and improve the quality of sleep. Sleeping well during pregnancy is an important factor in promoting maternal and fetal health because pregnant women are "sleeping for two." During daytime, pregnant women are busy in their daily activities, so sleep time is the best time to nourish your fetus. When you fall asleep is important and you should make it a habit to fall asleep by 11 pm every night.

Sleep is a vital indicator of overall health and well-being. "Sleep health" is important throughout our lifespan especially when you are pregnant. Sleep is actually a complex and far-from-passive process of active internal restoration, recuperation and reconsolidation which is essential for our health. Our nightly sleep is made up of several sleep cycles, each of which is composed of several different sleep stages, and the physiological and neurological differences between the two main types of sleep, non-REM and REM are almost as profound as the differences between sleep and wakefulness. Sleep helps your brain work properly. While you're sleeping, your brain is preparing for the next day. It's forming new pathways to help you learn and remember information. Our brain is still working when we are sleeping. This is helpful information for us so we should not tell ourselves to stop 'thinking' in order to fall asleep. Sleep problems are common during pregnancy because of physiological and endocrine changes at different trimesters. Emotional factors can also play a role. The excitement and anticipation of having a baby as well as the fears of impending motherhood and the anxiety about labor and delivery can all be stressful and affect their 'sleep health.'

One scientific study found that first-time mothers who got less than 6 hours of sleep at night were 4.5 times more likely to have a C-section and their average length of labor was 10 hours or longer compared with first-time mothers who slept 7 hours or more. When you fall asleep is also an important factor in promoting 'sleep health' and the golden time is around 11 pm. Scientific research shows that melatonin secretion and levels of melanocyte stimulating hormones are related to when you fell asleep. These hormones play an important role in physical and mental health.

4.2.8.1. Meditation Guidelines

- You should be well prepared for your sleep. You should fall asleep at 11 pm every night.
- Cut out caffeinated drinks like soda, coffee, and tea from your diet as much as possible. Restrict any intake of them to the morning or early afternoon.
- Avoid drinking a lot of fluids or eating a full meal within a few hours of going to bed.
- Avoid exercise right before you go to bed.
- Do not work, watch TV, play games or speak with others on the phone for at least half an hour before going to bed. Switch off all the electronics.
- Keep the room dark when you sleep. Don't switch on the light, not even a dim light. Sleep with your most comfortable posture (do not force yourselves to sleep in the left lateral position, because you will move and change positions when you sleep).
- Relax.
- Relax your mind and body.
- Relax your waist and hip, relax your neck muscles at the back, feel the weight of your body (the contact points between your body and your bed), find the feeling of falling asleep, sleeping in ….
- Remember to use your body to sleep, not your mind.
- Relax…Feel the Weight…Sleeping In

4.3. Four Immeasurables Meditation

Practice of Four Immeasurables Meditation in pregnant women means cultivation of the four immeasurable minds, loving kindness, compassion, empathetic joy and equanimity for all sentient beings, herself, her fetus, relatives and friends, unrelated persons and those disliked. Sending your blessings to others is an important practice of Immeasurables Meditation as a reminder to yourself that all sentient beings including those you love and hate are always in your mind and affecting you all the time, anywhere. Pregnant women have strong feelings on the meaning of life and appreciate the joy of giving birth. Pregnancy is the best time to do an intervention which can promote maternal health, fetal health and future child health. You should divide your practice of Four Immeasurables Meditation into three sections. The first section should be 15-20 minutes, basically the time the body, mind, and heart will take to settle down from the activities of daily life. Rest, in the experience of breathing or using other methods to let things settle is important. In the second section, the main part of the meditation session is to say the lines of the verse slowly, one by one. With each line, you experience what reactions arise. How does your body react to the line? What emotions arise? And what stories start to run? Don't try to change the reactions: just be open to the experience of them. When you have said all four lines, rest for a few minutes, experiencing what is arising, or, if nothing is arising, then just rest. Then say each line of the verse again, slowly, as before. Repeat this process for the main part of the meditation session. About 10 minutes before the end of the session, let the verses go, and just rest. Don't fall into distraction, don't try to control your experience, and don't work at anything. If you need to, rest in the experience of breathing.

4.3.1. Loving-Kindness Meditation

It is easy for pregnant women to cultivate the wish to be happy and enjoy their motherhood. It is a common belief that if you are happy, you can give birth to a cheerful baby. Loving-kindness is essentially a quality of mind, although it expresses itself in behavior. The definition of Loving-Kindness is "wants others to be happy." This love is unconditional, it requires a lot of courage and acceptance (including self-acceptance). The "near enemy" of love, or a quality which appears similar but is more an opposite, is conditional love (selfish love). The opposite wants others to be unhappy with anger and hatred. A result which one needs to avoid is attachment. The essential nature of loving-kindness is a yearning that the person on whom you are focusing your mind be well and happy.

Cultivation of loving-kindness is a behavioral intervention as it involves meditation and cultivation of positive psychology. This practice [20] will enable one to eliminate unwholesome attitudes and actions that produce unhappiness in one's life. This kind of spiritual power is expected to strengthen the maternal-fetal bonding and promote good maternal child development. This kind of positive emotion is best cultivated in the morning after waking up so that its influence can be extended to the whole day. Loving-kindness meditation is also one of the most efficient ways to cultivate forgiveness. Forgiveness is the ability to release from the mind all the past hurts and failures, all sense of guilt and loss. Forgiveness is the first step on the pathway to healing, enabling one to banish resentment. Without forgiveness, you cannot be happy. Studies have shown that the immune system was affected significantly by both happiness and sadness, in other words, by both positive and negative emotions. Happiness has its healing power. Cultivation of loving-kindness is the leading pathway to happiness. The practice of loving-kindness meditation can also neutralize the effects of anger, which will lead to ill health.

For pregnant women to practice the meditation on loving-kindness:

The pregnant woman should begin with oneself. You begin with yourself because without loving yourself it is almost impossible to love others. The verse is:

> May I be filled with loving-kindness
> May I be well
> May I be peaceful and at ease
> May I be happy

Say the lines of the verse slowly, one by one. With each line, experience what reactions arise. How does your body react to the line? What emotions arise? And what stories start to run? Don't try to change the reactions; just open to the experience of them. When you have said all four lines, rest for a few minutes, experiencing what is arising, or, if nothing is arises, then just rest. Then say each line of the verse again, slowly, as before. Practice this meditation repeatedly for a number of weeks until the sense of loving-kindness for you grows. When you feel ready, in the same meditation period you can gradually expand the focus of your loving-kindness to include others.

One should go on to develop it towards your fetus, then your close relative and friends.

One can move on to the more difficult task of developing, loving-kindness towards strangers, to all members of one's community and nation.

Finally, one then extends this attitude to persons for whom we naturally feel hostility or hatred or even our enemies.

4.3.2. Compassion Meditation

The definition of Compassion is "wants others to be free from suffering." This compassion happens when one feels sorry for someone, and one feels an urge to help. The near enemy is pity, which keeps the other at a distance. The opposite is wishing for others to suffer, or cruelty. A result which one needs to avoid is sentimentality. To develop compassion in daily life, means to prepare the mother psychologically to accept the suffering, both physical and mental, caused by the pregnancy. It also involves psychological preparation for any complications that may happen. For pregnant women to practice the meditation on compassion [21]:

The pregnant woman should begin with oneself. The verse is:

May I be free of suffering, harm, and disturbances.
May I accept things just as they are.
May I experience the world accepting me just as I am.
May I serve whatever arises.

Say the lines of the verse slowly, one by one. With each line, experience what reactions arise. How does your body react to the line? What emotions arise? And what stories start to run? Don't try to change the reactions; just open to the experience of them. When you have said all four lines, rest for a few minutes, experiencing what is arising, or, if nothing is arises, then just rest. Then say each line of the verse again, slowly, as before. Practice this meditation repeatedly for a number of weeks until the sense of compassion grows. When you feel ready, in the same meditation period you can gradually expand the focus of your loving-kindness to include others.

One should go on to develop it towards your fetus, then your close relative and friends.

One can move on to the more difficult task of developing, loving-kindness towards strangers, to all members of one's community and nation.

Finally, one then extends this attitude to persons for whom we naturally feel hostility or hatred or even our enemies.

4.3.3. Empathetic Joy Meditation

It is easy for pregnant women to develop empathetic joy as they can easily share and feel the happiness of pregnancy in bringing a new life to the earth with other pregnant women. The definition of Empathetic Joy is being happy with someone's fortune and happiness. Empathetic joy here refers to the potential of bliss and happiness of all sentient beings, as they can all become Buddha. The near enemy is hypocrisy or affectation. The opposite is jealousy. A result which one needs to avoid is spaced-out bliss. Empathetic joy is a great antidote to depression for oneself as well. The practice of empathetic joy meditation [22] may lead to more appreciation of life. This is particularly effective in pregnant women as a new life will be born in few months' time. The effect of cultivation of empathetic joy will lead to a happy life. It is an unselfish, very positive mental attitude which is beneficial for oneself and others. By rejoicing in others' progress on the spiritual path, one can actually share in their positive action. In this case, it also refers specifically to rejoicing in the giving birth of the next generation. In long term practice, this may have an anesthetic effect over physical suffering during pregnancy and labor pain. The verse for cultivation of empathetic joy is:

> May I enjoy the activities of life itself.
> May I enjoy things just as they are.
> May I experience the world taking joy in all that I do.

May I know what to do, whatever arises.

When one cultivates empathetic joy, pregnant women can begin with (1) one's own achievements (pregnancy is the greatest achievement). Thereafter, one can extend one's attitude of empathetic joy to (2) her fetus, close friends, relatives, (3) strangers, and (4) enemies.

4.3.4. Equanimity Meditation

The definition of Equanimity is not to distinguish between friend, enemy or stranger, but regard every sentient being as an equal. It is a clear-minded tranquil state of mind, not being overpowered by delusions, any mental dullness or agitation. The near enemy is indifference. The opposite is anxiety, worry, stress and paranoia. A result which one needs to avoid is apathy. Equanimity is the basis for unconditional, altruistic love, compassion, and joy for other's happiness and Bodhicitta (mind of awakening). Equanimity rounds off the other three immeasurables and brings them to a profound state of balance. Equanimity is an unselfish, detached state of mind which also prevents one from doing negative actions. Emotional transformation is facilitated by equanimity - the ability to experience provocative stimuli nondefensively and with minimal psychological disturbance. Equanimity is the opposite of reactivity and emotional liability, is highly valued across meditative traditions, and is said to be "the characteristic temperament of the sages" (Aurobindo, 1922, p.181). Equanimity is the basis of unconditional acceptance. This is particularly helpful for pregnant women in case there are complications that arise during pregnancy or they have found that their fetus and child have problems. Cultivation of equanimity is to practice non-attachment; it can be viewed as a kind of cognitive behavior approach. Equanimity meditation [23] helps us to cultivate altruism and this is the aim of the Four Immeasurables Meditation and what 'Immeasurables' means. The verse for cultivation of Equanimity is:

May I be free from preference and prejudice.
May I know things just as they are.

Benefits of Prenatal Meditation on Maternal Health, Fetal Health ... 37

> May I experience the world knowing me just as I am.
> May I see into whatever arises.

In cultivating equanimity, however, (1) one is advised to begin with a stranger because one is naturally free from strong feelings of clinging or aversion to him. (2) Then, one extends it to a person that one loves, including friends, relatives, and one's fetus. (3) Having aroused the wholesome attitude of equanimity, one can extend it to one's enemies, and (4) finally, to oneself.

4.4. Three Minutes Breathing Practice

- Aware of the Moment
- Relax & Bliss
- Let Go

"Aware of the Moment" is the essence of meditative practice. Just be aware of your mind but don't habitually follow your emotion. Relaxing will help you to relieve stress, control anxiety symptoms, improve sleep, and have a better quality of life. Making Bliss a habit will lead you through a joyful life. Let Go, you will have complete peace. You can practice "Three minutes Breathing practice" anytime, anywhere or when you have physical discomfort and feel upset.

CONCLUSION

Prenatal meditation leads to empowerment in all aspects of pregnancy; health, physical, mental, social and spiritual. Prenatal interventions can help pregnant women to reduce perinatal stress through their effect on coping mechanisms and improving physical discomfort in the postnatal period which are risk factors for maternal health, fetal health and child health. Pregnant women practicing meditation can provide the best in utero environment for fetal growth and development and fetal learning. Prenatal meditation can be added to present prenatal counselling and prenatal care systems to promote maternal health, child health and family health.

REFERENCES

[1] Jay, R. (2000). *Zen Meditations on Being Pregnant.* Italy: Sourcebooks, Inc.
[2] Barrett, E. S., Sefair, A. V., & O'Connor, T. G. (2017). Prenatal Maternal Stress in Context: Maternal Stress Physiology, Immunology, Neuroendocrinology, Nutrition and Infant Development. In *Diet, Nutrition, and Fetal Programming* (pp. 3-13). Humana Press, Cham.
[3] Sharma, D. S. (2016). Different Types of Meditation Techniques and Their Health Benefits (Review). *PARIPEX-Indian Journal of Research*, 4(9).
[4] Chan, K. P. (2010). Spirituality and Psychoeducation of pregnant Chinese women in Hong Kong: An evaluation of the effect of a Perinatal Eastern Based Meditative Intervention on maternal and fetal health status. *HKU Theses Online* (HKUTO).
[5] Duncan, L. G., & Bardacke, N. (2010). Mindfulness-based childbirth and parenting education: promoting family mindfulness during the perinatal period. *Journal of Child and Family Studies*, 19(2), 190-202.
[6] Braeken, M. A., Jones, A., Otte, R. A., Nyklíček, I., & Van den Bergh, B. R. (2017). Potential benefits of mindfulness during pregnancy on maternal autonomic nervous system functions and infant development. *Psychophysiology*, 54(2), 279-288.
[7] Isgut, M., Smith, A. K., Reimann, E. S., Kucuk, O., & Ryan, J. (2017). The impact of psychological distress during pregnancy on the developing fetus: biological mechanisms and the potential benefits of mindfulness interventions. *Journal of Perinatal Medicine.* DOI: https://doi.org/10.1515/jpm-2016-0189.

[8]   Tao, J., Chen, X., Egorova, N., Liu, J., Xue, X., Wang, Q., & Chen, L. (2017). Tai Chi Chuan and Baduanjin practice modulates functional connectivity of the cognitive control network in older adults. *Scientific Reports*, 7.

[9]   Zeng, X., Chan, V. Y., Liu, X., Oei, T. P., & Leung, F. Y. (2017). The four immeasurables meditations: differential effects of appreciative joy and compassion meditations on emotions. *Mindfulness*, 1-11.

[10] Chan, K. P. (2014). Prenatal Meditation influences Infant Behaviors. *Infant Behavior & Development*, 37, 556-561.

[11] Chan, K. P. (2014). Effects of Perinatal Meditation among pregnant Chinese women in Hong Kong: a randomized controlled trial. *Journal of Nursing Education & Practice*, 5(1), 1 - 18.

[12] Chan, K. P. (2015). Perceptions and experiences of pregnant Chinese women in Hong Kong on prenatal meditation: A qualitative study. *Journal of Nursing Education & Practice*, 6(3), 135 – 146.

[13] Lindsay, E. K. & Creswell, J. D. (2014). Helping the self help others: self-affirmation increases self-compassion and pro-social behaviors. *Front Psychol*, 12(5), 421.

[14] Fletcher, M. (2017). How to Incorporate Mindful Eating in Diabetes Care. *AADE in Practice*, 5(6), 34-38.

[15] Seguias, L., & Tapper, K. (2018). The effect of mindful eating on the subsequent intake of a high calorie snack. *Appetite*, 121, 93-100.

[16] Prakhinkit, S., Suppapitiporn, S., Tanaka, H., & Suksom, D. (2014). Effects of Buddhism walking meditation on depression, functional fitness, and endothelium-dependent vasodilation in depressed elderly. *J Altern Complement Med*, 20(5), 411-6.

[17] Gainey, A., Himathongkam, T., Tanaka, H., & Suksom, D. (2016). Effects of Buddhist walking meditation on glycemic control and vascular function in patients with type 2 diabetes. *Complementary Therapies in Medicine*, 26, 92-97.

[18] Todd, A. (2017). Mindfulness for Well-Being and Stress Management among College Students. *Counseling & Wellness: A Professional Counseling Journal*, 6.

[19] Hunter, B. (2017). Just Keep Breathing! Mindful Breath Awareness. *Understanding Child and Adolescent Grief: Supporting Loss and Facilitating Growth.*

[20] Williams-Orlando, C. (2016). Lovingkindness Meditation in Psychology. *Alternative and Complementary Therapies*, 22(3), 111-116.

[21] Jazaier, H., Lee, I., McGonigal, K., Jinpa, T., Doty, J. R., Gross, J. J. & Goldin, P. R. (2016). A wandering mind is a less caring mind: Daily experience sampling during compassion meditation training. *The Journal of Positive Psychology*, 11(1).

[22] Zeng, X., Chan, V. Y., Liu, X., Oei, T. P., & Leung, F. Y. (2017). The four immeasurables meditations: differential effects of appreciative joy and compassion meditations on emotions. *Mindfulness*, 1-11.

[23] Desbordes, G., Gard, T., Hoge, E. A., Holzel, B. K., Kerr, C., Lazar, S. W., Olendzki, A., & Vago, D. R. (2015). Moving beyond Mindfulness: Defining Equanimity as an Outcome Measure in Meditation and Contemplative Research. *Mindfulness* (NY), 6(2):356-372.

BIOGRAPHICAL SKETCH

Ka Po Chan

Affiliation: Centre of Buddhist Studies, University of Hong Kong

Education: MBBS(HK), PhD(HK)

Professional Appointments: Visiting Assistant Professor, Centre of Buddhist Studies, University of Hong Kong

Publications from the Last 3 Years

1. Chan, K. P. (2014). Prenatal meditation influences infant behaviors. *Infant Behavior and Development*, 37(4), 556-561.
2. Chan, K. P. (2014). Effects of perinatal meditation on pregnant Chinese women in Hong Kong: A randomized controlled trial. *Journal of Nursing Education and Practice*, 5(1), 1.
3. Chan, K. P. (2015). Perceptions and experiences of pregnant Chinese women in Hong Kong on prenatal meditation: A qualitative study. *Journal of Nursing Education and Practice*, 6(3), 135.
4. Chan, K. P. (2018). *Maternal Health and Fetus Education (Taijiao): Prenatal Eastern Based Meditative Intervention* (妊娠健康與胎教:產前健身健心運動) (in Traditional Chinese). HKSAR: Cosmos Books Ltd. In Publication.

In: Meditation
Editor: Lucia Brewer

ISBN: 978-1-53613-223-6
© 2018 Nova Science Publishers, Inc.

Chapter 2

THE DEGENERATION OF CONTEMPORARY MINDFULNESS: RE-ASSERTING THE ETHICAL AND EDUCATIONAL FOUNDATIONS OF PRACTICE IN MINDFULNESS-BASED INTERVENTIONS

Terry Hyland[*]
Free University of Ireland, Dublin, Ireland

ABSTRACT

The exponential growth of mindfulness-based interventions (MBIs) in recent years has resulted in a marketisation and commodification of practice – popularly labeled 'McMindfulness' – which divorces mindfulness from its ethical origins in Buddhist traditions. Using examples from education, the workplace and popular culture, this chapter critiques such commodification by utilising ideas and insights drawn

---

[*] Corresponding Author Email: hylandterry@ymail.com.

from work in educational philosophy and policy analysis. The 'McDonaldization' process is applied to the emerging populist versions of mindfulness, and analysed in some detail, alongside the capitalization and marketisation of MBIs on the 'McMindfulness' model. The central argument is that the crucial educational function of MBIs needs to be informed by the moral virtues which are at the heart of Buddhist mindfulness. Without such an ethical and educational foundation – actively connected with engaged Buddhist foundations aimed at individual and social transformation - mindfulness becomes just another fashionable self-help gimmick or popular psychological technique that is unlikely to be of any lasting benefit or value to practitioners or society.

Keywords: mindfulness-based interventions (MBIs), McMindfulness, commodification, McDonaldization, Buddhist ethics, education philosophy, education policy, social transformation

INTRODUCTION

In a recent article in the UK newspaper, *The Guardian*, Jon Kabat-Zinn (2015) – arguably, the person most responsible for the 'mindfulness revolution' (Boyce, 2011) which has influenced so many aspects of academia and popular culture in the last decade or so – noted the emergence of:

> ...concerns that a sort of superficial "McMindfulness" is taking over which ignores the ethical foundations of the meditative practices and traditions from which mindfulness has emerged, and divorces it from its profoundly transformative potential (p.1).

Kabat-Zinn was fully justified in referring to such concerns though his fairly anodyne remarks about the dangers of seeing mindfulness as a panacea fail to do justice to the enormity of the problems raised by the exponential growth of mindfulness-based interventions (MBIs) in recent years.

The *Guardian* piece was intended to coincide with the publication of *Mindful Nation UK* by the Mindfulness All-Party Parliamentary Group (MAPPG, 2015) in Britain. Recommendations – all generally favourable to mindfulness practices – were made in the Report for the introduction of MBIs in four key areas: health, education, the workplace and the criminal justice system. The fact that – in a time of economic austerity and severe cutbacks in public services – a group of British parliamentarians considered it worthwhile to promote mindfulness in this way is in itself ample testimony to the extent to which mindfulness has swept virus-like through academia, public life and popular culture over the last decade or so (Hyland, 2016). Mindfulness is a now a meme, a product, a fashionable spiritual commodity with enormous market potential and, in its populist forms, has been transmuted into an all-pervasive 'McMindfulness' (Purser & Loy, 2013) phenomenon.

The Degeneration of Mindfulness Practice

The reductionist, commodified forms of mindfulness practice – popularly known as McMindfulness – have been brought about by a number of processes operating within academia and the public socio-economic sphere. In the academic sphere, mindfulness has been taken up most energetically by psychologists, psychotherapists and educators, and there has been an exponential growth of publications measuring the impact of MBSR and related mindfulness-based cognitive therapy (MBCT) programmes on anxiety, depression and chronic pain sufferers, on addictions of various kinds, and to enhance mind/body well-being generally (Hyland, 2015a). Since his original MBSR programme has played such a large part in generating much of this research activity, Kabat-Zinn's criticisms of contemporary developments are understandably nuanced. Acknowledging the 'challenging circumstances relating to the major cultural and epistemological shifts' as Buddhist meditation was introduced into clinical and psychological settings, Williams & Kabat-Zinn (2013) observe that:

> Buddhist scholars, in particular, may feel that the essential meaning of mindfulness may have been exploited, or distorted, or abstracted from its essential ecological niche in ways that may threaten its deep meaning, its integrity, and its potential value (p.11).

Kabat-Zinn (2015) has been rather late in recognizing that there are 'opportunistic elements' for whom 'mindfulness has become a business that can only disappoint the vulnerable consumers who look to it as a panacea' (p.1). However, the 'opportunistic elements' warned against by Kabat-Zinn are surely underestimated here, and there is insufficient attention given to the ways in which such forces have managed to produce a grossly mutated version of mindfulness until it has now become a commodified consumerist product used to sell everything from colouring books and musical relaxation CDs to "apps" for mindful gardening, cooking and driving. Such commercial activity – arguably a paradigm case of McMindfulness – results in the *misuse* of mindfulness, whereas the inclusion of mindfulness in US army training regimes and by Google in staff development programmes (Stone 2014) clearly raises issues about the outright *abuse* of MBIs since foundational mindfulness values such as right livelihood, loving-kindness, compassion and non-materialism are self-evidently and fundamentally at odds with aspects of the core business of corporations and the military.

McDonaldizing Mindfulness

The process by which McMindfulness has been produced – McDonaldization – was originally coined and developed by Ritzer (2000) in the construction of a model informed by Weber's writings to describe and explain the increasing technical rationalization and standardization of more and more aspects of social, economic, political life and culture. As a form of policy analysis, Ritzer's model has been used extensively to critique developments in education (Hartley, 1995; Hyland, 1999) and other spheres of public life and culture (Alfino, Caputo & Wynyard, 1998)

The Degeneration of Contemporary Mindfulness 47

and its main stages can be usefully employed to map the emergence of McMindfulness. There are four main elements, and they are worth examining in some detail in relation to the evolution of the commodified versions of mindfulness practices.

Efficiency

Defined by Ritzer (2000) as 'choosing the optimum means to a given end' (p.40), efficiency results in streamlining, standardization and simplification of both the product and its delivery to customers. In terms of items sold under the mindfulness label, this process is relatively simple. If you want to maximize sales of a colouring book, you just put mindfulness on the front cover (e.g., Farrarons, 2014), and the same principle applies to all cultural products such as self-help and health/well-being manuals (arguably, the most lucrative sphere) and leisure activities such as cooking, gardening and sport. When it comes to mindfulness courses, the standardization process is greatly helped by having handy bite-sized MBSR/MBCT programmes to hand ready for delivery to potential consumers. Such courses are, of course, the original core vehicles for employing mindfulness practice to deal with depression, addiction, pain, and general mind/body afflictions. It is not suggested here that they are typical examples of McMindfulness. However, their 8-week structure – particularly as this is reduced, condensed and transmuted into "apps" and online programmes (see 'Control' element below) - clearly lends itself to these efficiency conditions and is undoubtedly complicit if not directly responsible for the exponential growth of MBIs and the McMindfulness brand over the last decade or so.

Calculability

This element of the process involves 'calculating, counting, quantifying' such that this 'becomes a surrogate for quality' (Ritzer, 2000, p.62). Ritzer describes how the business of reducing 'production and service to numbers' – examples of higher education, health care and politics are offered in illustration (ibid., pp.68-77) – results in regression to mediocre and lowest common denominator production and produce. The competence-based education and training (CBET) techniques informed by behaviourist principles provide a graphic illustration of how this obsession with measuring outcomes – at the expense of process and underlying principles – can distort, de-skill and de-professionalize education and training from school to university learning (Hyland, 1994, 2014). In a similar way, the drive to measure the outcomes of mindfulness has led to similar negative transmutations. Since the exponential development of the mindfulness industry, Grossman (2011) has been forceful in his criticisms of mindfulness measurement scales, particularly those relying upon self-reports by MBI course participants. The key weaknesses are that they de-contextualise mindfulness from its ethical and attitudinal foundations, measure only specific aspects of mindfulness such as the capacity to stay in the present moment, attention span or transitory emotional state and, in general terms, present a false and adulterated perspective on what mindfulness really is. Such developments are of precious little benefit to any of the interested parties whether they are, learners, teachers, mindfulness practitioners or external agencies interested in the potential benefits of MBIs. The position is summed up well by Grossman:

> Our apparent rush to measure and reify mindfulness—before attaining a certain depth of understanding—may prevent us from transcending worn and familiar views and concepts that only trivialize and limit what we think mindfulness is. The scientific method, with its iterative process of re-evaluation and improvement, cannot correct such fundamental conceptual misunderstandings but may actually serve to fortify them (2011, p.1038).

The proliferation of mindfulness scales which has accompanied the exponential growth of programmes has exacerbated this denaturing of the original conception, and it is now no longer clear precisely what is being measured. As Grossman & Van Dam (2011) note, such developments may prove counter-productive and unhelpful to all those working in the field. They argue further that:

The Degeneration of Contemporary Mindfulness 49

Definitions and operationalizations of mindfulness that do not take into account the gradual nature of training attention, the gradual progression in terms of greater stability of attention and vividness of experience or the enormous challenges inherent in living more mindfully, are very likely to misconstrue and banalize the construct of mindfulness, which is really not a construct as we traditionally understand it in Western psychology, but at depth, a way of being (ibid., p.234).

Along with the gradualness of mindfulness development, this 'way of being' is not susceptible to summative psychological testing. Instead, Grossman & Van Dam recommend formative assessment techniques employing longitudinal interviews and observations of MBI participants in specific contexts. More significantly, they go on to make the eminently sensible suggestion that 'one viable option for preserving the integrity and richness of the Buddhist understanding of mindfulness might be to call those various qualities now purporting to be mindfulness by names much closer to what they actually represent' (ibid.,p.234). There are also issues about the failure to record drop-out (hidden failure) rates of MBIs, and also the reporting of negative impacts of mindfulness experiences (Burkeman, 2016: Foster, 2016). On this crucial point, recent meta-analytical studies have discerned the positive skewing of results in 124 mindfulness treatment trials with the suggestion that wishful thinking may have led to negative outcomes going unpublished (Nowogrodzki, 2016). The dangers and pitfalls of summative measurement are returned to in later sections in relation to MBIs in educational contexts.

Predictability

In order to produce uniformity of outcomes in line with customer expectations, systems must be reasonably predictable and, to achieve this, a 'rationalized society emphasizes discipline, order, systematization, formalization, routine, consistency, and methodical operation' (Ritzer, 2000, p. 83). The standardization of MBSR/MBCT programmes fully satisfies these predictability criteria. Kabat-Zinn's original 8-week course has been modified slightly over the years but remains essentially similar to the 1979 MBSR version. This includes – as Williams and Penman (2011) describe – the standard ideas about switching off the autopilot, moving from 'doing' to being', and so on, realized through breath meditation, body scan, noting pleasant/unpleasant thoughts and feelings, and the like. Similar 'predictability' elements can be discerned in the strict control of teacher training for all those wishing to deliver such programmes (McCown, Reibel & Micozzi, 2011). Of course such 'routinization' and standardization is ultimately justified in pragmatic terms of what has been shown to 'work' in the sense of preventing relapse in depression sufferers, alleviating suffering for patients with chronic pain, and the other positive outcomes claimed for course participants. However, there is too little analysis of why it is just *these* standards and routines which need to be implemented and not potential alternatives. Why, for instance, is a course 8 but not 6 or 12 weeks long, and why so little attention given to the positive benefits of illness and the darker aspects of the human condition (Kashwan & Biswas-Diener, 2014)? Moreover, from an educational point of view, it may be more conducive to effective learning if flexibility of content and methods was allowed in accordance with the fostering of learner independence. Inflexibility linked to the strict adherence to prescribed routines, for example, has been cited as one of the reasons for the failure by the American Philosophy for Children programme to make any substantial impact on European educational systems (Murris, 1994; Hyland, 2003).

Control through Non-Human Technology

The chief aim of this control element is to diminish the 'uncertainties created by people' and 'the ultimate is reached when employees are replaced by nonhuman technologies' (Ritzer, 2000, p.121). On the face of it, MBIs seem to be quite some way from this form of control since they aim to foster values and dispositions which enhance human agency. However, the use of mindfulness in the military – particularly in the form of mindfulness-based mind fitness training (Purser, 2014) – is, arguably, a clear case of control of human capabilities directed towards particular purposes, in this case the production of efficient national warriors. Allied with the increasing use of nonhuman drone technology, it is entirely

The Degeneration of Contemporary Mindfulness 51

possible that mindfulness can be implicated here in the production of more effective killing machines, obviously in direct contradiction of core ethical precepts (Kabat-Zinn, 1990). Similarly, the use of mindfulness techniques by employers to influence employee attitudes and behaviour may be discerned in certain workplace applications (as discussed further below). Moreover, the increasing use of mindfulness "apps" such as 'Buddhify', 'Smiling Mind' and 'Headspace (http://www.independent.co.uk/extras/indybest/the-10-best-meditation-apps-8947570.html) – along with increasing use of online versions of MBSR/MBCT programmes – provides ample evidence of the full satisfaction of Ritzer's fourth McDonaldization criterion.

The Capitalization of Mindfulness

Within the framework of the McDonaldization process outlined above, the exploitation of mindfulness by industry and corporate culture has contributed massively to its degeneration in recent years. The appropriation of MBIs by corporations such as Google has been labelled the 'gentrification of the dharma' by Eaton (2014), who reports that 'many Buddhists now fear their religion is turning into a designer drug for the elite' (p.1). In a similar critical vein, Stone (2014) has observed that:

> Mindfulness meditation has exploded into an industry that ranges from the monastery to the military. Google, General Mills, Procter & Gamble, Monsanto and the U.S. Army are just a handful of the many enormous institutions that bring meditative practice to their workforce (p.1)

Arguments that the corporate takeover of mindfulness might work to change the culture and improve working conditions for employees are challenged by Purser & Ng (2015) who argue that many of the companies now offering MBIs as forms of stress reduction are actually responsible for causing such stress in the first place. As they contend:

Buddhist teachings about awakening to the reality of impermanence "as it is" become inverted in corporate mindfulness. Instead of cultivating awareness of the contingencies of present reality that cause suffering, and thereby developing the capacity to intervene in those conditions of suffering, corporate mindfulness goes no further than encouraging individuals to manage stress so as to optimize performance within existing conditions of precarity—which, curiously, are portrayed as inevitable even as they demand flexibility from individuals. (p.1)

The manic scramble by corporate organizations and workplace staff development firms to jump on the mindfulness bandwagon has direct parallels with the expropriation of the Protestant ethic to serve capitalist interests during the 18th century Industrial Revolution. Weber (1930/2014) described in some detail how the Calvinistic strands of Protestantism in particular were ideally suited to transform the 'other worldly' ascetic aspects of Christianity into an enlightened 'this worldly' materialistic principle which justified the new commercialism. Under the influence of the new trends the 'intensity of the search for the Kingdom of God commenced gradually to pass over into sober economic virtue' (p.100). Weber goes on to observe:

With the consciousness of standing in the fullness of God's grace and being visibly blessed by him, the citizen business man…could follow his pecuniary interests as he would and feel that he was fulfilling a duty in doing so. The power of religious asceticism provided him in addition with sober, conscientious, and unusually industrious workmen, who clung to their work as to a life purpose willed by God. Finally, it gave him the comforting assurance that the unequal distribution of the goods of this world was a special dispensation of Divine Providence… (ibid., pp. 101-2).

This handy multi-purpose nature of the religious ethic described by Weber is more than matched by the more recent appropriation of mindfulness spirituality on the part of contemporary business interests. In contemporary economic culture, corporate mindfulness – McMindfulness – now stands in for the Protestant ethic. As Slvoj Zizek (2001) has suggested

The Degeneration of Contemporary Mindfulness 53

'if Max Weber were alive today, he would definitely write a second, supplementary, volume to his *Protestant Ethic*, entitled *The Taoist Ethic and the Spirit of Global Capitalism*' (p.1). He goes on to argue that:

> although "Western Buddhism" presents itself as the remedy against the stressful tension of capitalist dynamics, allowing us to uncouple and retain inner peace and *Gelassenheit*, it actually functions as its perfect ideological supplement (ibid.).

The capitalization of mindfulness achieves a number of desirable objectives for corporate and industrial users:

1. Firms offering mindfulness have appreciated the enormous public relations potential of such provision. Mindfulness sessions in workplaces come to symbolize caring environments in which all the needs of employees – including psychological and spiritual, alongside the free coffees and employer-friendly arrangements of space – are catered for to the fullest extent. Such a badge of spirituality becomes a valuable marketing tool – as the Apple founder, the late Steve Jobs realized (http://www.mindfulness sresource.org/category/steve-jobs/) – as well as being a convenient way of deflecting workers' claims for compensation for stress-related illnesses. If employees are stressed, after all, facilities in the form of in-house therapeutic and mindfulness classes are available to all.

2. Marx saw clearly how religion – famously described as the 'sigh of the oppressed creature, the heart of a heartless world...the opium of the people' (McLellan, 1977, p.64) – functioned to support the socio-economic status quo with its class divisions and inequalities. With the nature of things endorsed as a form of divine providence – and with the eyes of the masses turned towards other worldly affairs – the tragic social injustices and fundamental immorality of capitalist production and relationships were thus maintained and reproduced through religion. McMindfulness –

now functioning to support the new 'hegemonic ideology of global capitalism' (Zizek, 2001, ibid.) -serves a similar purpose in the contemporary capitalist economy by offering forms of spiritual support for oppressive working conditions and unequal industrial relations (Eaton, 2014; Purser & Ng, 2015). Major corporations relish staff development and training which encourages employees – naturally through mindful present-moment awareness – to say 'yes' to all aspects of their experience no matter how painful and unpleasant (Amaranatho, 2015). Such 'training' will guarantee a docile workforce in which there are few challenges to the status quo and which is claimed to lead to 'improved productivity, improved creativity, less absenteeism, better communication and interpersonal relating' (ibid.). Now we can appreciate fully why Google has invested so much in mindfulness-based activities (Bush, 2014).

3. In addition to the substantial capitalist gains noted above, mindfulness has now been acknowledged as a valuable commodity in itself with enormous sales potential in a spiritually impoverished society. Kabat-Zinn's (2015) warning that MBSR 'can never be a quick fix', and that there are grave dangers in ignoring 'the ethical foundations of the meditative practices and traditions from which mindfulness has emerged' (ibid) has been completely ignored in the scramble to expropriate the mindfulness label to market just about any product imaginable. The proliferation of mindfulness "apps" and online programmes noted in the preceding section has contributing enormously to the marketising potential of this most lucrative spiritual commodity. Moreover, the virus-like spread of the meme now means that the mindfulness brand is now free-floating and available for use by anyone wishing to sell their products, whether these are colouring books or lifestyle programmes (for a satirical and humorous perspective on this crude commercialism see the *Ladybird Book of Mindfulness*, Hazeley & Morris, 2016).

The emergence of the McMindfulness phenomenon in recent years closely follows and fully satisfies the Ritzer model of the increasing technical rationalization of all aspects of life. Harvey (2014) has described in graphic detail how the voracious appetite of neo-liberal capitalism has come to devour all aspects of public and private spheres bringing about the total commodification of everyday life. As indicated above, the pseudo-spirituality of McMindfulness approaches has proved an invaluable vehicle – with far wider applications and purposes than its forerunner in the Protestant Ethic – for contemporary capitalist exploitation. It is crucial for committed practitioners to combat such developments, especially those who, like Stephen Batchelor, abhor a 'dharma that is little more than a set of self-help techniques that enable us to operate more calmly and effectively as agents or clients, or both, of capitalist consumerism' (2015, Kindle edition, loc. 340).

MINDFULNESS, ETHICS AND EDUCATION

It goes without saying that most serious and committed mindfulness practitioners and teachers would – along with Kabat-Zinn – deplore the McMindfulness developments noted above. What matters, however, is to inform the critiques of such degenerate interpretations with accounts of what is lost – by practitioners, the sangha and society in general - through the proliferation of mindfulness practices which are divorced from or at odds with the basic tenets of the Buddhist foundations. Predominant in this task must be the insistence that mindfulness becomes denatured and emasculated if practice is divorced from the ethical foundations inherent the universal dharma.

Mindful practices such as breath meditation, walking meditation and mindful movement have been demonstrated to have positive impacts on the behaviour of people of all ages from school to lifelong learning (Burnett, 2011; Langer, 2003; Hyland, 2011). On the basis of fifteen years of utilising mindfulness techniques in American schools and colleges, Schoeberlein & Sheth (2009) argue that:

Mindfulness promotes resilience and enhances social and emotional competence. Mindfulness combined with empathy, kindness and compassion supports constructive action and caring behaviour. Living mindfully begets greater mindfulness. The more you practice, the more mindfulness will infuse your experience of life, work and relationships (p.178).

The suggestion – in both Buddhist contemplative traditions and modern therapeutic interpretations – is that the practice of mindfulness leads naturally to the moral principles underpinning the noble eightfold path, and are instrumental in fostering a form of virtue ethics (Gowans, 2015). Direct connections are made between the inner clarity that Siegel (2010) calls 'mindsight' – the 'focused attention that allows us to see the internal workings of our own minds' (p.xi) – and the foundations of morality. This is brought out clearly in Kabat-Zinn's (2005) discussion of mindfulness and the moral life. As he suggests, the 'wholesome mind and body states' resulting from the practice include:

Generosity, trustworthiness, kindness, empathy, compassion, gratitude, joy in the good fortune of others, inclusiveness, acceptance and equanimity are qualities of mind and heart that further the possibilities of well-being and clarity within oneself, to say nothing of the beneficial effects they have in the world. They form the foundation for an ethical and moral life (p.103).

Although the process of ethical development within mindfulness practice can never be based on a simplistic input/output model (no more than any form of deep and rich teaching and learning), the centrality of the ethical dimension is clearly paramount. Schoeberlein & Sheth (2009) argue that 'mindfulness and education are beautifully interwoven' (p.xi), but the specifically *educational* nature of MBIs needs to be foregrounded at all times if practices are to remain true to the ethical foundations outlined by Kabat-Zinn and committed mindfulness practitioners.

In explaining and justifying his conception of education as the initiation into worthwhile activities, the philosopher of education R.S.

The Degeneration of Contemporary Mindfulness 57

Peters (1966) makes use of an analogy between activities of 'education' and those of 'reform' (this analysis is still widely respected; see Cuypers & Martin, 2009). He argues that education is like reform in that it 'picks out no particular activity or process' but, rather, it 'lays down criteria to which activities or processes must conform'. It is suggested that:

> Both concepts have the criterion built into them that something worthwhile should be achieved. 'Education' does not imply, like 'reform', that a man should be brought back from a state of turpitude into which he has lapsed; but it does have normative implications... It implies that something worthwhile is being or has been intentionally transmitted in a morally acceptable manner (p.25).

I suggest that a similar sort of analogy holds in respect of education and mindfulness practice. Neither process picks out any specific method or technique, yet both imply the achievement of a desirable state of mind. In the case of education, this state involves the development of knowledge and understanding, and in the case of mindfulness practice there is the goal of enhancing mental health and wellbeing by, for instance, removing delusions, breaking harmful habits or developing more wholesome or nourishing thoughts and actions.

It would be useful to look more closely at Peters' specific criteria of education as a way of further elaborating the extent of the connections between therapy and education. These are:

1. That education implies the transmission of what is worthwhile to those who become committed to it;
2. That education must involve knowledge and understanding and some kind of cognitive perspective, which are not inert;
3. That education at least rules out some procedures of transmission, on the grounds that they lack wittingness and voluntariness on the part of the learner (p.45).

Taking each of these in turn, we can determine how far MBI approaches satisfy each criterion.

Mindfulness may be considered worthwhile insofar as it involves the progression from a less to a more desirable state of mind and being. One core purpose of mindfulness-based practice is to free the mind from automatic, ruminative thought and action and this is equivalent to the Socratic method of freeing the mind from delusions and error in order to pave the way for genuine learning. Mindfulness cultivates the awareness – especially that which 'emerges through paying attention on purpose, in the present moment, and non-judgmentally to things as they are' (Williams et al, 2007, p.47) – which is a prerequisite for meaningful and productive teaching and learning.

Both spheres involve the attention to and modification of consciousness and modes of thinking and both aim at a form of enlightened awareness which pays due attention to values and feelings. Peters (1966) was perhaps the most distinguished and foremost advocate of a traditional liberal education grounded in forms of knowledge, but he took great care to leave room for individual development and personal relationships in teaching and learning. He observes that:

> the ability to form and maintain satisfactory personal relationships is almost a necessary condition of doing anything else that is not warped or stunted. If the need to love and be loved is not satisfied the individual will be prone to distortions of belief, ineffectiveness of lack of control in action, and unreliability in his allegiances. His attempt to learn things will also be hampered by his lack of trust and confidence. A firm basis of love and trust, together with a continuing education in personal relationships, is therefore a crucial underpinning to any other more specific educational enterprise (p.58).

Can mindfulness practices be said to incorporate the knowledge, understanding and active cognitive perspective required by Peters' second criterion? Certainly, there are clear differences in types of knowledge utilised and exemplified in the fields of education and mindfulness practice. These can be illustrated by examining the 'forms of knowledge' which, Hirst claims, cover the whole domain of human endeavour and provide the foundations of a liberal education, which has been traditionally viewed as a 'process which frees the mind from error' (Schofield, 1972, p.154). Originally, seven (or eight, depending on the particular interpretation) disciplines or forms – distinguishable from each other by their conceptual and logical frameworks, methodology and truth criteria – were identified by Hirst (1965): 'mathematics, physical sciences, human sciences, history, religion, literature and the fine arts, and philosophy' (p.131), in addition to theoretical and practical fields of knowledge which combined elements from the forms (and also incorporated morality). In later versions these were revised; history was subsumed into the human sciences,, mathematics and logic are called symbolics and literature and the fine arts are labelled aesthetics, doubt is cast about whether religion is a genuine form, and a new a new area 'awareness and understanding of our own and other people's minds' (Hirst and Peters, 1970, p.63) is identified.

In later comments on the forms of knowledge, Hirst (1974) was concerned to stress that the forms do not exhaust the aims or content of educational practice. He observed that:

> much commonsense knowledge and many forms of experience, attitudes and skills may be regarded as lying outside as lying outside all the disciplines we have...Many forms of education, including liberal education in my sense, will have objectives some of which come from within the disciplines and some of which do not (p.98).

The knowledge and understanding which guides mainstream MBIs may be characterised as that 'commonsense knowledge', experience, attitudes and skills referred to by Hirst. However, there is also clear evidence within dharma practice of the utilisation of aspects of the human and physical sciences and, especially, of the area labelled 'awareness and understanding of our own and other people's minds' (though this will be practical rather than theoretical, akin to Aristotle's concept of *phronesis* linked to the moral life). In addition, the aims of education and therapeutic mindfulness in terms of freeing the mind from error and delusion to make way for creativity and openness in learning are in close harmony. Thich

60 Terry Hyland

Nhat Hanh expresses this vision clearly, particularly in his conception of mindfulness and work. He advises us to:

> keep your attention focused on the work, be alert and ready to handle ably and intelligently any situation which may arise – this is mindfulness. There is no reason why mindfulness should be different from focusing all one's attention on one's work, to be alert and to be using one's best judgment. During the moment one is consulting, resolving, and dealing with whatever arises, a calm heart and self-control are necessary if one is to obtain good results...If we are not in control of ourselves but instead let our impatience or anger interfere, then our work is no longer of any value. Mindfulness is the miracle by which we master and restore ourselves (Hanh 1991, p.14).

This message applies to any form of work, including the 'work' of learning, teaching and education (these connections are explored below in the section on moral training).

The final criterion which needs to be satisfied for any activity to be educational concerns the use of methods which respect the wittingness and autonomy of learners. Obviously this rules out certain therapeutic practices such as hypnotherapy and behaviour modification but, equally, it rules out many educational practices involving coercion, punishment and indoctrination (Hirst and Peters, 1970). Practices which respect personal autonomy are, I would suggest, characteristic of a broad range of therapeutic mindfulness approaches aimed at mind/body wellbeing (and also in line with Buddhist scepticism about traditional authority, received opinion and revelation, see Bodhi, 2012, p.280ff.). Investigating the links between Buddhist practice and psychoanalysis, for example, Rubin (2003) explains the 'similarities between both traditions' and observes that:

> Both are concerned with the nature and alleviation of human suffering and each has both a diagnosis and 'treatment plan' for alleviating human misery. The three other important things they share make a comparison between tem possible and potentially productive. First, they are pursued within the crucible of an emotionally intimate

The Degeneration of Contemporary Mindfulness 61

relationship between either an analyst-and or a teacher and student. Second, they emphasise some similar experiential processes – evenly hovering attentions and free association in psychoanalysis and meditation in Buddhism. Third, they recognise that obstacles impede the attempt to facilitate change (pp.45-46).

This account is strikingly similar to the sort of learning and teaching encounter favoured in open and progressive education which emphasises student-centredness, autonomy and independent learning with the teacher acting as a facilitator, guide and resource person (Hyland, 2011). In addition, we can detect the idea of removing obstacles to learning, the freeing the mind from error that is characteristic of liberal education (Hirst & Peters, 1970).

Staying within the contemplative tradition, Salzberg and Goldstein (2001) explain how the 'function of meditation is to shine the light of awareness on our thinking'. The educational implications are brought out clearly in their description of how:

> The practice of bare attention opens up the claustrophobic world of our conditioning, revealing an array of options. Once we can see clearly what's going on in our minds, we can choose whether and how to act on what we're seeing. The faculty used to make those choices is called discriminating wisdom...the ability to know skilful actions from unskilful actions (p.48).

MBIs can have a potential impact on both the means and ends of education. Not only do they provide the foundations for productive learning, but also offer a blueprint to guide the direction of that learning. As Hanh (1999) observes:

> Mindfulness helps us look deeply into the depths of our consciousness ... When we practice this we are liberated from fear, sorrow and the fires burning inside us. When mindfulness embraces our joy, our sadness, and all our mental formations, sooner or later we will see their deep roots. ... Mindfulness shines its light upon them and helps them to transform (p. 75).

Against this background of normative criteria, it is easy to discern how McMindfulness practices fail to satisfy even the most basic educational requirements. There are no connections with the broad transformation of perspectives which allows for the fostering of wholesome thoughts and feelings and the reduction of harmful rumination and avoidance. Workplace and commercial applications of mindfulness are concerned only with specific strategic outcomes linked to productivity and persuasion. Moreover, many of the techniques employed at this level clearly fail to meet the autonomy criterion since they are directed at controlling and manipulating hearts and minds for ulterior purposes. On this account, the numerous mindfulness "apps" and products such as simplistic self-help and colouring books are – not simply ludicrous and exploitative mutations of mindfulness – but positively harmful to health in that they mislead people and construct obstacles to the sort of mindful transformation conducive to mind/body wellbeing. Authentic educational practice – rich and deep learning – cannot be divorced from ethical considerations (Peters, 1966; Palmer, 1998) and the same applies to mindfulness processes. McMindfulness applications fail miserably when they separate something called 'present moment awareness' (surrounded by a dangerous 'myth' exposed by Purser, 2014b) from moral principles such as compassion and loving-kindness. As Batchelor (2015) puts it in citing the *Kalama Sutta*, the 'transformation involved in the practice of the dharma is as much affective as it is cognitive', directed towards enabling us to 'dwell pervading the entire world with a mind imbued with loving kindness, compassion, altruistic joy, and equanimity'(loc.428).

Moreover, even the more orthodox MBIs – MBSR/MBCT programmes and mindfulness in schools – may suffer from some of the counter-educational defects noted above. The 'control' and 'standardization' elements noted in the McDonaldization analysis earlier may be unfavourably applied to certain aspects of the standard 8-week programmes to the extent that the drive for uniformity delimits the capacity for independent development on the part of participants. There does appear to be an element of prescriptive rigidity about the way in which participants are required to, for example, note pleasant/unpleasant events in week 4 and focus on thinking in week 6 (Williams, et al, 2007, pp.237-241). Furthermore, surely there are many ways for teachers to embody mindfulness in addition to those officially approved by centralised teacher training organisations such as MBI-TAC (2012). The fact that such formalised teaching criteria makes extensive use of 'competences' (ibid., pp.3-4) also tends to align them with discredited behaviourist assessment regimes (Hyland, 2014).

However, it is in the specification of outcomes that MBIs in education and workplaces run the risk of degenerating into McMindfulness practices. Problems in this area stem partly from the fact that – whereas MBIs in the health service and in therapeutic practice aimed at combating addictions and depression are essentially *remedial,* thus directly connecting them with foundational mindfulness principles concerned with relieving suffering – this is not quite the case in other spheres. In education and work there has been a tendency for this core *transformational* function to be co-opted in order to achieve specific *operational* objectives, and such pragmatic purposes have obscured the links with the foundational moral principles (Hyland, 2015a,b). The empirical research on mindfulness in schools is characterized by an instrumentalist concern with performative outcomes which appears remote from the original transformational intentions and goals of practice.

A review of Australian research on teaching mindfulness in schools, for example, concluded with the comment that 'mindfulness practices have been shown to help teachers: reduce their stress levels; assist with behaviour management strategies and improve self-esteem' (Albrecht, Albrecht & Cohen, 2012, p.11). Similarly, UK research linked to the *Mindfulness in Schools* (Misp or .b) project describes the outcomes of mindfulness lessons in secondary schools in terms of reducing 'negative emotion and anxiety' in students and contributing 'directly to the development of cognitive and performance skills and executive function' (Weare, 2012, p.2). The recent meta-analysis of work in this field by Zenner, Hermleben-Kurz & Walach (2014) concluded by noting that 'analysis suggests that mindfulness-based interventions for children and youths are able to increase cognitive capacity of attending and learning by nearly one standard deviation' (p.18). Such research does, of course, also include much anecdotal talk about enhancing emotional well-being and general mind/body health for both teachers and students (Schoeberlein & Sheth, 2009; Burnett, 2011) but the overriding impression is that mindfulness practice has in many instances been co-opted to achieve strategic instrumentalist ends in the pursuit of predominantly academic outcomes. This obsession with training attention and focus through mindfulness in a way which detaches it from foundational ethical principles has been noted by a number of philosophers concerned with MBIs in education (O'Donnell, 2015: Lewin, 2015).

MINDFULNESS AS MORAL TRAINING

A.N. Whitehead (1962 edn) once famously declared that there 'is only one subject matter for education, and that is Life in all its manifestations' (p.10). Similarly, if somewhat less grandiloquently, Peters (1973) argues that:

> When educationalists proclaim that 'education is of the whole man' (sic) they are enunciating a conceptual truth: for 'education' rules out narrow specialism just as it rules out a purely instrumental approach to activities... This transforming quality of education is what makes the contrast drawn between life and education ridiculous; for it is by education that mere living is transformed into a quality of life. For how a man lives depends on what he sees and understands... There is no end to this process... To be educated is not to have arrived at a destination; it is to travel with a different view (ibid., pp.19-20).

As suggested already above, the transforming quality of education through ethical development dovetails neatly with the transformation function of mindfulness practice in that both are intended to remove hindrances to the achievement of mind/body wellbeing and human flourishing. This journey may be conceived in part as a form of moral

The Degeneration of Contemporary Mindfulness 65

training and, in this respect, it is interesting how the conception of training is employed in Buddhist teachings and literature.

The key ethical tenets designed to foster benevolence, generosity, trust and responsibility are routinely referred to as 'trainings' in Hahn's writings on Buddhist mindfulness (Hahn 1999, 94-98) with the clear implication that a long-term course of practice and developmental work will be required. Similarly, many of the original Buddhist teachings use similes and analogies which refer to the nature of work and working people such as farmers, metalworkers, potters and other artisans, with *dharma* practitioners described as 'trainees' (Bodhi, 2000, pp 585-6, 688-9,1696-7). As Batchelor (2015) explains at length:

> On numerous occasions we find Gotama comparing the practice of the dharma to the skilled activity of the laborer or artisan...He compares the person who practices mindful breathing to a "skilled wood turner" who "when making a long turn understands 'I'm making a long turn'"...He likens the meditator who analyzes the elements of his body to a "skilled butcher who has killed a cow and is seated at a crossroads cutting it to pieces". The Buddha admires artisans' mastery of the skills they employ so effortlessly and effectively (loc.1238ff.)

Placing all this in an educational context, there are direct connections here with the traditional apprenticeship model of vocational learning (Hyland, 2015b), and also with moral education following the Aristotelian model of virtue ethics. In terms of Western moral philosophy, Buddhism has been standardly characterised as a form of 'virtue ethics...because Buddhism is first and foremost a path of self-transformation that seeks the elimination of negative states (vices) and their replacement by positive or wholesome ones' (Keown, 2005, p.25). This transformative perspective is present – not just in the popular writings on the practice (Hanh, 1999; Gunaratana, 2002) – but also in the therapeutic applications of mindfulness in education, health and psychotherapy. Gowans (2015) suggests that the dominance of Buddhist ethical perspectives which 'stress affinities specifically with Aristotle's eudaimonistic conception of virtue ethics can be explained by the idea that:

For Aristotle, a good life is oriented towards to the attainment of *eudaimonia*, a life of well-being centrally constituted by a set of virtues. Likewise for Buddhism it is plausible to suppose that a good life is oriented towards the attainment of enlightenment, arguably also a life of well-being centrally constituted by a set of virtues (p.138).

Although there are different orderings and priorities of particular virtues in the different traditions, the 'middle-way' between extremes is common to both as is the approach to education, a 'self-realization' through training and habit formation (Brumbaugh & Lawrence, 1963). For Aristotle (1981 edn) the virtues are:

engendered in us neither by nor contrary to nature; we are constituted by nature to receive them, but their full development in us is due to habit...Anything that we have to learn to do we learn by the actual doing of it: people become builders by building and instrumentalists by playing instruments. Similarly, we become just by performing just acts, temperate by performing temperate ones, brave by performing brave ones (pp.91-2).

Of course, learning to become virtuous by performing virtuous acts – just like the development of mindfulness traits and dispositions – also requires some degree of the right kind of instruction and guidance, and this is to be found in the moral development aspects of mindfulness applications noted earlier.

MINDFULNESS, EDUCATION AND CRITICAL SOCIAL ENGAGEMENT

The moral foundations of mindfulness training lead naturally to a progression from self-regarding to other-regarding virtues as greed, hatred and delusion are gradually replaced by generosity, kindness and understanding about the nature of the world and the human condition. Although the 'engaged Buddhist' movement is traditionally associated

The Degeneration of Contemporary Mindfulness 67

with the pioneering work of Thich Nhat Hanh from the 1960s (Kraft, 2000), it is, arguably, as old as Buddhism itself and takes its inspiration from the ethical elements of the eightfold path and the core virtues of compassion, non-harming and loving-kindness (Gowans, 2015). The Buddha's words from the *Mahavagga*: 'Come, friends...dwell pervading the entire world with a mind imbued with lovingkindness...compassion... altruistic joy...equanimity...without ill will' (Bodhi, 2000, p.1608) are interpreted by Olendzki (2010) as the origins of our duty of care to the world and its contents which provide a foundation for engaged Buddhism.

Other influential *dharma* strands have been suggested by Harvey (2000), and the theory and practice of socially engaged movements has expanded and diversified considerably over recent years. More significantly, there are now national and international Buddhist movements campaigning on a vast and diverse range of issues. The *International Learning Resource* Site on 'engaged practice' includes a wide range of articles and news about groups and meetings on topics as diverse as consumerism, the environment, race and gender, globalisation, work in prisons and hospices, in addition to peace-making in every part of the world (www.dharmanet.org/lcengaged.htm). The first world symposium on socially engaged Buddhism organised by Zen Peacemakers took place in Montague, Massachusetts in 2010 and the group regularly organizes 'bearing witness' retreats in areas of conflict, injustice and deprivation (http://zenpeacemakers.org/bw/).

Acknowledging Hanh's pioneering work in this area, Garfinkel (2006) set out to travel the world in search of socially engaged practice. From a Zen Hospice project in San Francisco (pp.2-3), a 'bearing witness' group remembering the Jewish holocaust at Auschwitz (pp.46ff), organisations challenging caste in equalities in India (pp.96ff) to NGOs fighting urban poverty in contemporary Japan (pp.221ff), Garfinkel demonstrates how engaged Buddhism is constantly striving to make a difference to the way the world is. As Garfinkel notes, 'right livelihood' (p.6) would be a most appropriate label for the modern applications of mindfulness he observed throughout his world tour in the footsteps of the Buddha.

Mindfulness practice is designed to promote well-being in ourselves and others or – in the language of the Buddhist noble truths – to work towards the reduction of the suffering of all living beings. What stands in the way of achieving such objectives? Clearly, the key *internal* obstacles are located in unwholesome instincts and the capriciousness of the emotions, and mindfulness can help in fostering the requisite control and, eventually, transforming these to promote generosity, kindness and compassion. Once this is achieved, however, there is a host of *external* factors which clearly contribute to what Schopenhauer (1970 edn) called the 'suffering of the world' (p.41) or, to express this in a less negative way, which militate against the promotion of human flourishing and well-being. Thus, the internal and external can be seen to come together in mindful engagement to bring about the desirable ends.

As Wilkinson and Pickett (2010) conclude in their analysis of levels of inequality around the world, 'further improvements in the quality of life no longer depend on further economic growth: the issue is now community and how we relate to each other' (p.254). The idea of education as the prime mover in the fostering of economic capital is now an empty and hollow slogan, particularly as countries around the world struggle with the consequences of the abject failure of neo-liberal economics. Yet, it is not only the economic consequences of Chicago school free marketeering (Klein, 2007) ideas that have turned out to be disastrous but also their impact on the social fabric in glorifying selfish and materialistic possessive individualism. The selfish capitalism which James (2008) and Gerhardt (2010) have criticised so forcefully has produced sickness – mental, physical and psychological – in all nations in which it has gone unchallenged by social-democratic and moral values concerned with societal well-being and the common good. Levels of public and community trust have plummeted in recent years (Seldon, 2009; Judt, 2010) and the fostering of social capital has never been more urgently needed from our education systems (Ergas & Todd, 2016).

The engaged Buddhist response to this global malaise stems – not just from the basic immorality of injustice, greed and social degeneration – but

The Degeneration of Contemporary Mindfulness 69

from its consequences in terms of poverty, conflict and the exacerbation of human suffering on a massive scale. A recent Oxfam report, for example, which reported solid evidence that the wealth of the richest 1% of the world will shortly exceed that of the other 99% (https://www.oxfam. org/en/pressroom/pressreleases/2015-01-19/) explained clearly why this was not just monstrously unjust and immoral but, more importantly, served to militate against the possibility of the economic, social and political reform which could ameliorate global problems of poverty, over-consumption and environmental destruction. This message has been reinforced in a number of recent economic analyses by Thomas Piketty (2013) and former World Bank Chief Economist, Joseph Stiglitz (2012), which point to the dangers for all of us of the growing gap between rich and poor throughout the world. The grotesque and obscene consequences of the neoliberal monopoly of global power networks since the 1970s is graphically illustrated in the recent work of George Monbiot (2016) who points out forcefully that:

> Without countervailing voices, naming and challenging power, political freedom withers and dies. Without countervailing voices, a better world can never materialize (Kindle edition, loc.128)

Stiglitz (2012) looks forward to the day when 'the 99% could come to realize that they have been duped by the 1%: that what is in the interest of the 1% is *not* in their interests', and this might lead to a 'society where the gap between the haves and have-nots has been narrowed, where there is a sense of shared identity, a common commitment to opportunity and fairness' (pp.359-60). In a similar vein, Seabrook (2015) has written extensively about the 'impoverishment of riches' by which the myth of material progress has led to tragic losses in terms of our humanity and the planet we inhabit. He talks of neoliberal capitalism as causing a 'wasting disease' which 'not only wears away the fabric of the world, it also consumes human resourcefulness from within' (p.208). Placing all this within a context of Buddhist values, Simmer-Brown (2002) explains how the 'crisis of consumerism' has impoverished and exacerbated human suffering in recent decades such that:

> we see the poor with not enough food and no access to clean drinking water…we see the sick and infirm who have no medicine or care; we see rampant exploitation of the many for the pleasure and comfort of the few; we see the demonization of those who would challenge the reign of wealth, power, and privilege' (p.3).

Socially engaged Buddhists are in common agreement with economists such as Stiglitz and social commentators such as Seabrook and Monbiot about both the causes of the present malaise and the ways to cure it. Myths about unconstrained growth and the need for ever-expanding consumerism need to be exploded in conjunction with the transformation of the craving which fuels this impoverishment. Seabrook (2015) argues with passion that:

> The raising of "the consumer" into human identity has been a fateful development. It demonstrates the power of an economic system to sustain its growth by expanding the capacity of humanity to ingest whatever it produces: without a voracious appetite for all available goods, that system would perish. As it is, people grow obese as the world shrinks (p.218).

His claim that capitalism has learned to 'render itself indistinguishable from human yearning' (ibid.) is interpreted within a Buddhist framework by Allan Hunt Badiner's (2002) argument that 'consumption has become one of the most urgent topics in our lives'. He goes on to suggest that:

> Revisiting our moral and spiritual values is an important part of our response to the fundamentally alienating ethic inherent in consumer culture. The Buddhist perspective offers not only a critique, but also practical ways to empower people to resist the prison of consumerism (p.ii).

CONCLUSION

Not only does the degeneration of spiritual practice through McMindfulness commodification stand in the way of the changes which socially engaged Buddhism is striving for, such commercialism serves to reinforce the consumerist craving which fuels such impoverishment and suffering. It is only by re-asserting the connections between mindfulness and its ethical roots in the *dharma* that the Buddhist project of transforming suffering can be achieved (cf recent work on 'critical mindfulness' by Ng & Purser, 2016). Fostering present-moment awareness in schools and colleges will not be sufficient to achieve this project without the ethical foundations and the moral training outlined above. The 'possessive individualism' which inspired and motivated early mercantilist capitalism asserts that the 'individual is essentially the proprietor of his own person and capacities, for which he owes nothing to society' (MacPherson, 1962, p.263) continues to drive the selfishness and greed of neoliberal economics. Rooted in human craving, this delusional egotism is immensely powerful as the Buddha observed in the teachings on the origination of identity in the *Majjhima Nikaya*:

> Now, Bhikkus, this is the way leading to the origination of identity...One regards the eye thus: 'This is mine, this I am, this is my self'. One regards forms thus; 'This is mine, this I am, this is my self'... . One regards craving thus: 'This is mine, this I am, this is my self' (Bodhi, 2009, p.1133).

In commenting on this teaching and the links with dependent origination generally, Olendzki (2010) observes that it:

> provides a model for understanding the profound interrelationship between all things, but it is a model that does not allow for a self. Nothing belongs to anybody: nobody has any self to protect; we all just co-arise with one another (p.136).

Expressing similar sentiments in more secular terms, Seabrook (2015) offers a vision of society which might stand as a mission statement for an ideal mindfulness in education project in this sphere. This vision entails the:

> retrieval of another version of wealth [which] is something we practice daily since it lies in the freely given, the acts of mercy and charity, the performance of duty, the endurance and patience of those who care for the infirm, sick and old, all the gifts of humanity not subject to the transaction of exchange, all that is shared voluntarily, the pooled resources and recognition of common vulnerability, the ability to see ourselves in others, a validation of the homely and familiar, the capacious storehouse of inner human resources to which the material treasures of the world are ancillary, the simplicity of our needs and the ease with which they can be satisfied outside the market (p.225).

REFERENCES

Alfino, M., Caputo, J.S. & Wynyard, R. (1998). *McDonaldization ReVisited: Essays on Consumer Culture*. London: Praeger.

Albrecht, N.J., Albrecht, P.M. & Cohen, M. (2012). Mindfully Teaching in the Classroom: A Literature Review; *Australian Journal of Teacher Education*, 37(12), pp.1-14.

Amaranatho (2015). *Learn to say 'Yes' - mindfulness in the workplace*, 8/9/15 http://www.rhhr.com/learn-to-say-yes-mindfulness-in-the-work place/accessed 3.12.15.

Aristotle (1981 edn). *The Ethics*. Harmondsworth: Penguin (trans. J.A.K. Thomson).

Badiner, A.H. (ed.) (2002). *Mindfulness in the Marketplace: Compassionate Responses to Consumption*. Berkeley, CA: Parallax.

Batchelor, S. (2015). *After Buddhism: Rethinking the Dharma for a Secular Age*. New Haven: Yale University Press (Kindle edition).

Bodhi, B. (2000). *The Connected Discourses of the Buddha* Boston, MA: Wisdom Publications.

Bodhi, B. (2009). *The Middle Length Discourses of the Buddha.* Boston, MA: Wisdom Publications.

Bodhi, B. (2012). *The Numerical Discourses of the Buddha: A Translation of the Anguttara Nikaya.* Somerville, MA: Wisdom Publications.

Boyce, B. (ed) (2011). *The Mindfulness Revolution.* Boston, MA, Shambhala Publications.

Brambaugh, R.S. & Lawrence, N.M. (1963). Aristotle: Education as Self-Realization; in *Philosophers on Education.* London: Harrap & Co. Ltd. (pp.49-75).

Burkeman, O. (2016). Colour Me Calm; *Guardian Review*, 9/1/16, p.5.

Burnett, R. (2011). Mindfulness in Schools: Learning Lessons from the Adults – Secular and Buddhist.; *Buddhist Studies Review*, 28.1, pp.79–120.

Bush, M. (2014). What's It Like to Take Google's Mindfulness Training? *Mindful: Taking Time for What Matters*, 30/7/14.

Cuypers, S.E. & Martin, C. (eds) (2009). *Reading R.S. Peters Today: Analysis, Ethics and the Aims of Education.* London: Wiley-Blackwell [Journal of Philosophy of Education, 43, Supplement 1, October 2009].

Eaton, J. (2014). Gentrifying the dharma: How the 1 percent is hijacking mindfulness. *Salon*, 5/3/14.

Ergas, O. & Todd, S. (eds) (2016). *Philosophy East/West: Exploring Intersections between Educational and Contemplative Practices.* Oxford: Wiley-Blackwell.

Farrarons, E. (2015). *The Mindfulness Colouring Book.* London: Boxtree.

Foster, D. (2016). Kind of Blue; *The Guardian Weekend*, 23/1/16, pp.46-9.

Garfinkel, S. (2006). *Buddha or Bust.* New York, NY: Three Rivers Press.

Gerhardt, S. (2010). *The Selfish* Society. London: Simon & Schuster.

Gowans, C.W. (2015). *Buddhist Moral Philosophy.* London: Routledge.

Grossman, P. (2011). Defining mindfulness by how poorly I think I pay attention during everyday awareness and other intractable problems for psychology's (re)invention of mindfulness: Comment on Brown et al. (2011). *Psychological Assessment, 23,* 1034 –1040.

Grossman, P. & Van Dam, T. (2011). Mindfulness, by any other name...Trials and Tribulations of *Sati* in Western Psychology and Science; *Contemporary Buddhism*, 12.1, 219-239.

Gunaratana, B.H. (2002). *Mindfulness in Plain English*. Boston: Wisdom Publications.

Hanh, Thich Nhat (1999). *The Heart of the Buddha's Teaching*. New York: Broadway Books.

Hartley, D. (1995). The McDonaldization of Higher Education: Food for Thought? *Oxford Review of Education*, 21(4), 409-423.

Harvey, D. (2014). *Seventeen Contradictions and the End of Capitalism*. London, Profile Books.

Harvey, P. (2000). *An Introduction to Buddhist Ethics: Its Teachings, History and Practices*. Cambridge: Cambridge University Press.

Hazeley, J.A. & Morris, J.P. (2016). *The Ladybird Book of Mindfulness*. Loughborough: Ladybird Books Ltd.

Hirst, P.H. & Peters, R.S. (1970). *The Logic of Education*. London: Routledge & Kegan Paul.

Hirst, P.H. (1974). *Knowledge and the Curriculum*. London: Routledge & Kegan Paul.

Hyland, T. (1994). *Competence, Education and NVQs: Dissenting Perspectives*. London: Cassell.

Hyland, T. (1999). *Vocational Studies, Lifelong Learning and Social Values*. Aldershot: Ashgate.

Hyland, T. (2003). Socrate est-il un andragogue ou un pedagogue?; in Jean Ferrari, et al. (eds): *Socrate Pour Tous*. (Paris: Librairie Philosophique J. Vrin) 73-92.

Hyland, T. (2011) *Mindfulness and Learning: Celebrating the Affective Dimension of Education*. Dordrecht: The Netherlands, Springer Press.

Hyland, T. (2014). Competence; in Phillips, D.C. (ed)(2014): *Encyclopedia of Educational Theory and Philosophy* (London, Sage) Vol.1, 166-167.

Hyland, T. (2015a). On the Contemporary Applications of Mindfulness: Some Implications for Education; *Journal of Philosophy of Education*, 49(2),170-186.

Hyland, T. (2015b). McMindfulness in the Workplace: Vocational Learning and the Commodification of the Present Moment; *Journal of Vocational Education and Training*, 67 (2), 219–234.

Hyland, T. (2016). Review of Mindful Nation UK; *Journal of Vocational Education and Training*, 68 (1), pp.133-136.

James, O. (2008). *The Selfish Capitalist*. London: Vermilion.

Judt, T. (2010). *Ill Fares the Land* London: Allen Lane.

Kabat-Zinn, J. (1990). *Full Catastrophe Living* London: Piatkus.

Kabat-Zinn, J. (2005). *Coming to Our Senses*. London: Piatkus.

Kabat-Zinn, J. (2015). Mindfulness has huge health potential – but McMindfulness is no panacea; *The Guardian*, 20.10.15; http://www. theguardian.com/commentisfree/2015/oct/20/mindfulness-mental-health-potential-benefits-uk, accessed 3.11.15.

Kashdan, T. & Biswas-Diener, R. (2014). *The Upside of Your Dark Side*. New York: Hudson Street Press.

Keown, D. (2005). *Buddhist Ethics*. Oxford: Oxford University Press.

Klein, N. (2007). *The Shock Doctrine* London: Penguin Books.

Kraft, K. (2000). New Voices in Engaged Buddhism. *Journal of Buddhist Ethics*, 7, 13-27.

Langer, E. (2003). A Mindful Education. *Educational Psychologist*, 28.1, pp.43–50.

Lewin, D. (2015). Heidegger East and West: Philosophy as Educative Contemplation; *Journal of Philosophy of Education*, 49(2), pp.221-239.

MacPherson, C.B. (1962). *The Political Theory of Possessive Individualism*. Oxford: Oxford University Press.

MAPPG (2015). Mindful *Nation UK – Report of the Mindfulness All-Party Parliamentary Group*. www.themindfulnessinitiative.org.uk accessed 6/11/15.

MBI-TAC (2012). The *Bangor, Exeter and Oxford Mindfulness-Based Interventions Teaching Assessment Criteria*. http:// mindfulness steachersuk.org.uk/pdf/MBI-TACJune2012.pdf, accessed 11/12/15.

McCown, D., Reibel, D. & Micozzi, M.S. (2011). *Teaching Mindfulness: A Practical Guide for Clinicians and Educators*. Dordrecht: Springer.

McLellan, D. (1977). *Karl Marx: Selected Writings.* Oxford: Oxford University Press.

Mindfulness Resource (2015). *Steve Jobs.* Arizona State University. http://www.mindfulnessresource.org/category/steve-jobs/accessed 19/11/15.

Monbiot, G. (2016). *How Did We Get Into This Mess? Politics, Equality and Nature.* London: Verso (Kindle Edition).

Murris, K. (1994). Not Now, Socrates...; *Cogito*, 8(1), 80-86.

Ng, E. & Purser, R. (2016). Mindfulness and Self-Care; Why should I care? *Patheos*, 4.4.16. http://www.patheos.com/blogs/americanbuddhist/2016/04/mindfulness-and-self-care-why-should-i-care.html, accessed 13.4.16.

Nowogrodzki, A. (2016). Power of positive thinking skews mindfulness studies; *Nature*, 21/4/16.

O'Donnell, A. (2015). Contemplative Pedagogy and Mindfulness: Developing Creative Attention in an Age of Distraction; *Journal of Philosophy of Education*, 49(2), pp.187-202.

Olendzki, A. (2010). *Unlimiting Mind.* Boston: Wisdom Publications.

Palmer, P.J. (1998). *The Courage to Teach.* San Francisco: Jossey-Bass Inc.

Peters, R.S. (1966). *Ethics and Education.* London: Allen & Unwin.

Peters, R.S. (1973). Aims of Education – A Conceptual Inquiry. In Peters, R.S. (Ed)(1973). *The Philosophy of Education.* (pp.11-57) Oxford: Oxford University Press.

Piketty, T. (2013). *Capital in the Twenty-First Century.* Cambridge, MA: Harvard University Press.

Purser, R. & Loy, D. (2013). Beyond McMindfulness; *Huffington Post*, 1/7/13, http://www.huffingtonpost.com/ron-purser/beyond-mc mindful ness_b_3519289.html; accessed 14/7/15.

Purser, R. (2014a) The Militarization of Mindfulness; *Inquiring Mind*, Spring; www.inquiringmind.com; accessed 7/12/15.

Purser, R. (2014b) The myth of the present moment, *Mindfulness*, 5 (4). doi:10.1007/s12671-014-0333-z).

Purser, R. & Ng, E. (2015). Corporate Mindfulness is Bullsh*t: Zen or No Zen, You're Working Harder and Being Paid Less. *Salon*, 25/9/15.

Ritzer, G. (2000). *The McDonaldization of Society: New Century Edition*. Thousand Oaks, CA: Pine Forge Press.

Salzberg, S. & Goldstein, J. (2001). *Insight Meditation*. Boulder, Colorado: Sounds True.

Schoeberlein, D. & Sheth, S. (2009) *Mindful Teaching and Teaching Mindfulness*. Boston: Wisdom Publications.

Schofield, H. (1972). *The Philosophy of Education - An Introduction*. London: Allen & Unwin.

Schopenhauer, A. (1970 edn). *Essays and Aphorisms*. Harmondsworth: Penguin Classics.

Seabrook, J. (2015). *Pauperland: Poverty and the Poor in Britain*. London: Hurst & Co.

Seldon, A. (2009). *Trust: How we lost it and how to get it back* London: Biteback Publishing.

Siegel, D.J. (2010). *Mindsight*. Oxford: Oneworld Publications.

Simmer-Brown, J. (2002). *The Crisis of Consumerism*; in Badiner, A. (ed) (2002);pp.3-8.

Stiglitz, J.E. (2012). *The Price of Inequality*. London: Penguin Books.

Stone, M. (2014). Abusing the Buddha: How the U.S. Army and Google co-opt mindfulness. *Salon*, 17.3.14.

Weare, K. (2012). *Evidence for the Impact of Mindfulness on Children and Young People* (.b Mindfulness in Schools Project/Exeter University Mood Disorders Centre).

Weber, M. (1930/2014). *The Protestant Ethic and the Spirit of Capitalism*. Bowdon: Stellar Books.

Whitehead, A.N. (1962 edn). *The Aims of Education* London: Ernest Benn.

Wilkinson, R. & Pickett, K. (2010). *The Spirit Level: Why Equality is Better for Everyone* London: Penguin.

Williams, M., Teasdale, J., Segal, Z. & Kabat-Zinn, J. (2007). *The Mindful Way through Depression*. London, The Guilford Press.

Williams, M. & Penman, D. (2011). *Mindfulness: An Eight-Week Plan for Finding Peace in a Frantic World*. New York: Rodale.

Williams, J.M.G. & Kabat-Zinn, J. (eds) (2013). *Mindfulness: Diverse Perspectives on its Meaning, Origins and Applications.* Abingdon, Routledge.

Zenner, C, Hermleben-Kurz, S. & Walach, H. (2014) Mindfulness-based interventions in schools—a systematic review and meta-analysis,. *Frontiers in Psychology*, 5, pp.1-20.

Zizek, S. (2001). From Western Marxism to Western Buddhism, *Cabinet*, Issue 2, http://www.cabinetmagazine.org/issues/2/western.php.

In: Meditation
Editor: Lucia Brewer

ISBN: 978-1-53613-223-6
© 2018 Nova Science Publishers, Inc.

Chapter 3

THE BUSINESS OF MEDITATION AND THE EXPECTATION OF "RESULTS": KUNDALINI RISING IN A CULTURE OF INSTANT GRATIFICATION

Melanie Saraswati Takahashi, PhD
Integral Yoga Institute, San Francisco, CA, US

ABSTRACT

This article examines the elusive primordial energy that the ancient yogis referred to as Kundalini. This energy when aroused, is said to ascend through each of the seven chakras from the base of the spine to the crown of the head. When the Kundalini reaches the crown chakra, cosmic consciousness, a restructuring of the psyche, and paranormal abilities have been reported. Many regard Kundalini as the next stage in the evolution of human consciousness and a necessary constituent in reaching one's highest potential. Kundalini is most often wakened from meditation and the yoga teachings pertaining to it, were traditionally veiled in secrecy, only being revealed orally from guru to discipline. In 1969, many of these techniques were revealed by Yogi Bhajan who introduced, developed, and popularized Kundalini yoga in the West. If an aspirant is mentally and physically unprepared for the awakening, the Kundalini encounters blocks during its ascension, as expressed by physical and emotional disturbances that psychologists refer to as a "spiritual emergency." It is argued that due to the unsupervised and unstructured appropriation of Eastern modalities in a Western context, the growing curiosity of Eastern expressions of spirituality, the commodification of these practices that promise extraordinary results, and a distracted technologically savvy population that expects them, spontaneous Kundalini awakenings are on the rise. Moreover, with Kundalini becoming the holy grail of New Age spirituality, many seekers are purposefully attempting to waken this energy unmediated by a teacher. Using a multidisciplinary approach and informed by my own personal experience with Kundalini, this paper will explore these issues in depth. How Kundalini is typically expressed and safely managed, and the importance among health care professionals to recognize the fine line between transcendence and spiritual emergency will also be reviewed.

Keywords: altered states of consciousness, chakras, cultural appropriation, energy, energy body, koshas, Kundalini, Kundalini yoga, life force energy, meditation, nadis, New Age spirituality, paranormal, Patanjali, phenomenology, prana, pranayama, psychic, sadhana, samadhi, serpent fire, Shakti, shaktipat, siddhis, spiritual emergency, spiritual tourism, transcendent, transpersonal, transpersonal psychology, transpersonal anthropology, yoga sutras

INTRODUCTION

This mechanism, known as Kundalini is the real cause of all genuine spiritual and psychic phenomena, the biological bases of evolution and development of personality, the secret origin of all esoteric and occult doctrines, the master key to the unsolved mystery of creation, the inexhaustible source of philosophy, art, and science, and the fountainhead of all religious faiths, past, present and future. (Gopi Krishna 1993:257)

Eastern practices of contemplation such as yoga, *pranayama*, meditation, Qigong, and Tai Chi, are no longer viewed as exotic esoteric

The Business of Meditation and the Expectation of "Results"   81

systems restricted to monks, yogis and wandering sadhus.[1] In the West, facilitated by the immediacy of digital technology, the resurgence of these techniques has propelled meditation and mindfulness into mainstream consciousness, and the subsequent rise of a billion-dollar industry. Travelling to far off lands in search of a Guru to learn and oversee these techniques can now be replaced by the click of a button in the comforts of home. Meditation websites, YouTube videos, and smartphone apps are exhaustive and readily available to the current technologically savvy generation. In 2015 there were over 1000 apps dedicated to meditation and mindfulness alone, with the top grossing app "Headspace" earning $30 million (Wieczner 2016). If not at home, yoga and meditation can also be accessed in the workplace as employers are increasingly realizing the benefits of meditation in improving office dynamics and work productivity. A mindfulness training program launched by Google "Search Inside Yourself Leadership Institute," has in one year, more than doubled its revenue in providing two-day meditation workshops to Fortune 500 companies and charging up to $35,000 for 50 participants (ibid).

Whether one likes it or not, meditation has gone corporate and like any other business, these programs are offering a service promising remarkable results, and those who participate are expecting to receive them. This anticipation of an experience, result, or goal, has its own built-in demise as it effectively undermines the core teachings of non-attachment and focusing one's awareness on the present moment. This approach also contradicts the fundamental spiritual teaching that we can never find happiness when we continue to search for it from sources outside of ourselves. To make meditation more palatable and less "woo-woo" to the Western mind, the spiritual context in which meditative traditions are drawn from, are often removed, and meditation gets stripped down to a technique. One of the consequences of culturally appropriating spiritual practices from their lineage traditions, is the removal of a supervised

---

[1] Sadhus are commonly found in India and Nepal. They dedicate their lives to spiritual growth adopting ascetic practices and renounce all worldly goods. Wandering from place to place sadhus rely on the generosity of others and food provided by temples for their daily survival.

checks and balances system by a community of support often referred to as "sangha." The workshop approach also seems to suggest that the benefits of meditation can be realized in a short amount of time and when this fails to happen, individuals will often move on to the next thing and consequently, the quest for enlightenment becomes a spiritual smorgasbord.

We don't usually associate meditation as being a catalyst for inducing anxiety, depression and illness since it is expected to reduce and prevent those afflictions and indeed most meditation practitioners achieve positive results. However, one largely unknown and unspoken casualty of this trend, is a growing number of individuals who have spontaneously encountered what is referred to as a Kundalini awakening.[2] Without proper preparation and guidance, physical and emotional disturbances can often ensue leaving seekers to deal with this powerful process on their own. Without the proper resources, these awakened individuals can be misdiagnosed with a variety of physical conditions, as well as mental illness diagnoses such as schizophrenia and bipolar disorder. Even more alarming, with the alluring promise of tapping into one's psychic abilities through Kundalini rising, there are numerous books and internet resources that offer step by step guides on how to awaken this powerful energy.

As a transpersonal anthropologist, experienced meditator, and certified yoga instructor, what I have come to respect most through my years of teaching and studying, is the extraordinarily transformative power of these practices. The techniques engage the subconscious, and direct the movement of subtle albeit potent energy systems in the body and should therefore be approached with caution, care, and respect. I can say this with confidence as I have personally experienced the spontaneous awakening of Kundalini energy and like many others was left misdiagnosed and lacking in resources to help interpret and integrate my experiences. Drawing from the fields of psychology, anthropology, the Hindu scriptures, as well as my own personal experience, this paper will examine this elusive energy referred to as Kundalini. How this energy is commonly expressed,

---

[2] Kundalini is identified as a Goddess in the Hindu scriptures, and will thus be capitalized.

The Business of Meditation and the Expectation of "Results" 83

activated and managed will be explored as well as the transformative potentials that can arise when managed safely. Finally, I will survey the complications that often accompany spontaneous awakenings, why they appear to be on the rise in the West, why Kundalini is so sought after, and what precautions should be followed to ensure one's safety.

WHAT IS KUNDALINI?

Kundalini comes from the Sanskrit word *kund* which means "to burn." *Kunda* means bowl, and *kundala* means "coiled up." Kundalini refers to a divine-feminine cosmic energy that lies dormant at the base of the spine as a serpent coiled three and a half times.[3] The three coils represent the states of consciousness-waking, sleeping, and dreaming- and the last half symbolizes cosmic consciousness through union with the divine. The three coils can also signify the past, present, and future with the remaining last half coil being the transcendence of time or transcendental consciousness. The root meaning of the Sanskrit words offers a clue as to the way in which Kundalini unfolds: the feminine creative force is said to lay dormant at the base of the spine in a bowl or womb, and when ignited, this forceful energy is unleashed up the spine (Arundale 1938:7). Just like a snake, this energetic fire can prove dangerous if the practitioner is unprepared, however if harnessed properly, it can be a vehicle for transformation and an evolution in consciousness.

Thus far, scientists have not been able to provide physical evidence for Kundalini's existence because its path travels in the subtle energy body through nerve channels referred to as *nadis*. [4] There are approximately 72,000 *nadis* in the human body and to grasp the workings of Kundalini, one needs to understand the yogic interpretation of the body. In yoga

---

[3] Other references to Kundalini include: Shakti, the Mother, the Goddess, Serpent Power, and the face of God.

[4] In Traditional Chinese Medicine, *nadis* are referred to as meridians.

philosophy tracing back to the early Upanishads[5], the human organism is viewed as multi-dimensional, comprised of five layers or sheaths known as *koshas*. The *koshas*-meaning illusion-begin with the outermost layer of the physical body, and work inward with each subsequent sheath being increasingly subtle compared to the previous. The physical body, the *annamaya kosha* deals with the physical structure of the body such as the tissues, organs, bones, connective tissue, muscles and skin. It also pertains to physical activities such as eating and sleeping. The second sheath is the *pranamaya kosha* and this refers to the energy body and the movement of *prana* or life-force energy which circulates the *nadis* via the body. From this paradigm, the energetic body influences our physiology as illness is believed to be caused from energetic blocks and imbalances in this system. *Prana* also has its influences on the mind; when the *prana* is regulated and controlled through breathing practices (*pranayama)* the mind becomes steady and calm. This is one of the reasons why in the yogic tradition, *pranayama* is an integral part of the preparation for meditation. The third sheath *manomaya kosha*, represents the mind, the ego, and the five senses. This layer allows us to perceive and make decisions informed by the outer world around us. Through this practice of yoga, *pranayama* and meditation, the chatter of the mind begins to dissipate and we become more in touch with our true nature or Self. The next layer, *Vijnanamaya kosha,* denotes the intellect or wisdom part of ourselves where a deeper awareness or inner knowing resides. Finally, the innermost layer the *anandamaya kosha,* is the foundation of our existence and refers to the bliss body where there are no longer feelings of separateness as subject and object become our True Self. From this perspective, the layers are illusions (*maya)* that veil our true nature, and must therefore be cultivated through contemplative and purification practices to arrive at the source.

When Kundalini is awakened, it travels up the spine through the central nerve channel *shushumna*, through each of the seven chakras. The goal is for the Kundalini to ascend to the crown chakra where she unites

---

[5] The Upanishads are ancient Sanskrit texts that comprise the key philosophical tenets of Hinduism. They are also referred to as Vedanta, meaning the final chapters of the Veda.

The Business of Meditation and the Expectation of "Results"   85

with the divine masculine Shiva, or Cosmic Consciousness. Along-side the *shushumna* channel, are the other two main *nadis,* the *ida* (feminine current) and the *pingala* (the male current). These outer channels intersect along the spine at the location of the seven chakras. For the Kundalini to rise successfully to the crown chakra, the chakras need to be free of blocks before it can traverse and continue its upward ascent. It is when the Kundalini gets blocked that many of the negative physical and emotional symptoms present themselves. The enigmatic psychic abilities that often accompany an awakening can also call one's mental health into question deterring many from seeking help. Nevertheless, Kundalini is an essential ingredient in experiencing God or Cosmic Consciousness: Sivananda describes it as "an electric fiery occult power, the great pristine force which underlies all organic and inorganic material" (Sivananda 1994: nd). Spiritual masters such as Ramakrishna and Swami Muktananda contend that the Kundalini must be roused to realize our true Self (Cousens 2005:6).

IGNITING AND MANAGING THE SERPENT FIRE

Numerous religious traditions acknowledge a divine energy that resides inside the human organism; In Japan, it is referred to as "*Ki,*" in China "*Chi,*" in Catholicism the "*Holy Spirit,*" in Tibetan Buddhism "*Dumo fire,*" and among the Kung bushmen this energy is referred to as "*n/um.*" There are also indications of Kundalini experiences being reported cross-culturally as evinced in the esoteric writings of the Assyrian, Egyptian, Taoist, Tibetan, Judaic, Native American, Christian mysticism, and African cultures to name a few (Greenwell :9). The widespread appearance of the serpent as a symbol of healing and transformation also alludes to some level of cognizance of this energy cross-culturally. In Indian mythology, Lord Vishnu rests on a thousand-headed snake where he sends out the first vibration from which the entire universe evolved. The ancient alchemists used the serpent to represent the process of psychic transformation, and in ancient Crete, snakes were worshipped as protectors of birth and regeneration. Although the serpent is associated with sin in the Judeo-Christian tradition, the Gnostics believed that the serpent in the Garden of Eden was endeavoring to free Adam and Eve from servitude to a limited external God and instead give them knowledge and access to the internal absolute (Svoboda 1993:83). Even the caduceus symbol used in modern medicine closely resembles the symbolic pathway of Kundalini; the staff can be interpreted as the central channel and the intersecting snakes on the staff are analogous to the *ida* and *pingala*. From a scientific perspective, the double helix of DNA mirrors the caduceus and the passage of Kundalini, suggesting the archetypal nature of this symbol and what it manifests. Here, the creation of the universe is echoed in the body as the same force igniting the cosmos but manifested at the microcosmic level (Mookerjee 1984:115).

While the recognition of Kundalini is not unique to yoga, no other tradition has approached Kundalini in such a systematic way. For roughly 3000 years, Kundalini practices were shrouded in secrecy until 1969 when Yogi Bhajan openly revealed these practices and introduced Kundalini yoga to the West (Shannahof-Khalsa 2012:1). [6] Historically it was a nomadic invasion of India that pushed these techniques underground; recognizing its potency and power, Kundalini practices were forbidden; the oppressors were cognizant of this energy's potential to empower individuals making them more difficult to control (ibid:). Prior to 1969, Kundalini remained underground and was taught and supervised by Gurus to a select few dedicated disciples.

The concealment of Kundalini techniques and the nature upon which they were historically transmitted, implies that there are certain established prerequisites and procedures necessary to safely initiate and guide this energy. In what is considered the authoritative text on classical yoga, *The Yoga Sutras* by Patanjali[7], Patanjali divides the text into four books with each book containing short aphorisms that are meant to prepare and guide

---

[6] The distinction should be noted between general Kundalini Yoga, versus the form practiced in the West. The latter is referred to as "Kundalini Yoga as taught by Yogi Bhajan."

[7] Dating back to the 2nd century BCE, the identity of Patanjali is uncertain and there are questions regarding whether the authorship was by one or several individuals.

The Business of Meditation and the Expectation of "Results"   87

an individual to experience "yoga," meaning union with the true Self. In Book I sutra 2, Patanjali defines yoga as "the restraint of the modifications of the mind-stuff is yoga." This sutra is the heart of R'aja Yoga,[8] and the foundation of the entire work. This sutra suggests that it is through the practice of quieting the mind that union with the divine can occur and one can thus abide in their true nature. The yoga sutras offer a methodical guide on how to restrain the mind to attain *samadhi,* or union with the divine. Patanjali introduces the eight limbs of yoga wherein Hatha (the physical postures) is the third of the eight limbs.[9] All modern forms of yoga-Ashtanga, Bikhram, Hatha, Kundalini, Vinyasa, and Yin for example- all fall under the umbrella Hatha. The postures that we now associate with yoga emerged eight centuries later; Patanjali's meaning of *asana* (steady and comfortable pose) thus referred to a sitting posture that enabled long periods of meditation. He therefore spends little time on Hatha and instead focuses his attention on the process of withdrawing the senses and turning awareness inward as outlined by the last three limbs: concentration, meditation and *samadhi.* Ironically, despite *pranayama* being the fundamental element of the energetic body and fourth limb, specific references to Kundalini are never mentioned in the work. However, Kundalini and *samadhi* are closely linked as evinced in the words of Sivananda: "No samadhi is possible without awakening the Kundalini" (1974:nd). While references to Kundalini are omitted from the yoga sutras, it is alluded to in Book III in the discussion of the *siddhis.* Patanjali outlines sixty-four minor *siddhis* and eight major ones. The *siddhis* are the supernatural and psychic accomplishments that result from a dedicated meditation practice.[10] These accomplishments are the same

---

[8] Also referred to as the "royal path," Raja yoga is the umbrella term for yoga philosophy. The first and most comprehensive text on Raja yoga is the Yoga Sutras of Patanjali.

[9] The eight limbs of Yoga are: (i) *Yamas* (rules of moral conduct or restraints), (ii) *Niyamas* (personal observances, iii) *Asana* (steady comfortable pose), (iv) *Pranayama* (breathing practices), (v) *Pratyahara* (withdrawal of the senses), (vi) *Dharana* (concentration), (vii) *Dhyana* (meditation), (viii) *Samadhi* (union with the divine).

[10] Buddhism also recognizes the siddhis resulting from meditation and the Buddha was known to have mastered them. This is evident in his name "Siddhartha Gautama" which means "he whose aim is to be accomplished."

psychic gifts that are associated with awakened Kundalini and hence like *samadhi* also work in concert.

In sutra 1.12 Patanjali asserts that mental modifications can be restrained through practice and non-attachment. From this approach, practice has a therapeutic value, and non-attachment a preventative one with both being necessary for success in Yoga (Carrera 2006:35). Patanjali says "Practice becomes firmly grounded when well attended to for a long time, without break and in all earnestness" (1.14). *Sadhana* comes from the Sanskrit word *sadhu* which means "to strive" and refers to a disciplined daily spiritual practice which includes diet, hatha yoga, *pranayama*, and meditation. A yogic diet[11] rids the body of toxins and a Hatha practice purifies the body but also facilitates longer periods of meditation since the body can sit more comfortably. Among the Western world, the third limb Hatha, has been embraced the most enthusiastically with a focus on fitness and flexibility. The association with fitness is a common misperception as somewhere along the way, it was overlooked that *asana's* purpose is to calm the mind and ease the body in preparation for meditation and the inward experience of union with the true Self. *Pranayama* calms the mind and strengthens the power of meditation by generating an intense energy in an enclosed space. The energy that is created awakens the Kundalini from its sleep; it is for this reason, that *pranayama* is given a heavy emphasis in the ancient texts (Mookerjee 1982:19). Therefore, *sadhana* is more than just a practice, but it is also a commitment to a disciplined way of life. Swami Satyananda argues: "The awakening, the rising and the union are all brought about through sadhana" (1967:109). According to Sivananda, the practice of daily *sadhana* should be supervised by a Guru and prescribed for that individual just like a doctor prescribes a treatment plan for a patient (1994:nd).

In the Guru/disciple relationship, there are no shortcuts or bypasses to fast forward this process. The teachings are passed down orally with the

---

[11] Traditionally a yogic diet is vegan with foods considered to be high in *prana*. It also includes refraining from anything that can disrupt the inward focus of meditation such as: alcohol, onions, and garlic.

Guru discerning when the disciple is ready to receive them. A typical *sadhana* suggested by Swami Satyananda reifies this point: "to begin with, five hours of *sadhana* is enough, though later on you will have to increase the time" (1967:11). Aspirants are also held accountable for their *sadhana* as they will often be expected to record and report on their daily practice to their Guru on a regular basis. A disciplined *sadhana* is intended to prepare the disciple by purifying the mind and body so that when the Kundalini does begin to stir, it can make its ascent to the crown chakra and avoid any major blocks. A Guru's power can also be transmitted to a disciple through exposure to *shaktipat*; this refers to the transmission of the Guru's *Shakti* (or energy) to the seeker. This *shaktipat* does not guarantee immediate activation as the Kundalini usually lies dormant for several years or lifetimes. In some instances, a *shaktipat* can ignite one's energy to rise immediately. A responsible Guru will only perform a *shaktipat* on someone who is ready to have their Kundalini stirred.

In addition to *sadhana*, as mentioned earlier, non-attachment is the second aspect of mastering the mind as outlined by Patanjali; this occurs when the mind shifts its core motivations from selfish to selfless, and the contentment of inner peace replaces sense-seeking pleasures (Carrera 2006:43). Non-attachment is the capacity to keep selfish motives away from actions, relationships, and learning; practice that lacks non-attachment can result in an overly inflated ego "that relishes using power to satisfy self-interest regardless of consequences" (Carrera 2006 :35). In Book III of the yoga sutras, the supernatural and psychic accomplishments that are said to result from a dedicated meditation practice are examined.[12] This can include clairvoyance, telepathy, precognition, psychokinesis, invisibility, and levitation, to name a few. This is where many spiritual seekers get trapped as they can easily get side tracked with the attachment and pursuit of the *siddhis* as the goal. The *siddhis* are only meant to be byproducts of meditation rather than something to strive for. Sivananda

---

[12] Buddhism also recognizes the siddhis resulting from meditation and the Buddha was known to have mastered them. This is evident in his name "Siddhartha Gautama" which means "he whose aim is to be accomplished."

goes as far to say that "Siddhis are a great hindrance to spiritual progress, and so long as one is within the realm of Siddhis and does not try to rise above it and march onwards, there is not the least hope of God-realization" (1965:nd). It is the ego that thirsts for the *siddhis* and this defeats the purpose of the practice as the "I," only becomes bigger by identifying with the ego (Satchidananda 1978:199). This only reinforces a separate sense of self and the aspirant fails to realize that fulfillment of the Kundalini process is the recognition that there is no "I" (Greenwell 2009:33). It is easy to massage the ego if one begins to see themselves and be treated by others as "extraordinary." If it isn't fame that one is after, the other is usually fortune; if one could forecast future events or read the minds of others, how tempting it would be to use this power for personal gain. The seeker can easily become spiritually arrogant and even corrupt. In Hindu mythology, there are many demons who were once accomplished yogis who fell from grace through attachment and abuse of the *siddhis* (Carrera 2006: 35). There's the added problem that even if an individual experiences a *siddhi* as a natural outcome of meditation, they can easily become attached to that experience and focus on recreating it which also becomes a diversion. Any attempt to repeat an inner experience is futile since reality never repeats itself in moment to moment happenings (Selby 2009:78). Even Patanjali cautions the seeker of these pitfalls in Book III sutra 51: "By non-attachment even to that [all these siddhis], the seed of bondage is destroyed and thus follows *Kaivalya* (Independence)." To attain true liberation, one must even let go of the desire for the *siddhis* since they are products of the mind and are therefore binding. As stated by Gopi Krishna "The object to be realized is the experience of the Self, beyond all price, beyond all thought and beyond everything the earth can offer" (1972 :90).

The role of a spiritual master is twofold: preparing the disciple's awakening, and being available afterwards (Krishna 1972:101). Kundalini supervision is necessary to help the disciple deal with any subsequent blocks encountered upon its assent, as well as helping the aspirant interpret and integrate the process. Further elaborated in the next section, the physical and psychological effects of awakening can be overwhelming,

The Business of Meditation and the Expectation of "Results"   91

harmful, and in some cases, even fatal. Even Gurus have been known to experience challenges upon wakening Kundalini and this further underscores the importance of being guided by an experienced teacher as well as being mentally stable enough to handle it.[13] Despite the secrets of Kundalini being divulged by Yogi Bhajan, most Hatha traditions avoid in depth discussions of Kundalini, let alone how to activate it. Most Raja yoga teacher trainings avoid books III and IV of the yoga sutras which deal with the more esoteric aspects of yoga like the *siddhis*. There seems to be an unspoken ethical awareness and responsibility among yoga teachers toward the delicate nature of the Kundalini process and the importance of wanting to avoid igniting this energy in someone who isn't ready. Similarly, the commentaries in Patanjali's yoga sutras become sparse in the latter two books. Patanjali's omission of Kundalini from the yoga sutras may have been quite intentional on his part; he is trying to prevent the aforementioned pitfalls that only serve as obstacles, and instead of chasing *shakti*, he prescribes going inward and cleaning the mind through the observance of the eight limbs. He is suggesting that the work to be done is a gradual restructuring of the subconscious through stillness where the mind shifts from externalization to internalization.

KUNDALINI AWAKENINGS IN THE WEST

While the yogic tradition delineates a methodical path to follow, there are numerous ways to ignite Kundalini, many of which the West has embraced. A regular meditation practice is the most common trigger for a Kundalini awakening, but it has also been known to stir spontaneously from breath work, psychedelic drugs, an impassioned love of God, Near Death Experiences (NDE's), intense sexual encounters, trauma and childbirth. In the West, reports of spontaneous awakenings are on the rise and this can be attributed to the accessibility of numerous spiritual, and

---

[13] See Krishnamurti, Muktananda, Motoyama and Gopi Krishna who have written about their experiences.

therapeutic healing modalities that deal with the subtle body. Spiritual teachers, therapists, body workers, and homeopaths often integrate meditation, yoga, visualization, sound healing and intense breath work as part of their approach (Greenwell 2002:6). There also exists an underground shamanic community of healers who administer psychedelic drugs such as ayahuasca, MDMA, psilocybin, salvia divinorum, LSD and peyote as part of the therapeutic process.[14]

The rise of spontaneous awakenings may also reflect an increased interest in spirituality as a way of coping with the feelings of alienation and disillusionment that many experience in the West (ibid). In a study that examined Millennial use of social media, it was found that its addictive nature can compromise the ability to sustain relationships (Basset et al. 2016). Additionally, anxiety and depression were correlated with increased engagement with social media, the primary symptoms being withdrawal from activities and social encounters, feelings of isolation, moodiness, stress caused from inconsequential matters, and an addictive personality (ibid). The authors conclude that the relationship Millennials have with social media is not always a healthy one. On average Millennials spend three plus hours/day on this medium, and the preoccupation with "likes," "follows," and "shares" further isolate the user (ibid). In many instances, the quest for a spiritual practice may be fueled by a search for connectedness and community.

Impatience and a lack of commitment to one practice is another factor behind the surge of spontaneous awakenings in the West. Our cultural work ethic is not conducive to the 5 hours of *sadhana* as suggested by Swami Satyananda; in my experience as a yoga instructor, the majority of students find it a stretch to commit to even one hour of regular practice. To turn the cell phone off, sit still, and shift one's awareness to the internal landscape, is a challenge particularly with the younger generations who operate in a gadget driven culture where bombardment of the senses and

---

[14] Although this method was not recommended by Patanjali, the use of drugs is mentioned in Book IV sutra 1, as one of the ways of procuring the *siddhis*. The exact contents of these herbs are unknown; it is likely these elixors were made from the psychedelic class of drugs that would have been available in the Himalayas at that time.

The Business of Meditation and the Expectation of "Results"   93

multitasking has become the norm. It's not an accident that among the eight limbs of yoga, Hatha has been the most readily accepted, with the subtle practices most often being omitted from yoga classes. Not only do students have difficulty committing to one practice, but sticking with one style of yoga is rare. Yoga has adapted to this stimulus driven population by constantly adding new innovative features to the class such as recorded and live music, live DJ sets, mirrors, lighting systems and fancy props to prevent boredom. The recent "trends" of hot rooms, naked yoga, ganga[15], acro[16] and aeriel[17] yoga also provide novelty and similarly guide one's focus on an outward experience of the discipline.

The digital age has also created a culture of immediate gratification as digital technology and smartphones facilitate information and services to be accessed instantaneously. Companies like Amazon Prime offer same day delivery services such that books, magazines, movies, music and TV shows can be immediately downloaded online. One can order ride services with vehicles arriving in less than three minutes, take-out and groceries can be ordered and delivered quickly, and purchasing tickets and booking flights are executed with a quick click of a button. We have been effectively socialized to expect instant gratification and become quickly irritated when we are forced to wait. The same can be said for meditation and spirituality; there is an expectation of a "quick fix" and something to be gained. As stated by Gopi Krishna: "The discriminating power of a balanced intellect, considered indispensable by the ancient masters for the right choice of the teacher and the path adopted, has been replaced by what is the most powerful incentive in this age: the possibility of gain." (1972:74). With a multitude of paths, if the expected results are not achieved, the solution is to try something else rather than persevere. As Perrin explains, "The problem isn't that there are so many paths; the problem is the promiscuous nature of the people who follow them"

---

[15] This new trend popular in San Francisco combines smoking cannabis with yoga poses

[16] Acro is a form of trust based partner yoga that blends acrobatics, Thai massage and yoga. The partner on the floor (called the base) supports the flier (partner in the air).

[17] This is a new form of yoga originating in New York that incorporates pilates, dance, and yoga with the use of a hammock that works as a kind of trapeze.

94 Melanie Saraswati Takahashi

(2009:50). Jumping from workshop to workshop, while unmediated by a teacher, there is no regulator for the mystical and psychic buttons being unknowingly pushed in the process of shopping around.

The business of spirituality is another factor in spontaneous awakenings. Traditionally teachings were passed down orally and were available for free. In today's current climate, there is an opportunity to make money and many are capitalizing by making "futile attempts to adapt the ancient teaching to the present highly artificial and competitive social order, often with disastrous consequences" (Krishna 1972:71). In a society that promotes the material wealth, meditation and yoga have become commodities where it's normal and expected for teachers to self-promote and build a following. For a price, some even claim to offer "shortcuts" to enlightenment with the common boon being a bypass of commitment with the promise of instant results from wakened Kundalini. This is evident in the following example in relation to *shaktipat*:

> Meditation in itself is a vast subject. One of the joys of Shaktipat is that you do not need to practice meditation for twenty years to achieve self-realisation and enlightenment. When you receive shaktipat and the kundalini awakens, meditation becomes a natural and effortless practice. You basically do not need to do anything. Only sit. This has to be the fastest and surest way to self-realization and to experience divinity. From your act of reading this page you are already getting the free ticket, to take you on the journey of your life.[18]

The common theme of these marketing strategies is the allure of skipping the in-depth methodical process for an immediate outcome. Rarely are there guidelines for initiate preparation or post-initiation follow-up. The authenticity of these teachers is questionable as it is common for the credentials of the "Guru" offering these services to be omitted; in some cases, the "Guru" even remains anonymous. One anonymous teacher offers *shaktipat* for $200 with additional online courses that can be purchased

---

[18] This quote is taken from a website where the author is unknown http://kundalini-shaktipat. com/kundalini_shaktipat.html.

The Business of Meditation and the Expectation of "Results" 95

later. Other websites are very detailed about the results of *shaktipat* but are vague around the cost. One such site requires the purchase of a membership as a prerequisite before obtaining a *shaktipat,* but like many others, fails to mention the price. An interested individual must send an email inquiry and in one such case, the membership fee was $1000 USD. Subsequent emails followed including one in which the Guru claimed that he coincidently "happened" to live in the same city as mine and on the same street, even though the original fee was quoted to me in Rupees! Furthermore, the methods of transmission enable these services to be rendered to a global market of consumers; claims are made that *shaktipat* does not need to be administered in person; these services can be delivered by phone, fax, email, regular mail, the internet and CD. One website sells a series of 3 CD's for $97 claiming "You can experience deep meditation & bliss in your own home simply by listening to a bliss-inducing Kundalini Shaktipat CD."[19] This is not to say that the experience of *shaktipat* is not real, but I would argue that it is very easy for this type of experience as a scam to be pulled off without any accountability. If you read the fine print, these websites usually have disclosures saying they are not responsible if the intended results are not procured, and similarly not accountable for any potential negative effects of the experience. Whereas most rituals have a preparation, initiation and reintegration phase, these are "one-trick ponies" where the aspirant is left to their own devices.

Another commonly used lure is to capitalize on our innate curiosity with the occult and gaining access to secret knowledge. A New York Times bestseller claims to offer an underground five-minute meditation technique that will yield the following results in 1-2 months: look younger, improved efficiency (a 4 hour task can be reduced to 30 minutes), financial gain, paranormal abilities, increased intelligence, and hyper-dimensional consciousness [to name a few] (Pepin 2012). The author openly acknowledges drawing from the "best" systems and integrating them into one secret technique. While promising what sounds like the holy grail of rewards, this technique tinkers with esoteric practices stripped from their

---

[19] http:\\www.bliss-music.com/kundalini_shaktipat.htm.

cultural context while negating the essential groundwork and precautions that are inherent to these traditions, including the need for a teacher. More often than not, this sets up one to fail as it encourages seekers to attach themselves to these rewards, expect them, and effectively effaces the splendor of the present moment by focusing on the result; this is not an oversight by the author as he argues "in the end, it's the results that matter" (2012:nd). Even if these rewards are tapped into through the arousal of Kundalini, if the mainstream culture fails to recognize subtle energy systems, the psychological and physical effects of this awakening can result in a spiritual emergency.

KUNDALINI AWAKENINGS AND SPIRITUAL EMERGENCY

In 1980, psychologists Stanislov and Christine Grof founded SEN (spiritual emergency network), an organization that connects individuals who have had difficulty processing a spiritual experience with knowledgeable professionals familiar with these states. The acronym was later changed to spiritual emergence network to acknowledge and identify the positive transformations that can arise during the crisis. In recognizing the rising interest in Eastern spiritual practices, there became a need for such a support network as an increasing number of individuals were reporting psycho-spiritual crises resulting from meditation and other forms of spiritual exploration. Kundalini awakenings are included in this category largely due to the work of Dr. Lee Sannella who was the first to bring attention to Kundalini-related spiritual emergencies. [20] In addition to founding the *Kundalini Clinic* in San Francisco, his book *The Kundalini Experience: Psychosis or Transcendence,* provides the most comprehensive clinical data on spontaneous awakenings through an examination of close to 1000 reported cases. Depending on the individual's

---

[20] Other forms of spiritual emergency include: shamanic journey, psychological renewal through activation of the central archetype, psychic opening, emergence of a karmic pattern, and possession states (Grof and Grof, 1993:139).

The Business of Meditation and the Expectation of "Results"   97

preparation, existing energetic blocks, and support systems in place, the Kundalini phenomenon and the way it unfolds is unique for everyone. Even without a set blueprint however, there are symptoms that have been repeatedly reported that Sannella groups into four categories: motor, sensory, interpretive and non-physiological phenomena (1987:93). Motor phenomena can involve: unusual sensations and movements with the eyes, shaking, muscle twitching and spasms, assuming yoga postures without any prior experience with yoga, spontaneous crying, laughing, screaming and whistling, unusual patterns of breathing, and paralysis during meditation (ibid:94-95). Sensory phenomena include: tickling, tingling, and vibratory sensations, feeling temperature extremes (particularly heat), inner lights and visions, visual distortions, inner sounds such as ear ringing, whistling, hissing, humming and chirping, eye pain, and headaches (ibid:95-98). Among the interpretive phenomena: unusual and extreme emotions, distortions in thought processing, detachment, dissociation and single seeing[21] (ibid 98:101). Non-physiological phenomena encompass: out-of-body-experiences (OBE's) and the varieties of psychic perceptions such as clairvoyance, clairaudience, clairsentience, precognition, and telepathy.

The recognition of spiritual emergency among transpersonal psychologists and psychiatrists, has had a positive impact clinically as the Diagnostic Statistical Manual was revised in DSM IV to differentiate meditative and trance related experiences as non-pathological under the classification "Spiritual or Religious Problem." This new classification was intended to rectify and prevent misdiagnoses that only cause more harm to the individual:

> … how many creative people in our culture are suffering because of diagnostic mistakes? I feel that the healing profession has a special obligation to make every effort to correct these mistakes. Recognition of the kundalini phenomenon as a nonpsychotic process is a part of this. It is tragic that potentially charismatic folks like shamans trance mediums, and

---

[21] This refers to the ability to see inwardly and outwardly at the same time.

God-intoxicated individuals… might actually find themselves in custodial care in our society. Possibly there are many now who, despite their eccentricities, should be released so they can enrich our lives (Sannella 1987:112-113).

Despite the changes to DSM IV, it is doubtful that there has been much of a clinical impact in this regard as the Kundalini phenomenon continues to remain largely unknown within the mental health community (Whitfield, 2009:132). Historically transpersonal crises were treated using a spiritual framework by cultural authorities well versed in these areas and drawing from a rich cultural map of phenomenology (ibid: 131-132). With the appropriation of Eastern spirituality in the West, shamans, Gurus, monks and the like, have been replaced by psychologists and psychiatrists, many of whom have little understanding or experience with contemplative practices (ibid). Moreover, unlike polyphasic cultures who socially sanction altered states of consciousness (ASC's) and whose worldviews are informed by these states, the West has operated with an ethnocentric bias towards monophasia (Laughlin et al. 1993:191). Monophasic cultures prioritize the waking phase as the appropriate state to garner knowledge from and discount those experiences informed by ASC's, as well as prohibit access to substances known to induce them. Since 90% of the world's cultures are considered polyphasic (Bourguignon 1973: 9-11), among transpersonal anthropologists who study these cultures, it is paramount that they have training in phenomenology. This does not assume that the anthropologist's experience will mirror that of their informants, but it does allow the researcher to ask relevant questions, and establish rapport that will facilitate a more in depth understanding of the experience. This is particularly relevant in the study of transpersonal phenomena as many of these encounters transcend rational thought thus making it difficult to articulate an experience in a cogent way without sounding mentally unstable. Someone who has had personal experience with these states will have a better tool kit to ask probing questions that will elicit responses, assess the situation, and avoid a misdiagnosis.

Due to this monophasic bias in our culture, Sannella notes that many cases go unreported as individuals fear that they will be labeled as unstable and find themselves hospitalized, institutionalized, or medicated (ibid 113). Perhaps this reflects the limitations of treating spiritual emergency from a psychological framework instead of a spiritual one. In a study that surveyed over 6000 reports of religious experiences from the RERC (Religious Experience Research Center) database, only 27 accounts specifically identified their experience as Kundalini related (Lockley nd: 6). The author suggests these findings are not a reflection of the rarity of the phenomenon, but more likely a failure for Kundalini experiences to be correctly identified from using terminologies other than Kundalini as a descriptor (ibid 12). The reported awakenings were also independent of cultural and religious background indicating that the context in which many cases occur are diverse and similarly lack the knowledge and support structure to recognize and deal with it appropriately (ibid: 5).

Looking back on my own Kundalini awakening, it was a gradual process that took two years to fully unfold. Despite being a transpersonal anthropologist, yoga and meditation instructor, Kundalini was the last thing on my mind and it wasn't until the symptoms subsided that I finally understood what was happening. I was fortunate to have a mentor and colleague adept in the field of consciousness studies, recognize the symptoms and suggest resources to help me interpret the experience. I was also blessed to be an instructor a yoga institute where I had access to the guidance of Swamis who offered spiritual council. Prior to that I had only heard anecdotal stories of yogis who activated their Kundalini from intense breath work, and given that Kundalini and spiritual emergency were never brought up in my teacher trainings, I was uncertain of its legitimacy. The phenomenon is so experientially based that until one encounters it for themselves, it is easy to regard it with skepticism. My early symptoms were so peculiar and seemingly random that I didn't have a reference point for comparison and when the episode dissipated, I quickly forgot about it. The first symptom was a ringing and pulsing sound in the ears. The ringing was so distracting at times that the only way I could escape it was to put headphones on and listen to music at a volume that would drown out the ringing. My eyes also felt strange as if they were constantly trying to focus and it felt like there was too much visual stimulation for my eyes to absorb everything at once. I could see clearly but the odd sensations made my stomach feel queasy.

Following that episode, I experienced no further physical symptoms until a few months later while on a trip to Europe. This trip proved challenging emotionally, physically and mentally; despite being on a fabulous vacation, I didn't feel like myself. Emotionally I felt vulnerable, reactive and in complete despair. Physically, my ears were ringing intermittently, my eyes had the same disconcerting sensation, but in addition to these symptoms, I felt nauseated most of the time, experienced hot flashes and my hands began to shake. Mentally I was forgetful having no recollection of what we did the day before and simple routine tasks like operating my phone or sending an email eluded me. One of the accommodations we stayed in had a grand piano and despite being a piano teacher for over twenty-five years, the keys felt unfamiliar and I was convinced that European pianos must have different sized keys than North America (which they do not). The occurrences were so bizarre that I assumed the cause was jet-lag and blamed myself for being a hypochondriac. That episode eventually subsided until the Christmas holidays when the symptoms became acute and I was completely debilitated for almost two months. My eyes continued to bother me and my vision became distorted. It was like wearing a new pair of glasses with the wrong prescription and these sensations resulted in a sensitivity to light and motion. I felt hot and clammy, my hands continued to shake, and my hands and feet would become numb and ice cold. My depth perception and balance was affected, I experienced tingly sensations, an aversion to food, and difficulty sleeping. The mental confusion amplified to the point where I would have bouts of not knowing where I was or what I was doing. I was forgetful and at times couldn't play the piano as the music would look completely foreign to me. The symptoms would begin mildly and become more heightened as the day progressed. It wasn't until I started hallucinating that I finally went to the doctor in fear that I had a brain tumor or early stages of dementia. An MRI and CT scan at Stanford

The Business of Meditation and the Expectation of "Results"   101

University Hospital ruled out a brain tumor and multiple sclerosis which were initially suspected by the neurologist. The symptoms continued resulting in a second trip to the hospital where I ended up in the psychiatric ward and was asked if I had suicidal thoughts or plans of hurting anyone. After several more tests, the neurologist wrote me a prescription and concluded that I was suffering from atypical silent ocular migraines.[22] Throughout the entire process, I increased my meditation practice as an attempt to feel grounded, not realizing that being in this state of mind, meditation was only exacerbating the condition.

I continued to experience periodic symptoms-though much less severe-for another year but these stretches were also accompanied by profound mystical experiences of the kind I had only read about. It was then that I started to suspect a connection with spirituality as the ear ringing and some of the other symptoms began to coincide with my yoga and meditation practice. It was also at that time, that I started to experience aspects of the paranormal and numerous synchronicities that my rational mind could not explain. Given the previous encounter with the biomedical system, I kept all of this to myself and even refrained from telling my husband as I feared that I was losing my mind. It was at that time that I finally divulged these incidents to my colleague and when he identified it as a Kundalini awakening, everything started to make sense. My fears and sense of isolation were dispelled and over time I adapted to the new sensory experiences so that they rarely bother me now. It felt like I finally started to wear a pair of glasses with the right prescription customized for my heightened senses. It has been suggested that a Kundalini awakening stimulates the dormant potentials of the right brain which allows consciousness to experience itself in a new and profound way (Greenwell 2009:30). In my case I have found this to be true and as terrifying as the process was, I am grateful for it. By tuning in to my inner world, my brain feels like it has been re-wired. I have become more aware of patterns and conditioning from my unconscious, and by tuning out the noise of the material world, I have a much stronger connection with my true Self.

---

[22] The absence of a head ache is referred to as a silent migraine.

FINAL THOUGHTS

This paper examined the transpersonal difficulties associated with Kundalini as a spiritual emergency. The mechanisms involved in inducing and managing the serpent fire was discussed and the importance of a teacher and committing to one path was emphasized. The dangers of haphazard experimentation of practices removed from their original cultural contexts and the clinical biases resulting from a monophasic emphasis was also reviewed. The curiosity with Eastern spirituality will inevitably continue to grow and in tandem, we can expect a rising number of Kundalini awakenings. Some of these will be unknowingly spontaneous among unsuspecting individuals, and others will be purposeful. Instructional books, videos, websites and CDs on how to specifically waken Kundalini are rampant and the fascination with the promised psychic abilities plays into our culture's preoccupation with the material world.

The digital age has resulted in a population with a very different functioning brain in comparison to earlier generations. The constant interruptions of text messaging, email and social media has created a "Millennial brain" masterful at multitasking but lacking in focus. In the last 5 years, the average attention span has declined from 12 to 8 seconds which is one second lower than a goldfish (Loeb 2015:1). Distraction has become such an issue among youth that spinners and devices such as fidget rings and fidget cubes have become the recent big trends aimed at focusing the distracted mind. These gadgets could easily be replaced by meditation as the focus required could potentially counter these interruptions by supporting improved concentration. Meditation could also alleviate the physiological addiction to social media as the dopamine known to be released from each tweet, like, tag, text or share, could be replaced by the dopamine that yoga and meditation are known to produce. The mere practice of turning inward and experiencing oneness over the "I," could also counteract the self-absorption associated with the "selfie" generation. In a sense, we are facing a double-bind; the Millennial generation more than any other, can benefit the most from meditation, however one could argue that they are also the least likely to successfully commit to a dedicated practice. Our culture's immediate expectation of a result, addiction to social media, brains wired for distraction, and preoccupation with self, work as impediments to a regular practice being formed. The spiritual landscape has also become a business with meditation and yoga becoming commodified. This commodification encourages competition, self-promotion and the assurance of results without having to put in the necessary mileage, thus leaving the seeker completely unprepared when their Kundalini is stirred, or disappointed when it doesn't.

This paper is not intended to scare seekers away from spirituality and meditation. Having gone through the process myself, I see Kundalini as a vehicle through which an individual can achieve their highest human potential. My objective is to educate spiritual seekers, mental health professionals, and spiritual teachers in recognizing that this process is real. It is important to know how it unfolds, how to safely prepare for it, and how to integrate the experience in a constructive manner. Spiritual teachers need to be aware that Kundalini is no longer a secret and that students are deliberately trying to waken it without the proper guidance. I have been fortunate on my path to have been trained in a lineage tradition that values all eight limbs of yoga by devoting one third of the class to the subtle practices. *Pranayama* is taught in a cautious and conservative way wherein students have specific stages they must master before they are encouraged to move toward a deeper form of the technique. As a non-profit yoga center, access to this knowledge is not dependent on finances as students can take their classes for free through a work-exchange program. As an ashram, students have access to resident Swamis who are available for support and spiritual council. Residents at the ashram abide by the yogic lifestyle which includes diet, daily hatha, *pranayama* and meditation. As a lineage tradition, the teachings honor their culture of origin and centers such as these are more than yoga studios that tend to only focus on one of the eight limbs (Hatha). These institutions are holistic spiritual centers that provide structure for a seeker on the spiritual path. This lifestyle most closely approximates the traditional way in which the teachings were originally transmitted without having to travel to India. For those curious about spirituality, I would advocate finding a center with a similar kind of support structure in place. Students need to be cautious of fads, unsupervised breath work, or claims to secret techniques that promise enlightenment at a cost.

So how does one quiet the mind in a gadget driven culture with distracted brains needing constant rewards? The long answer to this question goes beyond the scope of this paper but a starting point is for teachers to meet individuals where they are at. Just like the traditional Guru/disciple relationship, a teacher should customize a practice and help set goals that are realistic and achievable. In some cases, this might mean suggesting to begin with a five-minute practice, with the goal of increasing the time gradually. Many educational institutions now incorporate meditation into the classroom and some have even replaced detention with the practice. Early exposure to meditation is a more enduring solution where the experience of committing to the practice is enforced early on and thus becomes a habit. Spiritual teachers also have a responsibility to avoid making promises of what the student "should" or "will" experience. Unlike everything else in our culture, enlightenment is the one thing that cannot be bought. Discipline, non-attachment, humility, patience, purity of the mind and heart are the necessary ingredients. Ultimately we don't meditate for ourselves; the universe is a projection of our consciousness thus the peace cultivated in the inner world is reflected in the outer. One needs to remember that meditation is not about personal power and gain but rather, it is an act of selfless service.

REFERENCES

Arundale, G. S. (1938). *Kundalini: An Occult Experience*. Adyar India: Theosophical Publishing House.

Bassett, L., Dickerson, E., Jordan, T. & Smith, L. (2016). Millennials' Social Media Engagement and its Effect on Mental Health. *Public Relation Research,* Dec 5th, pg 1-39.

The Business of Meditation and the Expectation of "Results"   105

Bourguignon, E. (1973). *Religion, Altered States of Consciousness, and Social Change*. Columbus: Ohio State University Press.

Carrera, R. J. (2006). *Inside the Yoga Sutras: A Comprehensive Sourcebook for the Study and Practice of Patanjali's Yoga Sutras*. Yogaville: Integral Yoga Publications.

Cousens, G. (2005). *Spiritual Nutrition: Six Foundations for Spiritual Life and the Awakening of Kundalini*. Berkeley: North Atlantic Books.

Greenwell, B. (2009). Kundalini: The Role of Life-Force Energy and Self-Realization. In G. K. Khalsa, A. Newberg, S. Radha, & K. Wilber (Eds.), *Kundalini Rising: Exploring the Energy of Awakening* (pp. 22-26). Boulder, Colorado: Sounds True.

Greenwell, B. (2002). *Energies of Transformation: A Guide to the Kundalini Process*. New Delhi: Shri Jainendra Press.

Grof C. & Grof S. (1993). Spiritual Emergency: The Understanding and Treatment of Transpersonal Crises. In R. Walsh & F. Vaugham (Eds.), *Paths Beyond Ego: The Transpersonal Vision* (pp. 137-144). Los Angeles: The Putnam Publishing Group.

Krishna, G. (1972). *Kundalini-The Secret of Yoga*. Ontario: F. I. N. D. Research Trust.

Krishna, G. (1993). *Living with Kundalini*. Boston: Shambala.

Laughilin C. D., J. McManus & J. Shearer (1993). Transpersonal Anthropology. In R. Walsh & F. Vaugham (Eds.), *Paths Beyond Ego: The Transpersonal Vision* (pp. 190-195). Los Angeles: The Putnam Publishing Group.

Lockley, M. (nd). *Kundalini Awakening, Kundalini Awareness*. http://www.studyspiritualexperiences.org/uploads/3/6/6/5/3665804/ku ndalini-lockley.pdf.

Loeb, H. (2016). In Search of an Attention Span. *Huffington Post*. October 7th, 2016 http://www.huffingtonpost.com/harlan-loeb/in-search-of-an-attention_b_8254864.html.

Louchakova, O. (2009). Kundalini and Health: Living Well with Spiritual Awakening. In G. K. Khalsa, A. Newberg, S. Radha, & K. Wilber (Eds.), *Kundalini Rising: Exploring the Energy of Awakening* (pp. 22-26). Boulder, Colorado: Sounds True.

Mookerjee, A. (1984). Kundalini: The Awakening of the Inner Cosmic Energy. In S. Groff & M. L. Valier (Eds.), *Ancient Wisdom and Modern Science* (pp. 115-154). Albany: State University of New York Press.

Pepin, E. (2012). *Meditation within Eternity: The Modern Mystics Guide to Gaining Unlimited Spiritual Energy, Accessig Higher Consciousness and Meditation Techniques for Spiritual Growth.* Portland: Higher Balance Publishing.

Perrin, S. (2009). Life, Happiness, and Kundalini Yoga. In G. K. Khalsa, A. Newberg, S. Radha, & K. Wilber (Eds.), *Kundalini Rising: Exploring the Energy of Awakening* (pp. 22-26). Boulder, Colorado: Sounds True.

Sannella, L. (1987). *The Kundalini Experience: Psychosis or Transcendence?* California: Integral Publishing.

Saraswati, S. S. (1967). *Taming the Kundalini*. Bihar, India: Bihar School of Yoga.

Satchidananda, S. S. (1978). *The Yoga Sutras of Patanjali: Translation and Commentary by Sri Swami Satchinanda.* Yogaville: Integral Yoga Publications

Shannahoff-Khalsa, D. (2012). *Sacred Therapies: The Kundalini Yoga Meditation Handbook for Mental Health.* New York: W. W. Norton & Company.

Selby, J. (2009). Beyond Kundalini Awakening. In G. K. Khalsa, A. Newberg, S. Radha, & K. Wilber (Eds.), *Kundalini Rising: Exploring the Energy of Awakening* (pp. -73-84). Boulder, Colorado: Sounds True.

Sivananda, S. S. (1965). *Satsanga and Svadhyaya: The Glory, the Importance and the Life-transforming Power of Holy Company and Spirtual Books.* Himalayas: The Divine Life Society. http://www.dlshq.org/download/satsanga.htm.

Sivananda, S. S. (1994). *Kundalini Yoga* (10th edition). Himalayas India: The Divine Life Society.

Svoboda, R. E. (1993). *Aghora II: Kundalini.* Albuquerque: Brotherhood of Life Publishing.

The Business of Meditation and the Expectation of "Results"   107

Walsh, R. & Vaughan, F. (1993). Problems on the Path: Clinical Concerns. In G. K. Khalsa, A. Newberg, S. Radha, & K. Wilber (Eds.), *Kundalini Rising: Exploring the Energy of Awakening* (pp. 131-137). Boulder, Colorado: Sounds True.

Wheeler, J. H. (2015). Kundalini Shaktipat. *Kundalini Shakitpat and Kundalini Awakening* [http://kundalini-shaktipat.com/kundalini_shakti pat.html].

Whitfield, C. L. (2009). Spiritual Energy: Perspective from a Map of the Psyche and the Kundalini Recovery Process. In G. K. Khalsa, A. Newberg, S. Radha, & K. Wilber (Eds.), *Kundalini Rising: Exploring the Energy of Awakening* (pp. -73-84). Boulder, Colorado: Sounds True.

Wieczner, J. (2016). *Meditation Has Become a Billion-Dollar Business. Fortune.* http://fortune.com/2016/03/12/meditation-mindfulness-apps/.

ABOUT THE AUTHOR

Melanie Saraswati Takahashi, PhD, has been a dedicated practitioner of meditation and yoga for over 25 years. Having a keen interest in spirituality and its various expressions cross-culturally, she received her PhD in Religious Studies from the University of Ottawa in 2004. Being a piano teacher since the age of 16, much of her research focusses on the relationship between music and trance. She was one of the first anthropologists to conduct fieldwork at raves and recognize them as contemporary manifestations of ritual and spirituality in technocratic societies. She has published articles on rave and the subset of electronic dance music cultures that evolved from the movement. Her most recent forthcoming publication examines the impact of digital technology on the DJ as "technoshaman" in the genre referred to as EDM (Electronic Dance Music). She was a full-time professor of anthropology at Heritage College from 2004-2008 before moving to San Francisco California. She has served as a specialized research faculty at the Institute of Transpersonal Psychology in Palo Alto, and the Board of Directors at the Integral Yoga

Institute in San Francisco. She is currently the head of teachers at the Integral Yoga Institute and is also working on her second doctorate in the field of parapsychology at the University of Metaphysical Sciences.

In: Meditation
Editor: Lucia Brewer

ISBN: 978-1-53613-223-6
© 2018 Nova Science Publishers, Inc.

Chapter 4

A COMPARISON OF MINDFULNESS MEDITATION AND TAI CHI/QI GONG IN THE MODERATION OF CANCER PAIN IN ADULTS

Carol A. Rizer[*]
School of Nursing, The University of Texas at Tyler, Tyler, TX, US

ABSTRACT

Background: Pain is a ubiquitous and often debilitating symptom that can seriously affect the quality of life and daily functioning of adults with cancer. Tai chi, qi gong, and mindfulness practices have been shown to improve the pain experience associated with multiple etiologies. In March 2016, the Department of Health and Human Services released a National Pain Strategy encouraging recognition of the different types of pain, accelerating efforts to collect quality data, and encouraging patients' self-management of pain. Objective: The objective for this review was to determine whether evidence existed that directly compared the utility of tai chi/qi gong and mindfulness meditation in the treatment of cancer pain in adults. Methods: A literature search was conducted using CINAHL,

---

[*] Corresponding Author Email: crizer@uttyler.edu.

Medline, UpToDate, and the Cochrane database, as well as the reference lists of retrieved articles. The search included articles in English published 2003-2016. Findings: Several articles described the benefits of tai chi/qi gong on the pain experience of adult cancer patients, and multiple articles discussed the positive effects of mindfulness practices on pain. However, no articles were found that directly compared the utility of tai chi/qi gong and mindfulness meditation in the treatment of cancer pain.

Keywords: mindfulness, MBSR, mindfulness-based stress reduction, tai chi, qi gong, cancer, and pain

IMPLICATIONS FOR PRACTICE

1) Nurses should be aware of the National Pain Strategy. This was presented in March 2016, and suggests that patients should be made aware of and become active in strategies to help manage their pain. 2) Several complementary and alternative medical therapies, including Tai chi/Qi gong and mindfulness meditation practices, have shown certain levels of success in cancer pain control. 3) Tai chi/Qi gong, mindfulness meditation practices, and other complementary medical therapies may assist in offsetting the difficult sequelae of opioid use/misuse associated with opioid therapy.

Pain is a ubiquitous and often debilitating symptom, which can seriously affect quality of life and daily functioning. The National Institute of Health's National Center for Complementary and Integrative Health (NCCIH) estimates that almost 50 million adults in the United States (US) suffer from significant chronic pain [Nahin, 2012; NIH-NCCIH, 2015]. Cancer-related chronic pain affects thousands of people worldwide, with a milieu of side effects ranging from mild to devastating. These side effects often contribute to patient morbidity and mortality [National Pain Strategy, 2016].

The Department of Health and Human Services released a national strategy [National Pain Strategy, 2016] to coordinate efforts in reducing the physical, psychological, social, and economic burden of pain experienced by millions of Americans. In response to the Institute of Medicine (IOM) report in 2011, the "Blueprint for Transforming Pain Prevention, Care, Education, and Research", the National Pain Strategy (NPS) was developed by a diverse team of national experts to take steps toward achieving a system of high quality and evidence-based care for all people. This strategy incorporated complementary and alternative modalities, as well as traditional pharmacologic and surgical approaches [National Institute of Health, The Interagency, 2016]. The Institute of Medicine (IOM, 2011) created a report that addressed key recommendations outlining the need for recognizing the different types of pain, tailoring treatment strategies appropriately, addressing the lack of current data, accelerating efforts to collect data, and encouraging patients' self-management of pain. Some of the IOM's underlying principles that drove the formation of the NPS included the idea that chronic pain can, itself, be a disease [NPS, 2016]. It is now being recognized that pain results from a combination of biological, psychological, and social factors, and hence, pain treatment approaches should employ comprehensive and interdisciplinary input [NPS, 2016]. Examples of these include: complementary and alternative modalities, physical and behavioral medicine, neuromodulation, and traditional pharmacologic and interventional, and/or surgical approaches [NPS, 2016].

Mindfulness practices, tai chi, and qi gong are among the most notable complementary and alternative medical practices that have been shown to improve the pain experience in patients with a variety of pain etiologies, including cancer. The purpose of this paper is to present evidence from the literature regarding: (a) pain in persons with cancer, and (b) any direct comparison of evidence as to the utility of tai chi/qi gong and mindfulness meditation in the treatment of cancer pain in adults.

METHODS

A literature search was conducted using CINAHL, Medline, UpToDate, and the Cochrane database, as well as the reference lists of retrieved articles. The search included articles in English, published from 2003-2016. Several articles were found that described the relationships and effects of mindfulness practices, Tai chi, and/or Qi gong, and the degree of effect on cancer-related pain in adults. Search terms included the following: mindfulness, mindfulness-based stress reduction, MBSR, tai chi, gi gong, cancer, and pain.

Cancer and Cancer Pain

The American Cancer Society [2015] and the National Cancer Institute [2014] state that about 1.4 million Americans will receive a cancer diagnosis each year and almost 70% will survive the 5-year mark. The cancer diagnosis can mean weeks, months, or years of physical, mental, and emotional symptoms, regardless of whether/when treatment is initiated. Persons with cancer often face many confounding and deleterious symptoms, such as pain, fatigue, sleep disturbance, depression, stress, anxiety, and a decrease in functional status. These symptoms may lead to a considerable negative impact on the health-related quality of life (HRQOL), depending on the severity of the disease and the duration of illness [Kurucová, et al., 2014; Teunissen, et al., 2007; Salonen, et al., 2011].

Recent research [Hooper and Gerber, 2014] suggests that the pain experience from cancer and/or its related treatments remains one of the most common symptoms contributing to a diminished HRQOL. To effectively facilitate the most efficacious treatment plan for pain therapy, an appropriate, applicable, and evidence-based definition of pain must be determined [Page, 2015]. The NPS uses the scientific definition that pain is a protective mechanism, which causes the individual to react and/or remove a stimulus that is perceived as causing or potentially causing tissue damage [NPS, 2016]. Acute pain is sudden in onset and time limited, whereas chronic pain is defined as pain that occurs at least half the time during a period of six months or more [NPS, 2016].

Research has determined that pain can be described as either nociceptive, resulting from neural pathway activities secondary to actual or potential tissue-damaging stimuli, or neuropathic, a type of chronic pain initiated by lesions or dysfunction in the nervous system, which can cause greater sensitivity to pain and worsen the quality of life [Nicholson, 2006; Rayment, et al., 2013]. Neuropathic pain is commonly associated with conditions such as diabetic peripheral neuropathy, painful post-herpetic neuralgia, and cancer [Nicholson, 2006; Rayment, et al., 2013]. Most practitioners consider the patient to be the identifier and describer of their own pain, basing treatments accordingly. However, since pre-term neonates, non-verbal children, and incompetent adults may also experience pain, the clinical assessment of pain should continually evolve, and should be based on the most current science available [Anand, Emory, and Craig, 1996]. The complexity and subjectivity of pain is multidimensional and contributes to the diversity of symptomatology presented among individual patients and may make diagnosis and treatment plans more challenging [Portenoy and Abrahms, 2016; Portenoy and Dhingra, 2016].

Portenoy and Dhingra [2016] discuss the two general categories of pain syndromes, including those that are acute (may accompany some type of diagnostic or therapeutic intervention, or have symptoms related to the cancer/tumor itself) and those that are chronic, in which the symptoms are usually related to the cancer or the treatment of the cancer. Portenoy and Abrahms [2016] found that early identification of the pain syndrome may help determine the etiology of the pain, as well as the diagnosis, treatment plan, and prognosis of the pain and/or disease.

Both physical and psychological symptoms vary with the type of cancer and the different treatments available. Physical symptoms commonly associated with cancer and/or its treatments include pain, nausea, fatigue, mucositis, and stomatitis (inflammation or ulceration of the mucous membranes of the mouth and/or the gastrointestinal tract), and urinary/fecal incontinence [Kurucová, et al., 2014]. Anxiety, fear, sleep disturbances, depression, loneliness, remorse, and sadness are some of the most common psychological symptoms [Nemcová, 2008; Kurucová, et al., 2014; Teunissen, et al., 2007]. Functional aspects of performing daily activities, such as the ability to continue to work or to go back to work after cancer treatments, can affect the patient's sense of identity and social role. This may contribute to the continued distress of the cancer experience [Hwang, Lokietz, Lozano, and Parke, 2015; Strada, et al., 2010]. Cancer patients often express psychosocial distress as manifested by lack of sexual desire and/or decreased performance, as well as ongoing fear and anxiety about the cancer experience itself, even after physical symptoms may have dissipated [Hwang, Lokietz, Lozano, and Parke, 2015; Strada, et al., 2010]. Often, psychological symptoms remain even after the patients' attempts to find healthy ways to relieve them [Hwang, Lokietz, Lozano, and Parke, 2015].

The experience of pain is personal and individualized, and is dependent on multiple physical, psychological, emotional, and spiritual factors [NPS, 2016; Portenoy and Dhingra, 2016]. Because recent decades have seen higher rates of survivability of patients with cancer, the potential for opioid misuse has become more of an issue than ever before, even in patients with terminal illness [Pergolizzi, et al., 2016]. Some risk of misuse and/or dependency is inherent among patients exposed to opioid use as well as a risk of acquiring aberrant drug-related behaviors and/or participating in illicit drug use [Fishbain, et al., 2008]. Another cause for concern among care providers who prescribe opioids is the risk of intentional dose escalation and self-medication of pain and other negative symptoms by the patient without medical supervision [Anghelescu, Ehrentraut, and Faughnan, 2013; Fishbain, et al., 2008; Garland and Black, 2014].

Treatment options for chronic pain generally include drugs and other pharmacologic measures, physical therapies, behavioral therapies, neuromodulation, and interventional and/or surgical approaches [Rosenquist, 2016]. The best outcomes for patients with chronic pain have been shown to come from the use of a combination of treatment modalities used in concert [Kamper, et al., 2015]. The addition of a complementary adjunctive therapy (for example, Mindfulness and Tai chi/Qi gong) has been shown to moderate many negative symptoms of pain, even if addictive behaviors are already present [Garland and Black, 2014].

Mindfulness and Mindfulness-Based Stress Reduction (MBSR)

Among the most widely utilized complementary and/or alternative medical practices to offset the symptoms and side effects of cancer and its treatments are mindfulness meditation practices, including Mindfulness-Based Stress Reduction (MBSR). Mindfulness meditation was born of Eastern meditation traditions, but has since become a significant and popular part of Western complementary medical therapies [Baer, 2003; Hawtin and Sullivan, 2011]. The practice of mindfulness may be applied to the experience of pain by first understanding that the suffering associated with pain is often secondary, and riddled with psychological and emotional associations that often grow the negative aspects of the experience out of proportion, as opposed to simply engaging the primary pain itself [Beynon-Pindar, 2014; Burch and Penman, 2013; Kabat-Zinn, 1982]. Mindfulness can be practiced individually, in groups, or with guided meditations, which can often be found online and free of charge.

Mindfulness-Based Stress Reduction, established by Jon Kabat-Zinn [1990], is a formalized program of mindfulness meditation in which participants attend 8 weeks of training (2 hours/week), with a 'retreat' day of meditation practice incorporated towards the end of the program. Participants of MBSR learn its basic tenets, including the nonjudgmental observation of bodily sensations, emotions, and thoughts, as well as internal and environmental states/events [Kabat-Zinn, 1990]. These tenets are based on the early work of Kabat-Zinn [2003] showing that 'paying attention on purpose' promotes a spontaneous, although brief, "uncoupling of the sensory component of the pain from the affective and cognitive dimensions" [Kabat-Zinn, 1982, p. 35] resulting in a deconditioning of the reactivity to painful stimuli. In the decades since this early research, the work surrounding mindfulness meditation and MBSR has amassed a body of evidence that examines the relationship of these techniques in moderating multiple aspects of negative and potentially harmful conditions affecting human beings, including stress, pain, attentional deficits, sleep, anxiety, depression, and others [Beaulac and Bailley, 2015; Lengacher, et al., 2009; Mishra, et al., 2012]. MBSR seeks to utilize ancient and potentially transformative meditative practices as a complement to the patient's medical plan of care [Baer, 2003; Kabat-Zinn, 1993].

Tai Chi and Qi Gong

Tai chi is the ancient art of slow and deliberate dance-like exercises and positions designed to enhance the flow of vital energy force, or qi [Smith and Bauer-Wu, 2012; Overcash, Will, and Weisenburger Lipetz, 2013]. Practiced in group settings or alone, it can be used for self-defense, exercise, and meditation [Williams, 2003]. Qi gong involves a combination of movement, meditation, breathing, and self-massage, and its origins predate recorded history [Overcash, Will, and Weisenburger Lipetz, 2013; Qi gong Institute, 2016]. Its theoretical roots have been compared to the relaxation response theory created by Benson and Klipper in1992 [Benson and Klipper, 1992; Overcash, Will, and Weisenburger Lipetz, 2013]. Its theoretical roots have also been compared to the theory of psychoneuroimmunology by Ader, Cohen, and Felten [1995].

Tai chi and qi gong are considered closely related (some sources say 'identical') in the most important health and wellness aspects of traditional Chinese medicine, and part of a unique category of exercise that includes meditative movements [Jahnke, et al., 2010; Larkey, et al., 2009]. For this reason, the discussion of the benefits of tai chi and qi gong, in all their forms will be described individually, but viewed as pooled evidence for the purposes of this review and will henceforth be discussed as 'tai chi/qi gong'. To avoid confusion, it should be noted that a specific sequence of exercises exist that are collectively known as tai chi qi qong (TCQQ), consisting of 18 movements, and utilizing parts of both tai chi and qi gong [Thongteratham, et al., 2015]. This form, though popular in many parts of the world, has not been studied extensively and when discussed specifically in this review, it will be referred to as TCQQ [Thongteratham, et al., 2015].

Another form of qi gong includes Zhineng qi gong, which is differentiated from other forms because of the integration of the qi (inner energy), and medical qi gong (MQ), which includes controlled breathing, postures, and meditation, along with specific movements [Overcash, Will, and Weisenburger Lipetz, 2013]. Tai chi Chuan, based on Chinese Tao philosophy, is a form of tai chi that focuses on slow, gentle movements, while keeping a tranquil mind [Lan, Lai, and Chen, 2002].

The notable health and wellness benefits of tai chi [Chen, et al., 2015; Zhang, et al., 2016a] and qi gong [Chen, et al., 2013; Oh, et al., 2010] include improvements in both psychological and physiological symptoms (including pain) in patients with or without cancer [Ernst, 2016; Thongteratham, et al., 2015]. A preponderance of evidence has found tai chi to decrease stress and anxiety, improve depressive symptoms and self-esteem, reduce fatigue, and lower cortisol levels [Galantino, 2013; Galantino, et al., 2013; Larkey, et al., 2015; Mustian, et al., 2004; Oh, et al., 2010; Tsang, et al., 2013a; Tsang, et al., 2013b]. Participants also show improvements in physical conditioning, muscular strength, flexibility, cardiovascular condition, and microvascular functioning [Arce-Esquivel, et al., 2016; Thongteratham, et al., 2015]. Of some concern, several reviews of the existing evidence point out methodological flaws in some studies that indicate the need for more high-quality research in this area [Jahnke, et al., 2010; Mitchell, et al., 2014].

Effects of Mindfulness on Cancer Pain

Several evidence-based neuroscientific and contemplative epistemological concepts of the benefits of mindfulness meditation practices in the moderation of chronic pain occur through several mechanisms: 1) ameliorating negative emotional perceptions of pain through improved interoceptive awareness [Zeidan, et al., 2012]; 2) moving intentional focus from the painful condition to a more contemplative and accepting view of body and mind habitus and negativity [Froeliger, et al., 2015; Garland and Howard, 2014]; 3) decreasing attentional bias [Garland, et al., 2010] and cravings [Bowen, et al., 2009]. A systematic review of randomized controlled trials provided substantive evidence of the benefits of mindfulness-based therapies in the moderation of cancer-related somatic symptoms, as well as improvement in HRQOL markers such as anxiety, depression, fear of cancer spread or recurrence, emotional well-being, fatigue, physical function, and physical health [Zhang, et al., 2016b]. The review also described positive, but not statistically significant improvements in stress, spirituality, pain, and sleep.

Pain can potentially and negatively impact the HRQOL of persons with cancer. Lengacher and colleagues [2009] found that psychological status and quality of life in patients within 18 months of breast cancer treatments were significantly and positively affected by 6 weeks of MBSR, as compared with usual care. Chiesa and Serretti [2011] found that mindfulness meditation has positive, but non-specific effects for decreasing pain, while Ussher and colleagues (2014) described a significant difference between a 10-minute body scan meditation conducted in the clinic (positive results) vs. the participant's home (no difference).

Grant and colleagues [2011] found that meditators were better able to neutrally view painful stimuli via a "functional decoupling of the cognitive-evaluative and sensory-discriminative dimensions of pain" [p. 155], thereby decreasing higher order evaluative processes and diminishing the perception of pain. However, in several experimental studies, it was found that although mindfulness meditation can decrease perceptions of pain, it often requires a considerable investment of time to be able to see consistent results in the management of chronic pain and brief mindfulness interventions may be less effective [Gotink, et al., 2015; Brown and Jones, 2010; Buhle and Wager, 2010; Sharpe, et al., 2013].

Effects of Tai Chi and Qi Gong on Cancer Pain

Multiple studies have outlined positive effects and benefits related to the use of tai chi/qi gong for cancer patients [Chen, et al., 2015; Galantino, et al., 2013; Mishra, et al., 2012; Thongertham, et al., 2015; Will, 2013]. One study by Mishra and colleagues [2012] examined 40 trials with 3694 participants randomized to an exercise (n = 1927) with a comparison (n = 1764) group, finding that exercise may have beneficial effects on HRQOL, including cancer-specific concerns, body image/self-esteem, emotional well-being, sexuality, sleep disturbance, social functioning, anxiety, fatigue, and pain. However, these authors pointed out that the study was limited because of a risk of bias, as well as by the similarity of exercise groups. A small Thai study examined the impact of tai chi on several negative effects of breast cancer in women, finding reductions in fatigue, cortisol levels, self-esteem, and quality of life [Thongteratham, et al., 2015].

A systematic review of the literature examined 35 systematic reviews to evaluate whether there were any improvements of medical conditions or clinical symptoms found with tai chi intervention [Lee and Ernst, 2011]. Lee, et al., [2007a; 2010b; 2011c] repeatedly found that the only improvements were in the categories of fall prevention and psychological health, and did not show overall improvements in cancer-related symptomatology in the two systematic reviews utilizing breast cancer patients. Pan, et al., [2015] examined breast cancer patients (n = 322) who participated in tai chi Chuan exercises and found no difference in pain levels.

Several studies did find improvements in pain levels of breast cancer survivors, such as improved pain in patients with cancer and/or non-cancer pain conditions, and joint arthralgias [Brisemme, et al., 2007; Song, et al., 2007; Tsai, et al., 2013; Wang, et al., 2009]. Overall, tai chi has mostly been shown to be effective in decreasing pain in patients with osteoarthritis, low back pain, and fibromyalgia, but not as effective in rheumatoid arthritis or headache, even though the studies are lacking in number and quality [Peng, 2012; Schulenberg, 2015]. In a systematic review of the literature, Mitchell et al., [2014] found that the effectiveness of tai chi/qi gong for cancer pain, although promising, has not yet been adequately established.

Most studies reviewed for this work expressed the need for further research using high quality methodologies to further identify the specific benefits of tai chi/qi gong for cancer pain. In a review of randomized controlled trials by Jahnke and colleagues [2010], methodological flaws were identified in most of the relatively few randomized controlled trials reviewed, thus providing little evidence to suggest that tai chi was effective in improving psychosomatic symptoms.

RESULTS

A notable collection of evidence exists that describes the benefits and/or potential benefits of mindfulness practices on the pain experience of adults with cancer. Several studies describing the effects of tai chi/qi gong on cancer pain, although fewer in number and less conclusive than those utilizing mindfulness, were of value to this review. Many studies regarding these alternative therapies described benefits to the overall HRQOL, including improvements in the levels of anxiety/depression/fatigue associated with cancer, which could indirectly affect the pain experience. There were no articles found that directly compared the utility of tai chi/qi gong and mindfulness meditation in the treatment of cancer pain in adults. Although each of these therapies have shown positive effects, this review found that the benefits of tai chi/qi gong in the moderation of cancer pain are somewhat less well-documented than are the benefits of mindfulness practices, and more studies with substantial methodological rigor are needed.

An important sidebar to the information gained from this review is the potential effect that these and other complementary medical therapies may have in minimizing the need for pharmacological intervention and consequently offsetting the potential negative sequelae associated with opioids. The NPS recommends that a thorough clinical assessment be conducted for every patient receiving chronic opioid therapy so that a thorough evaluation of the risks of potential misuse can be accomplished [NPS, 2016]. In addition, a discussion of alternative and complementary therapies should be a part of routine patient education so that all available and viable non-medical options for pain control can be considered [Anghelescu, et al., 2013].

CONCLUSION

Several benefits of both tai chi/qi gong and mindfulness meditation in the moderation of cancer pain have been noted clinically and studied experimentally. However, the comparison of both groups as separate interventions in the same study has yet to be formally examined and compared. There appear to be multiple nonspecific and potentially confounding factors that may cause methodological problems in this context.

Since several reviews describe methodological flaws in the existing evidence, further study utilizing more rigorous methodology should be done. The use of an active control group, which could address nonspecific effects (instead of a wait-list control), or the addition of an active control in a three-arm trial may move future research in a more definitive direction [Bishop, 2002; Crane-Okada, et al., 2012; Grossman, et al., 2004; MacCoon, et al., 2012; Rosenkranz, et al., 2013]. This review suggests that by ensuring the use of methodological quality, researchers may make more efficient progress toward understanding which/how each of these complementary medical therapies will provide the most efficacious additions to the plan of care for the management of pain in persons with cancer.

The existing evidence speaks to the potential benefits of tai chi/qi gong and mindfulness practices on the moderation of cancer pain, and healthcare providers should be knowledgeable of and incorporate complementary therapies into the therapeutic pain regimen. The use of complementary praxes can encourage the patient to take an active role in their own care, as suggested by the National Pain Strategy, and may offset many of the problems associated with long-term opioid use, including misuse and addiction.

REFERENCES

[1] Ader, R., Cohen, N. & Felten, D. (1995). Psychoneuroimmunology: Interactions between the nervous system and the immune system. *The Lancet, 345*(8942), pp. 99-103.

[2] American Cancer Society. (2015). *What is cancer?* Available at: http://www.cancer.org/cancer/cancerbasics/what-is-cancer.

[3] Anand, K. J. S. & Craig, K. D. (1996). New perspectives on the definition of pain. *Pain-Journal of the International Association for the Study of Pain, 67*(1), pp. 3-6.

[4] Anghelescu, D. L., Ehrentraut, J. H. & Faughnan, L. G. (2013). Opioid misuse and abuse: Risk assessment and management in patients with cancer pain. *Journal of the National Comprehensive Cancer Network, 11*(8), pp. 1023-1031.

[5] Arce-Esquivel, A. A., Ballard, J. E., Haas, B. K., Hermanns, M. L., Rizer, C. A., Kimmel, G. T. & Wang, Y. T. (2016). Effect of tai chi on vascular function among patients with peripheral neuropathy. *Journal of Heart and Cardiology, 2*(4), pp. 1- 7.

[6] Baer, R. A. (2003). Mindfulness training as a clinical intervention: A conceptual and empirical review. *Clinical Psychology: Science and Practice, 10*(2), pp. 125-143.

[7] Beaulac, J. & Bailly, M. (2015). Mindfulness-Based Stress Reduction: Pilot study of a treatment group for patients with chronic pain in a primary care setting. *Primary Health Care Research and Development, 16*(04), pp. 424-428.

[8] Benson, H. & Klipper, M. Z. (1992). *The relaxation response.* New York: Harper Collins.

[9] Beynon-Pindar, C. (2014). Mindfulness for health: A practical guide to relieving pain, reducing stress, and restoring wellbeing. *British Journal of Occupational Therapy, 77*(5), pp. 264-265.

[10] Bishop, S. R. (2002). What do we really know about mindfulness-based stress reduction? *Psychosomatic Medicine, 64*(1), pp. 71-83.

[11] Bowen, S., Chawla, N., Collins, S. E., Witkiewitz, K., Hsu, S., Grow, J., Clifasefi, S., Garner, M., Douglass, A., Larimer, M. E. & Marlatt,

A. (2009). Mindfulness-based relapse prevention for substance use disorders: A pilot efficacy trial. *Substance Abuse, 30*(4), pp. 295-305.

[12] Brown, C. A. & Jones, A. K. (2010). Meditation experience predicts less negative appraisal of pain: Electrophysiological evidence for the involvement of anticipatory neural responses. *Pain, 150*(3), pp. 428-438.

[13] Buhle, J. & Wager, T. D. (2010). Does meditation training lead to enduring changes in the anticipation and experience of pain? *Pain, 150*(3), pp. 382-383.

[14] Burch, V. & Penman, D. (2013). *Mindfulness for health: A practical guide to relieving pain, reducing stress, and restoring wellbeing.* Hachette, UK.

[15] Chen, Y. W., Hunt, M. A., Campbell, K. L., Peill, K. & Reid, W. D. (2015). The effect of tai chi on four chronic conditions—cancer, osteoarthritis, heart failure and chronic obstructive pulmonary disease: A systematic review and meta-analyses. *British Journal of Sports Medicine*, pp. bjsports-2014. doi:10.1136/bjsports-2014-0943 88.

[16] Chen, Z., Meng, Z., Milbury, K., Bei, W., Zhang, Y., Thornton, B., Liao, Z., Wei, Q., Chen, J., Guo, X. & Liu, L. (2013). Qigong improves quality of life in women undergoing radiotherapy for breast cancer. *Cancer, 119*(9), pp. 1690-1698.

[17] Chiesa, A. & Serretti, A. (2011). Mindfulness-based interventions for chronic pain: A systematic review of the evidence. *The Journal of Alternative and Complementary Medicine, 17*(1), pp. 83-93.

[18] Crane-Okada, R., Kiger, H., Sugerman, F., Uman, G. C., Shapiro, S. L., Wyman-McGinty, W. & Anderson, N. L. (2012). Mindful movement program for older breast cancer survivors: A pilot study. *Cancer Nursing, 35*(4), pp. E1-E13.

[19] Ernst, E. (2016). *Complementary and alternative therapies for cancer.* [online]. Available at: http://www.uptodate.com/contents/complementary-and-alternative-therapies-for-cancer?source= search_result&search=Complementary+and+alternative+therapies+for+cancer&selectedTitle=1~150.

[20] Fishbain, D. A., Cole, B., Lewis, J., Rosomoff, H. L. & Rosomoff, R. S. (2008). What percentage of chronic nonmalignant pain patients exposed to chronic opioid analgesic therapy develop abuse/addiction and/or aberrant drug-related behaviors? A structured evidence-based review. *Pain Medicine, 9*(4), pp. 444-459.

[21] Froeliger, B. E., Garland, E. L., Modlin, L. A. & McClernon, F. J. (2015). Neurocognitive correlates of the effects of yoga meditation practice on emotion and cognition: A pilot study. *Frontiers in Integrative Neuroscience*. [online] Available at: https:// www.ncbi. nlm.nih.gov/pmc/articles/PMC3405281/.

[22] Galantino, M. L. (2013). Tai chi for well-being of breast cancer survivors with aromatase inhibitor-associated arthralgias: A feasibility study. *Alternative Therapies in Health and Medicine, 19*(6), pp. 38-44.

[23] Galantino, M. L., Callens, M. L., Cardena, G. J., Piela, N. L. & Mao, J. J. (2013). Tai chi for well-being of breast cancer survivors with aromatase inhibitor-associated arthralgias: a feasibility study. *Alternative Therapies in Health and Medicine, 19*, pp. 38–44.

[24] Garland, E. L. & Black, D. S. (2014). Mindfulness for chronic pain and prescription opioid misuse: Novel mechanisms and unresolved issues. *Substance Use & Misuse, 49*(5), pp. 608-611.

[25] Garland, E. L., Gaylord, S. A., Boettiger, C. A. & Howard, M. O. (2010). Mindfulness training modifies cognitive, affective, and physiological mechanisms implicated in alcohol dependence: Results of a randomized controlled pilot trial. *Journal of Psychoactive Drugs, 42*(2), pp. 177-192.

[26] Garland, E. L. & Howard, M. O. (2013). Mindfulness-oriented recovery enhancement reduces pain attentional bias in chronic pain patients. *Psychotherapy and Psychosomatics, 82*(5), pp. 311-318.

[27] Gotink, R. A., Chu, P., Busschbach, J. J., Benson, H., Fricchione, G. L. & Hunink, M. M. (2015). Standardised mindfulness-based interventions in healthcare: An overview of systematic reviews and meta-analyses of RCTs. *PLoS One, 10*(4), p.e0124344.

Mindfulness, Tai Chi/Qi Gong in Cancer Pain 125

[28] Grant, J. A., Courtemanche, J. & Rainville, P. (2011). A non-elaborative mental stance and decoupling of executive and pain-related cortices predicts low pain sensitivity in Zen meditators. *Pain*, *152*(1), pp. 150-156.

[29] Grossman, P., Niemann, L., Schmidt, S. & Walach, H. (2004). Mindfulness-based stress reduction and health benefits: A meta-analysis. *Journal of Psychosomatic Research*, *57*(1), pp. 35-43.

[30] Hawtin, H. & Sullivan, C. (2011). Experiences of mindfulness training in living with rheumatic disease: An interpretative phenomenological analysis. *The British Journal of Occupational Therapy*, *74*(3), pp. 137-142.

[31] Hooper, G. & Gerber, E. (2014). Measuring the quality of life in men with prostate cancer. *Urologic Nursing*, *34*(4), pp. 177-184.

[32] Hwang, E. J., Lokietz, N. C., Lozano, R. L. & Parke, M. A. (2015). Functional deficits and quality of life among cancer survivors: Implications for occupational therapy in cancer survivorship care. *American Journal of Occupational Therapy*, *69*(6), 6906290010p1-6906290010p9. doi: 10.5014/ajot.2015.015974.

[33] Institute of Medicine, National Center for Biotechnology and Information. (2011). *Relieving Pain in America: A blueprint for transforming prevention, care, education, and research.* [online] Available at: http://www.ncbi.nlm.nih.gov/books/NBK92525/ 2011.

[34] Jahnke, R., Larkey, L., Rogers, C., Etnier, J. & Lin, F. (2010). A comprehensive review of health benefits of qigong and tai chi. *American Journal of Health Promotion*, *24*(6), pp. e1-e25.

[35] Kabat-Zinn, J. (1982). An outpatient program in behavioral medicine for chronic pain patients based on the practice of mindfulness meditation: Theoretical considerations and preliminary results. *General Hospital Psychiatry*, *4*(1), pp. 33-47.

[36] Kabat-Zinn, J. (1990). *Full catastrophe living: Using the wisdom of your body and mind to face stress, pain, and illness.* Delta Trade Paperbacks.

[37] Kabat-Zinn, J. (1993). Mindfulness Meditation: Health benefits of an ancient Buddhist practice. In: D. Goleman and J. Garin, eds. Yonkers, NY: *Consumer Reports*, pp. 259-276.

[38] Kabat-Zinn, J. (2003). Mindfulness-based interventions in context: Past, present, and future. *Clinical Psychology: Science and Practice*, *10*(2), pp. 144-156.

[39] Kamper, S. J., Apeldoorn, A. T., Chiarotto, A., Smeets, R. J. E. M., Ostelo, R. W. J. G., Guzman, J. & van Tulder, M. W. (2015). Multidisciplinary biopsychosocial rehabilitation for chronic low back pain: Cochrane systematic review and meta-analysis. *British Medical Journal, 350*, p. 444. CD000963. doi: 10.1002/14651858.CD000963. pub3. doi: http://dx.doi.org/10.1136/bmj.h444.

[40] Kurucová, R., Ziaková, K., Gurková, E. & Srameková, G. (2014). Occurrence of annoying symptoms of patients with cancer. *Central European Journal of Nursing and Midwifery*, (6)*1*, pp. 185–190.

[41] Lan, C., Lai, J. S. & Chen, S. Y. (2002). Tai chi Chuan. *Sports Medicine, 32*(4), pp. 217-224.

[42] Larkey, L., Jahnke, R., Etnier, J. & Gonzalez, J. (2009). Meditative movement as a category of exercise: implications for research. *Journal of Physical Activity and Health, 6*(2), pp. 230-238.

[43] Larkey, L. K., Roe, D. J., Weihs, K. L., Jahnke, R., Lopez, A. M., Rogers, C. E., Oh, B. & Guillen-Rodriguez, J. (2015). Randomized controlled trial of qigong/tai chi easy on cancer-related fatigue in breast cancer survivors. *Annals of Behavioral Medicine, 49*(2), pp. 165-176. doi: 10.1007/s12160-014-9645-4.

[44] Lee, M. S., Choi, T. Y. & Ernst, E. (2010a). Tai chi for breast cancer patients: A systematic review. *Breast Cancer Research and Treatment, 120*, pp. 309-316.

[45] Lee, M. S. & Ernst, E. (2011b). Systematic reviews of tai chi: An overview. *British Journal of Sports Medicine*, (46)bjsports80622, pp. 713-718. doi:10.1136/bjsm.2010.080622.

[46] Lee, M. S., Pittler, M. H. & Ernst, E. (2007c). Is Tai chi an effective adjunct in cancer care? A systematic review of controlled clinical trials. *Support Care Cancer., 15*, pp. 597–601.

[47] Lengacher, C. A., Johnson-Mallard, V., Post-White, J., Moscoso, M. S., Jacobsen, P. B., Klein, T. W. & Goodman, M. (2009). Randomized controlled trial of mindfulness-based stress reduction (MBSR) for survivors of breast cancer. *Psycho-Oncology, 18*(12), pp. 1261-1272.

[48] MacCoon, D. G., Imel, Z. E., Rosenkranz, M. A., Sheftel, J. G., Weng, H. Y., Sullivan, J. C., Bonus, K. A., Stoney, C. M., Salomons, T. V., Davidson, R. J. & Lutz, A. (2012). The validation of an active control intervention for mindfulness based stress eduction (MBSR). *Behaviour research and therapy, 50*(1), pp. 3-12.

[49] Mishra, S. I., Scherer, R. W., Geigle, P. M., Berlanstein, D. R., Topaloglu, O., Gotay, C. C. & Snyder, C. (2012). Exercise interventions on health-related quality of life for cancer survivors. *Cochrane Database of Systematic Reviews., 15*(8), CD008465. doi: 10.1002/14651858.CD008465.pub2.

[50] Mitchell, S., Hoffman, A., Clark, J., DeGennaro, R., Poirier, P., Robinson, C. & Weisbrod, B. (2014). Putting evidence into practice: An update of evidence-based interventions for cancer-related fatigue during and following treatment. *Clinical Journal of Oncology Nursing*, (18.6 Suppl), pp. 38-58.

[51] Mustian, K. M., Katula, J. A., Gill, D. L., Roscoe, J. A., Lang, D. & Murphy, K. (2004). Tai chi chuan, health-related quality of life and self-esteem: A randomized trial with breast cancer survivors. *Supportive Care in Cancer, 12*(12), pp. 871-876.

[52] Nahin, R. L. (2012). Estimates of pain prevalence and severity in adults: United States, 2012. *Journal of Pain, 16*(8), pp. 769-780.

[53] National Cancer Institute. (2014). *Understanding cancer prognosis.* Available at: http://www.cancer.gov/about-cancer/diagnosis-staging/ prognosis.

[54] National Institute of Health, The Interagency. (2016). *Pain Research Coordinating Committee.* Available at: https://iprcc.nih.gov/.

[55] National Pain Strategy, Interagency Pain Research Coordinating Committee. (2016). *National pain strategy: A comprehensive population health-level strategy for pain.* Washington, DC:

Department of Health and Human Services. https://iprcc.nih.gov/docs/HHSNational_Pain_Strategy.pdf.

[56] Nemcová, J. (2008). Assessment in palliative care. *Diagnosis in Nursing*, *4*(5), pp. 26-30.

[57] Nicholson, B. (2006). Differential diagnosis: Nociceptive and neuropathic pain. *The American Journal of Managed Care*, *12*(9 Suppl), pp. S256-262.

[58] NIH-NCCIH (*National Center for Complementary and Integrative Health*), 2015. NIH analysis shows Americans are in pain. [online] Available at: https://nccih.nih.gov/s news/press/08112015.

[59] Oh, B., Butow, P., Mullan, B., Clarke, S., Beale, P., Pavlakis, N., Kothe, E., Lam, L. & Rosenthal, D. (2010). Impact of medical qigong on quality of life, fatigue, mood, and inflammation in cancer patients: A randomized controlled trial. *Annals of Oncology*, *21*(3), pp. 608-614.

[60] Overcash, J., Will, K. M. & Weisenburger Lipetz, D. (2013). The benefits of medical qi gong in patients with cancer: A descriptive pilot study. *Clinical journal of Oncology nursing*, *17*(6), pp. 654-658. doi: 10.1188/13.CJON.654-658.

[61] Page, S. (2015). Neuroanatomy and physiology of pain perception in the developing human. *Issues in Law and Medicine*, *30*(2), pp. 227-236.

[62] Pan, Y., Yang, K., Shi, X., Liang, H., Zhang, F. & Lv, Q. (2015). Tai chi chuan exercise for patients with breast cancer: A systematic review and meta-analysis. *Evidence-Based Complementary and Alternative Medicine*, 2015, pp. 1-15. doi: 10.1155/2015/535237.

[63] Peng, P. W. (2012). Tai chi and chronic pain. *Regional Anesthesia and Pain Medicine*, *37*(4), pp. 372-382.

[64] Pergolizzi, J. V., Zampogna, G., Taylor, R., Gonima, E., Posada, J. & Raffa, R. B. (2016). A guide for pain management in low and middle income communities: Managing the risk of opioid abuse in patients with cancer pain. *Frontiers in Pharmacology*, *7*(42). doi: 10.3389/fphar.2016.00042.

Mindfulness, Tai Chi/Qi Gong in Cancer Pain 129

[65] Portenoy, R. K. & Dhingra, L. K. (2016). Overview of cancer pain syndromes. *UpToDate.* Available at: http://www.uptodate.com/ contents/overview-of-cancer-pain-syndromes?source=search_ result &search=Overview+of+cancer+pain+syndromes&selectedTitle=1~1 50.

[66] Portenoy, R. & Abrahm, J. (2016). Assessment of cancer pain. *UpToDate.* Available at: http://www.uptodate.com/contents/ over view-of-cancer-pain-syndromes?source=search_result&search= Overview+of+cancer+pain+syndromes&selectedTitle=1~150.

[67] Qi gong Institute. (2016). *What is qi gong?* Available at: http://www. qigonginstitute.org/.

[68] Rayment, C., Hjermstad, M. J., Aass, N., Kaasa, S., Caraceni, A., Strasser, F., Heitzer, E., Fainsinger, R., Bennett, M. I. (2013). European Palliative Care Research Collaborative, Neuropathic cancer pain: Prevalence, severity, analgesics, and impact from the European Palliative Care Research Collaborative–Computerised Symptom Assessment study. *Palliative Medicine, 27*(8), pp. 714-721.

[69] Rosenkranz, M. A., Davidson, R. J., MacCoon, D. G., Sheridan, J. F., Kalin, N. H. & Lutz, A. (2013). A comparison of mindfulness-based stress reduction and an active control in modulation of neurogenic inflammation. *Brain, Behavior, and Immunity, 27*, pp. 174-184. doi: 10.1016/j.bbi.2012.10.013.

[70] Rosenquist, E. (2016). Evaluation of chronic pain in adults. *UpToDate.* Available at: http://www.uptodate.com/contents/ evaluation-of-chronic-pain-in-adults.

[71] Salonen, P., Kellokumpu-Lehtinen, P. L., Tarkka, M. T., Koivisto, A. M. & Kaunonen, M. (2011). Changes in quality of life in patients with breast cancer. *Journal of Clinical Nursing, 20*(1-2), pp. 255-266.

[72] Sharpe, L., Nicholson Perry, K., Rogers, P., Refshauge, K. & Nicholas, M. K. (2013). A comparison of the effect of mindfulness and relaxation on responses to acute experimental pain. *European Journal of Pain, 17*(5), pp. 742-752.

130 Carol A. Rizer

[73] Smith, M. E. & Bauer-Wu, S. (2012). Traditional Chinese medicine for cancer-related symptoms. *Seminars in Oncology Nursing*, (28)*1*, pp. 64-74.

[74] Song, R., Lee, E. O., Lam, P. & Bae, S. C. (2007). Effects of a Sun-style Tai Chi exercise on arthritic symptoms, motivation, and the performance of health behaviors in women with osteoarthritis. *Taehan Kanho Hakhoe Chi*, *37*(2), pp. 249-256.

[75] Strada, E. A., Portenoy, R. K., Hesketh, P. J. & Savarese, D. M. F. (2010). Psychological, rehabilitative, and integrative therapies for cancer pain. *UpToDate*. Available at: http://www.uptodate.com/ contents/psychological-rehabilitative-and-integrative-therapies-for-cancer-pain?source=search_result& search=Psychological% 2C+ rehabilitative%2C+and+integrative+therapies+for+cancer+pain&sele ctedTitle=1%7E150.

[76] Teunissen, S. C., Wesker, W., Kruitwagen, C., de Haes, H. C., Voest, E. E. & de Graeff, A. (2007). Symptom prevalence in patients with incurable cancer: A systematic review. *Journal of Pain and Symptom Management*, *34*(1), pp. 94-104.

[77] Thongteratham, N., Pongthavornkamol, K., Olson, K., Ratanawichitrasin, A., Nityasuddhi, D. & Wattanakitkrilert, D. (2015). Effectiveness of tai chi qi gong program for Thai women with breast cancer: A randomized control trial. *Pacific Rim International Journal of Nursing Research*, pp. 280-294.

[78] Tsai, P. F., Chang, J. Y., Beck, C., Kuo, Y. F. & Keefe, F. J. (2013). A pilot cluster-randomized trial of a 20-week Tai Chi program in elders with cognitive impairment and osteoarthritic knee: effects on pain and other health outcomes. *Journal of Pain and Symptom Management*, *45*(4), pp. 660-669.

[79] Tsang, H. W., Lee, J. L., Au, D. W., Wong, K. K. & Lai, K. W. (2013a). Developing and testing the effectiveness of a novel health qigong for frail elders in Hong Kong: A preliminary study. *Evidence-Based Complementary and Alternative Medicine*. Available at: https://www.ncbi.nlm.nih.gov/pmc/articles/PMC3784263/.

[80] Tsang, H. W., Tsang, W. W., Jones, A. Y., Fung, K. M., Chan, A. H., Chan, E. P. & Au, D. W. (2013b). Psycho-physical and neurophysiological effects of qigong on depressed elders with chronic illness. *Aging and Mental Health, 17*(3), pp. 336-348.

[81] Ussher, M., Spatz, A., Copland, C., Nicolaou, A., Cargill, A., Amini-Tabrizi, N. & McCracken, L. M. (2014). Immediate effects of a brief mindfulness-based body scan on patients with chronic pain. *Journal of Behavioral Medicine, 37*(1), pp. 127-134.

[82] Wang, C., Schmid, C. H., Hibberd, P. L., Kalish, R., Roubenoff, R., Rones, R. & McAlindon, T. (2009). Tai Chi is effective in treating knee osteoarthritis: A randomized controlled trial. *Arthritis Care & Research, 61*(11), pp. 1545-1553.

[83] Will, K. M. (2013). The benefits of medical qi gong in patients with cancer: A descriptive pilot study. *Clinical Journal of Oncology Nursing, 17*(6), pp. 654-658.

[84] Williams, T. (2003). *Complete illustrated guide to Chinese medicine: Using traditional Chinese medicine for harmony of mind and body.* London: Harper Thorsons.

[85] Zeidan, F., Grant, J. A., Brown, C. A., McHaffie, J. G. & Coghill, R. C. (2012). Mindfulness meditation-related pain relief: Evidence for unique brain mechanisms in the regulation of pain. *Neuroscience Letters, 520*(2), pp. 165-173.

[86] Zhang, L. L., Wang, S. Z., Chen, H. L. & Yuan, A. Z. (2016a). Tai chi exercise for cancer-related fatigue in patients with lung cancer undergoing chemotherapy: A randomized controlled trial. *Journal of Pain and Symptom Management, 51*(3), pp. 504-511.

[87] Zhang, J., Xu, R., Wang, B. & Wang, J. (2016b). Effects of mindfulness-based therapy for patients with breast cancer: A systematic review and meta-analysis. *Complementary Therapies in Medicine,* (26), pp. 1-10. [online] Available at: <http://www. complementarytherapiesinmedicine.com/article/S0965-2299(16) 30021-8/abstract>.

BIOGRAPHICAL SKETCH

Carol A. Rizer

Affiliation: The University of Texas at Tyler

Education: DNP, APRN, CRNA-ret.
Doctor of Nursing Practice-in Clinical Nursing Practice 2013
Oklahoma City University, Oklahoma City, OK
Clinical Dissertation: Proving Competence: Evidence of Excellence in Nurse Anesthesia Practice
Master of Science- in Nursing; certificate in nurse anesthesia 1994
University of Texas Health Science Center, Houston, TX
Bachelor of Science- in Nursing 1988
The University of Texas at Tyler, Tyler, TX
Bachelor of Science- in Biomedical Science 1980
Texas A&M University, College Station, TX

Business Address: 3900 University Blvd., Tyler, TX 75799

Research and Professional Experience: Evidence to Clinical Practice Applications.
Mindfulness meditation and biomedical relationships
Mindfulness meditation and pain
Mindfulness based stress reduction
Pain and Tai Chi
Pain and Mindfulness meditation

Professional Appointments: *Quality Improvement Coordinator-consultant-* Lakeland Anesthesia Associates, Athens, TX, 2001-present
Bethesda Health Clinic-Consultant, Tyler, TX; 2013-present.
*Medical Missions-*Green Acres Baptist Church, Tyler, TX; 2001-present
Dove Medical Press Peer Reviewer; February 2014-present.

Jones & Bartlett Publishing, Textbook proposal reviewer, July, 2015 & May, 2015.
University of Utah's Academy of Health Science Educators-External Reviewer; 2015- present.

Honors: Established the Pat Chandler Tiller Memorial Nursing Scholarship; the University of Texas at Tyler, 2009-Present
The Nurses' Health Study II, 1989-present; participant
Winner of 2013 poster competition, Sigma Theta Tau International, Iota Nu Chapter, The University of Texas at Tyler

Publications from the Last 3 Years:

'Screening and Initial Management of Alcohol Misuse in Primary Care'; *the Journal for Nurse Practitioners*, November/December 2017; Carol A. Rizer; Marcie D. Lusk.
'Effects of Tai Chi Training on Muscle Strength, Mobility, and Quality of Life in Patients with Peripheral Neuropathy'; Submitted to *Journal of Sport and Health Science*, May 2017; Arturo A. Arce-Esquivel, Barbara K. Haas, Melinda L. Hermanns, Joyce E. Ballard, Carol A. Rizer, Gary T. Kimmel, Yong T. Wang.
'Effects of Light Therapy on Vascular Function in Patients with Diabetic Peripheral Neuropathy'; Submitted to *Journal of Integrative Cardiology*, Spring, 2017.
Effect of Tai Chi on Vascular Function Among Patients with Peripheral Neuropathy'; Published *Journal of Heart and Cardiology*, 2(4): 1-7; Arturo A. Arce-Esquivel, Joyce E. Ballard, Barbara K. Haas, Melinda L. Hermanns, Carol A. Rizer, Gary T. Kimmel, and Yong T. Wang; Fall 2016.
'The Role of Perceived Stress and Health Beliefs on College Students Intentions to Practice Mindfulness Meditation', published in *American Journal of Health Education*; January 2016. DOI:10.1080/1932503 7.2015.1111176.

'Documenting Competence: Evidence of Excellence in Nurse Anesthesia Practice'. *The European Scientific Journal (ESJ)*. Published May 2015. Doi: 10.13140/RG.2.1.4607.4961.

'Pre-op Evaluation Challenges for the PCP: Interpreting the New ACC/AHA Guidelines'; *Nurse Practitioner Perspectives/Advance*; Published June 2016.

In: Meditation
Editor: Lucia Brewer

ISBN: 978-1-53613-223-6
© 2018 Nova Science Publishers, Inc.

Chapter 5

CONCENTRATIVE MEDITATION AS A FIRST STEP OF MINDFULNESS: THE EFFECTS ON WORRY, DISPOSITIONAL MINDFULNESS, DECENTERING, AND ATTENTION

Keisuke Tanaka[1] and Yoshinori Sugiura[2]
[1]Joetsu University of Education, Japan
[2]Hiroshima University, Japan

ABSTRACT

Concentrative Meditation (CM), which focuses exclusively on focused attention, is often employed as an introductory practice for mindfulness meditation. This paper examined the effects of CM on worry, attention, dispositional mindfulness, and decentering. Twenty-six university students (Mean age = 19.7 years, SD = 1.73) were alternately assigned to two groups (CM or controls) according to self-reported worry scores. The CM group (n = 13) participated in a two-week CM program consisting of five sessions every two or three days, and daily homework; we compared them with non-intervention controls (n = 13). Both groups completed self-report questionnaires (worry, mindfulness, and decentering) and the Attention Network Test (a performance-based task measuring attentional functions) before and after the intervention. Results showed that the CM group indicated reduced worry, and improved nonjudging and describing facets of dispositional mindfulness than the control group. Furthermore, the CM group indicated a trend for improvement in decentering and orienting (selective attention) than the control group. Correlations between change-scores in the CM group showed that the more selective attention improved, the more decentering increased. These results suggest that short-term uses of concentrative meditation are likely to be effective for worry, which may be associated with enhanced selective attention and decentering.

Keywords: concentrative meditation, mindfulness, worry, decentering, attention

INTRODUCTION

Chronic and excessive worrying has negative effects on psychological health. Worry is defined as "a chain of thoughts and images, negatively affect-laden and relatively uncontrollable (Borkovec, Robinson, Pruzinsky, and DePee, 1983)." While pathological worrying is the chief symptom of generalized anxiety disorder (GAD), it is a common phenomenon, and is present in other anxiety and emotional disorders (Purdon & Harrington, 2006). Therefore, worry is considered a transdiagnostic factor (Kertz, Bigda-Peyton, Rosmarin, & Bjorgvinsson, 2012; Starcevic et al., 2007). Therefore, an intervention aimed at alleviating worry may have wide-ranging implications for the treatment of emotional problems.

Mindfulness meditation has been used to treat emotional disorders, through such therapies as mindfulness-based stress reduction (Kabat-Zinn, 1990), dialectical behavior therapy (Linehan, 1993), and mindfulness-based cognitive therapy (Segal, Williams, & Teasdale, 2002). In a meta-analysis, Hoffmann, Sawyer, Witt, & Oh (2010) showed that mindfulness-based therapy is effective for anxiety and mood problems in the clinical population. Moreover, two open-trials showed that mindfulness training reduced worry in individuals with GAD (Craigie, Rees, Marsh, & Nathan,

2008; Evans et al., 2008). Furthermore, Delgado et al. (2010) found that mindfulness training reduced worry to the same extent as progressive muscle relaxation in a university student sample. Mindfulness training, therefore, seems a promising way to reduce chronic worry.

In spite of evidence supporting its efficacy, the working mechanism of mindfulness has not received sufficient investigation. Dispositional mindfulness, decentering, and attentional control have been postulated as mediators of its effects. Mindfulness is defined as "paying attention in the present moment on purpose with nonjudgmental attitudes" (Kabat-Zinn, 1990). This definition refers to the mental state rather than the training methods used to enhance it. Therefore, studies have, at times, treated mindfulness as a trait with measurable individual differences (e.g., Baer, Smith, Hopkins, Krietemeyer, & Toney, 2006). Dispositional mindfulness has been shown to be a multi-faceted construct; most of its facets have negative relationships with psychological symptoms, and positive relationships with positive psychological functions (Baer et al., 2006).

Decentering, one of the putative mediators of mindfulness training, refers to the capacity to deal with one's thoughts and feelings as temporary, objective events in the mind (Fresco et al., 2007). Decentering, as measured by the Experiences Questionnaire (EQ; Fresco et al., 2007), is negatively associated with rumination and depression symptoms (Fresco et al., 2007). Carmody, Baer, Lykins, & Olendzki (2009) found that dispositional mindfulness and decentering were highly correlated, and that mindfulness training improved both dispositional mindfulness and decentering. It was also showed that improvements in both mindfulness and decentering mediated reduction of symptoms (Carmody et al., 2009).

The self-regulation of attention appears to be the core mediator in mindfulness techniques (Bishop et al., 2004; Brown & Ryan, 2003). In a review, Chiesa, Calati, and Serretti (2011) found evidence that mindfulness meditation practices enhanced attentional functions. A study conducted by Jha, Krompinger, and Baime (2007) demonstrated, particularly clearly, that attention is related to different aspects of meditation. The study (a) assessed the effect of concentrative meditation (CM), which relates exclusively to orienting function on the Attention Network Test (ANT;

Fan, McCandliss, Sommer, Raz, & Posner, 2002), a widely used multidimensional assessment of attentional functions (i.e., alerting, orienting, and executive attention). The ANT is a reaction time (RT)-based flanker task involving the cueing of timing and place of target appearance. Alerting is defined as achieving and maintaining an alert state, otherwise known as "sustained attention"; it is indexed by subtracting RTs on double-cue trials from those on no cue trials. Double-cue informs for participants that targets will immediately appear while no-cue do not inform timing of targets appearance. In the no-cue trials, targets are suddenly provided. Thus, alerting score refers to alerting the target appearance. Orienting is defined as the selection of information from sensory inputs, also known as "selective attention"; it is indexed by subtracting RTs on spatial-cue trials from those on center-cue trials. Spatial cue informs for participants both places and timings of targets appearances while center-cue informs only timings. Thus, orienting score refers to selective attention to a spatial cue. Finally, executive attention refers to the ability to resolve conflicts; it is indexed by subtracting RTs on congruent target trials from those on incongruent target trials. In the incongruent target trials, the target, an arrow, is surrounded by the arrows which indicates the direction opposite to the target direction. In the congruent target trials, the target is surrounded by the arrows which indicates the direction same to the target direction. Thus, executive attention score refers to resolving the conflicts from incongruent and competitive information.

Jha et al. (2007) compared (a) naive participants who participated in an eight-week mindfulness training to (b) a group experienced in concentrative meditation (CM) who participated in a retreat, and to (c) a control group that had never been exposed to mindfulness. At pre-retreat, the experienced group demonstrated higher executive attention compared to participants with controls; this difference was likely due to previous CM experience. After the intervention, the training group showed higher orienting abilities, and the experienced group showed improved alerting. In addition, when a post hoc analysis of the orienting and alerting scores was conducted, researchers found that the MBSR group showed reduced RTs for spatial-cue trials, while the experienced group demonstrated reduced

Concentrative Meditation as a First Step of Mindfulness 139

RTs for the no-cue trials. Jha et al. (2007) concluded that training group improved the selective attention. On the other hand, Jha et al. inferred that for experienced CM practitioners, a retreat allowed for the development of receptive attentional controls.

Jha et al. (2007), however, had a rather complex design that somewhat obscured their results: namely, in their study, the observed attentional changes may have been attributed to a combination and/or interaction of CM and mindfulness meditation, not solely to the length of meditation experience. Mindfulness meditation itself consists of various techniques; frequently, for example, meditation begins with focused attention, thus adopting CM techniques. Therefore, it may be useful to tease apart the components of mindfulness meditation and examine them in isolation. In addition, using multidimensional measurements of putative mediators (including attentional control) may further assist in clarifying the possible underlying mechanisms.

Two review articles support the usefulness of separating CM from mindfulness. First, Lutz, Slagter, Dunne, and Davidson (2008) discriminated between focused attention (FA) meditation and open monitoring (OM) meditation. Lutz et al. (2008) defined FA as a voluntary focused attention on a chosen object, while OM involves non-reactive monitoring of the present moment experiences. OM reflects the features of what is now a widely practiced form of mindfulness meditation, while FA is similar to CM. Second, Rapgay, Bystritsky, Dafter, and Spearman (2011) explored the differences between traditional mindfulness meditation and its modern version; the traditional form emphasizes concentration, while the modern type emphasizes insight. These reviews suggest that concentrative (or FA) meditation is distinguishable from insight (or OM) meditation. However, CM and insight meditation have numerous things in common. For example, no differences have been found between CM and OM meditators in performance on executive attention, orienting (Chan & Woollacott, 2007), or sustained attention when the stimulus was expected (Valentine & Sweet, 1999). On the other hand, OM may also improve sustained attention for an unexpected stimulus, which is linked to receptive attention (Jha et al., 2007; Valentine & Sweet, 1999).

Since CM is often employed as introductory practice for mindfulness, examining the change in mindfulness-related variables induced by CM may allow us to examine meditation's more basic components. For example, in breath counting meditation, participants focus on their breathing and count the breaths. Participants are asked to return their attention to their breath if it wanders at any point. If simple training based on counting breaths has effects on worry, mindfulness, decentering, and/or attentional control, it is clinically useful. However, there have been few studies that examine the effects of CM on these variables. Thus, the purpose of the present study was to examine whether short-term (two weeks), simple CM intervention (i.e., counting breaths) leads to enhanced attentional control, mindfulness, decentering, and reductions in worry. We also explored the type of change, if any, that occurred in these indices before and after the intervention, since attentional skills may enable individuals to observe their experiences, while refraining from automatically responding to them in their habitual patterns (Carmody, 2009).

METHODS

Participants

Participants were recruited from a psychology class at a Japanese university. We first excluded participants who had low worrying scores (i.e., below the average) on the Penn State Worry Questionnaire (PSWQ), which had been completed during their classes. Following this exclusion process, 26 students (M_{age} = 19.7 years, SD = 1.73) participated. Then, we allocated participants to a meditation (CM) or a control group; to balance the two groups in terms of worrying score, participants were alternately assigned to the groups in the order of their PSWQ scores. The average worrying score across both groups (M = 56.2) was higher than that of a non-clinical sample (e.g., Molina & Borkovec, 1994). Half of the participants (3 men, 10 women, M_{age} = 19.8, SD = 1.73) were assigned to the CM group, while the other half (2 men, 11 women, M_{age} = 19.7, SD = 1.80) were assigned to the non-intervention control group.

The two-week CM program comprised five sessions every two or three days, and daily homework. On the first day, participants completed the self-reported questionnaires and the attention task (pre-test). After the pre-test, the CM group participated in a two-week CM program. The first training session was conducted soon after the pre-test. Participants then took part in meditation sessions three times before the post-test. They completed the post-test after the fifth training session, on the last day. All sessions and homework were guided, using 15-minute pre-recorded audio files.

Intervention Program

We used counting breath meditation as the CM technique. A single session lasted about fifteen minutes. Participants were asked to complete five sessions over the course of two weeks; this period was chosen because four to seven days of brief meditation may be expected to improve perceptual and cognitive skills (Mirams, Poliakoff, Brown, & Lloyd, 2012; Zeidan, Johnson, Diamond, David, & Goolkasian, 2010). We employed the same counting breath procedure as that which was used by Katsukura, Ito, Nedate, and Kanetsuki (2009), who have shown that counting breath meditation reduced depression and improved interview-based metacognitive awareness in a Japanese student sample. Participants were asked to count their breaths, from one to ten, repeatedly. When their mind wandered from their breathing to thoughts, emotions, sensations, sights, or sounds, they were asked to return it to their breath. This procedure involved elements also featured in mindfulness. For example, participants were asked to "gently" bring their attention back to their breath if their attention wandered. CM, however, may be considered a simpler intervention than mindfulness training, because it does not emphasize a wide range of experiences.

Measures

Penn State Worry Questionnaire (PSWQ)

The PSWQ (Meyer, Miller, Metzger, & Borkovec, 1990) is a 16-item questionnaire to measure the frequency and intensity of worry. It has excellent psychometric properties (Molina & Borkovec, 1994). The Japanese version of the PSWQ by Sugiura and Tanno (2000) was used in the present study. The Japanese version has also demonstrated good psychometric properties among a student population (Sugiura & Tanno, 2000). Items were rated on a 5-point Likert scale, ranging from 1 (*not at all true*) to 5 (*very true*).

Five-Facet Mindfulness Questionnaire (FFMQ)

The FFMQ (Baer et al., 2006) includes 39 items in five subscales assessing an individual's tendency to be mindful in daily life. The five subscales included observing, describing, acting with awareness, nonreactivity, and nonjudging. Observing refers to attending to or noticing internal (e.g., sensations, emotions, cognitions) and external stimuli (e.g., sights, sounds, smells). Describing refers to describing and labeling internal experiences with words. Acting with awareness refers to paying attention to one's current actions without behaving automatically or inattentively. Nonjudging refers to being non-evaluative of one's cognitions and emotions. Finally, nonreactivity refers to the tendency to not react to one's thoughts and feelings, thereby allowing them to come and go without being caught up in them. For the Japanese version of the FFMQ (Sugiura, Sato, Ito, & Murakami, 2012), all subscales have demonstrated acceptable reliability (Cronbach's α = 0.67–0.85). Furthermore, the subscales have demonstrated good construct validity by showing correlations with various relevant variables (Sugiura et al., 2012). Items were rated on a 5-point Likert scale ranging from 1 (*never or very rarely true*) to 5 (*very often or always true*).

Concentrative Meditation as a First Step of Mindfulness 143

Experiences Questionnaire (EQ)

The Japanese version of the EQ (Fresco et al., 2007; Kurihara, Hasegawa, & Nedate, 2010) is a 15-item scale assessing decentering. The Japanese version of the EQ has good reliability (Cronbach's α = 0.78; Kurihara et al., 2010). We used the 10-item decentering sub-scale. The decentering subscale of the EQ demonstrates adequate construct validity, as shown by its correlations with acceptance, affective control, rumination, and cognitive control (Kurihara et al., 2010). Items were rated on a 5-point Likert scale ranging from 1 (*never*) to 5 (*all the time*).

Attention Network Test (ANT)

We used a Java version of the ANT (Fan et al., 2002) on Fan's web page (https://www.sacklerinstitute.org/cornell/assays_and_tools/ ant/ jin.fan/). The ANT is an RT-based attentional task that measures three attentional subsystems (alerting, orienting, and executive attention). Participants were seated in front of a computer screen at distance of 65 cm. Participants were asked to press the button that corresponded to the direction of the central arrow (left or right) and not to mind surrounding arrows. Also, participants were instructed to respond to the central arrow as quickly and as accurately as possible.

The ANT consisted of a combination of three target conditions (congruent, incongruent, and neutral) and four cue conditions (no cue, double cue, center cue, and spatial cue). In the congruent target condition, the surrounding arrows pointed in the same direction as the central arrow. While in the incongruent target condition, the surrounding arrows pointed in the opposite direction of the central arrow. The central arrow was not flanked in the neutral target condition. In the no-cue condition, no cue was presented, and arrows suddenly appeared. In the double-cue condition, arrows appeared after two asterisks were presented both above and below the fixation. In the center-cue condition, a single asterisk appeared at the fixation. In both double-cue and center-cue conditions, cue asterisks informed participants when the target would appear, but not where the target would appear. In the spatial-cue condition, an asterisk appeared at the location of the upcoming target. The spatial cue condition involves that participants can gain both temporal and spatial information.

The cues initially were presented for 100 ms, in every trials. The arrows were presented for 400 ms immediately following cue offset. The target disappeared after participants responded. The inter-trial interval (ITI) was randomized, lasting anywhere from 400 to 1,600 ms. The ANT consisted of 24 practical trials and 288 experimental trials (72 per cue condition). All trial types was randomly presented.

The RT scores for the correct trials were used in the analysis. ANT scores were calculated using the RT difference between the target conditions or cue conditions. Alerting was indexed by the RT on no cue condition – the RT on double cue condition. Orienting was indexed by the RT on center cue condition – the RT on spatial cue condition. Executive attention was indexed by the RT on no incongruent target condition – the RT on congruent target condition.

RESULTS

ANT Manipulation Checks

We conducted within-participants t-tests (RT in no cue vs. double cue, center cue vs. spatial cue, incongruent target vs. congruent target) to check for successful manipulation on the pre-training ANT score. Consistent with our predictions, the no cue condition showed longer RTs than the double cue condition; the center cue condition showed longer RTs than the spatial cue condition; the incongruent target condition showed longer RTs than the congruent target condition, ts (25) > 8.45, ps < .001.

Table 1. Pre-post scores for each group on study variables

Measures	Pre				Post				Interactions	
	CM		Controls		CM		Controls		F	η_p^2
	M (SD)		M (SD)		M (SD)		M (SD)			
PSWQ	56.2	(9.71)	56.2	(12.56)	51.2	(6.97)	56.8	(11.39)	7.20 *	0.23
Observing	21.5	(5.30)	23.6	(4.81)	22.0	(6.20)	23.2	(4.97)	0.37	0.02
Describing	21.7	(5.81)	21.2	(5.40)	23.0	(5.40)	20.1	(4.89)	6.54 *	0.21
Acting with awareness	22.1	(5.25)	22.5	(5.24)	24.1	(4.63)	23.2	(5.30)	1.38	0.05
Nonjudging	25.2	(6.88)	19.4	(6.61)	27.5	(6.80)	18.2	(5.40)	6.96 *	0.22
Nonreactivity	17.2	(2.91)	17.8	(4.07)	18.3	(4.48)	17.6	(3.93)	1.76	0.07
EQ	26.9	(4.01)	26.6	(5.16)	29.3	(4.33)	26.7	(4.73)	3.49 †	0.13
ANT-Alerting	46.3	(29.34)	36.2	(19.47)	46.6	(23.28)	52.9	(23.33)	2.64	0.10
ANT-Orienting	49.6	(21.56)	39.2	(20.93)	40.4	(13.84)	43.2	(11.47)	3.45 †	0.13
ANT-Executive Attention	109.5	(20.33)	95.0	(25.66)	81.8	(19.03)	81.4	(24.21)	3.01 †	0.11

Note. $†p < .10$, $*p < .05$

Pretreatment Differences

Between-groups comparisons revealed no differences on sex and age. Means and standard deviations of all study measures at pre- and post-test are displayed in Table 1. Furthermore, no significant pretreatment differences between groups were found for all self-report measures and ANT subsystems, except for FFMQ-nonjudging, t (24) = 2.21, $p < .05$), where the CM group (M = 25.2) showed higher levels of FFMQ-nonjudging than controls (M = 19.4).

The Effects of CM on Worry, Mindfulness, and Decentering

A mixed designed group (CM/controls) × time (pre/post) ANOVA was conducted for each self-report measure to evaluate the effects of CM. These results are displayed in Table 1. Group × time interactions were significant for PSWQ [F (1, 24) = 7.20, $p < .05$, η_p^2 = 0.23]. As a result of follow-up tests, we observed that the CM group indicated significantly reduced PSWQ from pre- (M = 56.2) to post-test (M = 51.2). CM group showed medium effect (d = 0.63).

Group × time interactions were significant for FFMQ-nonjudging and describing, F (1, 24) = 6.96, $p < .05$, η_p^2 = 0.23; F (1, 24) = 6.54, $p < .05$, η_p^2 = 0.21. We observed that CM group showed significantly improved FFMQ-nonjudging from pre- (M = 25.2) to post-test (M = 27.5), and improved on FFMQ-describing from pre- (M = 21.7) to post-test (M = 23.0). CM group showed small effects for nonjudging and describing (respectively, d = -0.46, d = -0.32). Furthermore, we observed a marginal interaction on EQ, F (1, 24) = 3.49, p = .07, η_p^2 = 0.13. The CM group showed marginal increments on the EQ from pre- (M = 26.9) to post-test (M = 29.3). CM group showed medium effect (d = -.70).

There were no significant interactions on FFMQ-nonreacting, observing, and acting with awareness, F (1, 24) < 1.04, $n.$ $s.$, η_p^2 < 0. 04. Effect sizes in CM group were respectively d = -0.40, d = -0.23, and d = -0.52.

The Effects of CM on Attention Network

The same mixed ANOVA was conducted for each ANT score (alerting, orienting, and executive attention). These results are displayed in Table 1. We did not observe a significant interaction effect on orienting, $F(1, 24) = 3.45$, $p = .08$, $\eta_p^2 = 0.13$. However, the CM group showed a marginal decrease in their orienting score from pre- ($M = 49.6$) to post-test ($M = 40.4$). Effect sizes for alerting, orienting, and executive attention in CM group were respectively $d = -0.02$, $d = 0.70$, and $d = 1.64$. Figure 1-A shows the scores of orienting for each group. In addition, we divided the orienting score into spatial cue RTs and center cue RTs. Then, we conducted time (pre- vs. post-test) × condition (spatial cue vs. center cue) comparisons in the CM group to clarify whether the change in orienting was driven by RTs in the center cue or spatial cue condition. From this comparison, we observed a marginal interaction ($F(1, 24) = 3.45, p < .10$) and CM was found to decrease RTs in both spatial cue and center cue conditions ($ps < .01$). Figure 1-B shows RTs on both two conditions at pre- and post-treatment in the CM group and under the center cue condition, slope was steeper.

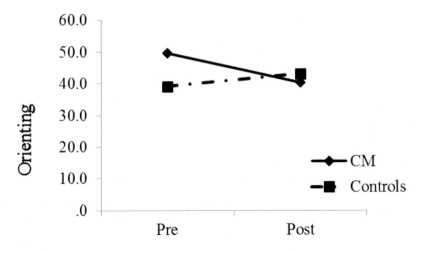

Figure 1-A. Orienting mean scores: Pre-post changes in mean scores for the CM group and controls.

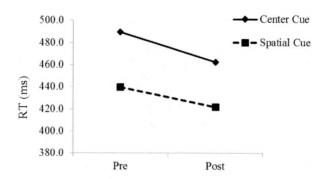

Figure 1-B. Mean scores of decomposed RT on orienting: Pre-post changes in the CM group.

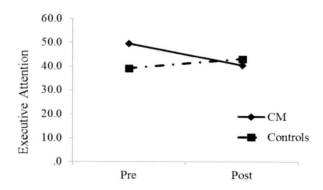

Figure 2-A. Executive attention mean scores including pre-post changes in mean scores for the CM group and controls.

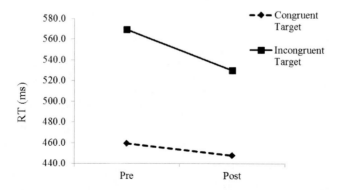

Figure 2-B. Mean scores of decomposed RT on executive attention: Pre-post changes in the CM group.

Concentrative Meditation as a First Step of Mindfulness   149

In addition, we observed no significant interaction effect on executive attention, F (1, 24) = 3.01, p = .10, η_p^2 = 0.11. The CM group (Figure 2-A) showed a marginal decrease in executive attention from pre- (M = 109.5) to post-test (M = 81.8). On executive attention, the control group also showed a marginal decrease from pre- (M = 95.0) to post-test (M = 81.4), d = 0.59. Using the divided time (pre- v. s. post-test) × condition (incongruent target v. s. congruent target) comparison in the CM group, we observed a marginal interaction (F (1, 24) = 3.01, p < .10) and CM decreased RTs in both the incongruent (p < .01) and congruent conditions (p < .01), with slightly steeper slope in the incongruent condition. Figure 2-B shows the RTs in the congruent target or incongruent target conditions at pre- and post-treatment for the CM group.

Finally, we could not observe a significant interaction for the alerting aspect, F (1, 24) = 2.64, $n.$ $s.$, η_p^2 = 0.10.

Table 2. Correlations between change scores in RT for each condition on ANT and self-report measures

	Alerting		Orienting		Executive Attention	
	No Cue	Double Cue	Center Cue	Spatial Cue	Congruent Target	Incongruent Target
PSWQ	-.12	-.16	-.18	-.16	-.18	-.22
Observing	.05	-.03	-.14	-.15	-.01	-.13
Describing	.10	-.14	-.20	.09	-.10	.10
Acting with awareness	-.35	-.10	-.16	-.43	-.28	-.16
Nonjudging	.20	.42	.43	.31	.36	.43
Nonreactivity	-.45	-.51†	-.46	-.51†	-.48	-.63*
EQ	-.49†	-.32	-.25	-.57*	-.38	-.35

Note. †p < .10, *p < .05

Correlation between Changes in ANT and Self-Report Measures

Finally, in order to explore the association between changes in attention and self-report measures from T1 to T2, we correlated change scores from T1 to T2 in the CM group. Changes in three attentional functions (orienting, executive attention, alerting) did not correlate with any self-report measures, but change in orienting marginally correlated with change in EQ ($r = .50$, $p < .10$). Furthermore, we examined correlations between divided ANT change scores and the change scores for the self-report measures (Table 2). A faster RT in the spatial cue condition was associated with higher EQ score ($r = -.57$, $p = .04$). On the other hand, the change score in center cue condition did not show any significant correlations with self-report measures. A faster RT in the incongruent cue condition was associated with higher nonreactivity ($r = -.63$, $p = .02$), while changed RT in the congruent cue condition did not show any significant correlations with self-report measures. The change score in the no-cue condition and that in double-cue condition showed no significant correlations with self-report measures.

DISCUSSION

Our main findings were as follows: (1) CM reduced worry, improved describing and nonjudging, and marginally improved decentering; (2) CM had no effects on ANT scores, but marginally improved attentional orienting and executive attention; and (3) change scores for performance in the spatial-cue condition were associated with change scores for decentering, and change scores for performance in the incongruent cue condition were associated with change scores for nonreactivity. These results were largely consistent with our predictions. They suggest that even a single-handed use of CM, which is often used as a starting point in mindfulness meditation, may be effective for mindfulness-related variables and worry in the short term.

The most interesting finding in our result is that the CM group reduced their worry from pre- to post-test to a significantly greater level than the control group. We posit that CM (i.e., focused breathing) may be an effective intervention for worry because it promotes the deliberate letting go of worried thoughts and focusing on present-moment experiences (Arch & Craske, 2006). Additionally, Rapgay et al. (2011) has suggested that attending to the target object without minding all other objects and experience is the initial phase of mindfulness practices. This type of meditation is called "samatha". They have presumed traditional mindfulness, which emphasizes the importance of concentration (in contrast to modern mindfulness interventions), can target the process behind GAD symptoms more directly. Our results suggest that concentration training using CM has potential for becoming a useful approach in the clinical setting.

We also observed significant CM effects on some facets of dispositional mindfulness (i.e., non-judging and describing). Furthermore, we observed a marginal improvement in decentering in the CM group. Thus, CM seems to promote adaptive relationships with emotions or cognitions. These results may be supported by Carmody (2009)'s attentional model of mindfulness. This model supposes that mindfulness practitioners learn not only to develop facility with attention, but also to implicitly recognize that internal experience comprises discrete components, such as thoughts, feelings, and sensations, which act in concert (Carmody, 2009). Notably, Carmody et al. (2009) have shown substantial increases in mindfulness and decentering following mindfulness training. Attention and decentering have also been thought to be the core mediators of mindfulness (Shapiro, Carlson, Astin, & Freedman, 2006). In the attentional model of Carmody et al. (2009), attentional skill is viewed as a central process in which it can be conceptualized as facilitating a process of recognition. We found no significant changes in ANT scores, although marginal changes ($p < .10$) were shown in orienting attention (i.e., attentional selectivity). Moreover, these improvements were correlated. According to Bishop et al. (2004), sustaining one's attention on the breath keeps one's attention anchored in the present moment, and it leads to the detection of thoughts, feelings, and sensations as they arise in the stream of consciousness. Thus, CM has a possibility of providing participants with the opportunity of meta-cognitive experiences through simple training of selective attention focused on their own breath. These improvements may lead to reductions in worry. These results imply that the single-handed use of CM may have the potential to provide participants with action processes similar to the sort of mindfulness meditation envisioned by Carmody et al. (2009). His interpretation is also consistent with the fact that we had largely focused on manipulating selective attention towards breath.

We also observed a marginal change in the executive attention of the CM group; this, however, might have resulted from task exposure effects, because controls also changed in their executive attention scores (Jha et al., 2007). However, a correlation between reduced responses to incongruent targets and nonreactivity in the CM group was observed. This indicates that individuals high on nonreactivity have greater cognitive control flexibility, consistent with research by Anicha, Ode, Moeller, and Robinson (2012).

We could not, however, find a significant improvement in acting with awareness and observing facets. One possibility for such null findings is that the full package of mindfulness training may be associated with various attention components and diverse mindfulness facets, while CM may largely be linked to enhancing attentional selectivity and decentering. For example, previous research has shown that observing was associated with perceptual skills (Anicha et al., 2012), and acting with awareness was associated with sustained attention, indicated by few exaggerated lapses of attention (Schmertz, Anderson, & Robins, 2009). Thus, improvements in the full range of dispositional mindfulness may require various attentional skills. It may, alternatively, need more practice to improve present-focused attention towards a participant's sum of activities, rather than simply breathing.

We will need more research to clarify these complications by improving on some of our experimental limitations. First, we may need to choose another attentional task because response time-based measures are likely to be affected by test effort (Jensen, Vangkilde, Frokjaer, & Hasselbalch, 2012). Second, we need to examine the effects of longer-term interventions, because attentional performance is positively related to meditation practice (Moore & Malinowski, 2009), and treating people with prolonged experiences has yielded greater improvements in alerting than in naïve individuals (Jha et al., 2007). Nevertheless, our brief, short-term intervention improved some of the variables related to worry. The changes indicated in the relatively short timeframe are promising for future efforts that engage participants in practice over longer periods, and suggest that the changes are due to specific techniques, rather than overall changes in one's daily life. Further study is needed to compare CM to the full package of mindfulness training in a setting of equal and comparable training conditions. Additionally, future studies should employ more stringent RCTs and include clinical samples. In sum, the single use of CM is likely to be effective for worry reduction, which may be associated with enhanced attentional control and decentering.

REFERENCES

Anicha, C. L., Ode, S., Moeller, S. K., & Robinson, M. D. (2012). Toward a cognitive view of trait mindfulness: Distinct cognitive skills predict its observing and nonreactivity facets. *Journal of Personality, 80*, 255–285.

Arch, J. J., & Craske, M. G. (2006). Mechanisms of mindfulness: Emotion regulation following a focused breathing induction. *Behaviour Research and Therapy, 44*, 1849–1858.

Baer, R. A., Smith, G. T., Hopkins, J., Krietemeyer, J., & Toney, L. (2006). Using self-report assessment methods to explore facets of mindfulness. *Assessment, 13*, 27–45.

Bishop, S. R., Lau, M., Shapiro, S., Carlson, L., Anderson, N. D., Carmody, J., … Devins, G. (2004). Mindfulness: A proposed operational definition. *Clinical Psychology: Science and Practice, 11*, 230–241.

Borkovec, T. D., Robinson, E., Pruzinsky, T., & DePree, J. A. (1983). Preliminary exploration of worry: Some characteristics and processes. *Behaviour Research and Therapy, 21*, 9–16.

Brown, K. W., & Ryan, R. M. (2003). The benefits of being present: Mindfulness and its role in psychological well-being. *Journal of Personality and Social Psychology, 84*, 822–848.

Carmody, J. (2009). Evolving conceptions of mindfulness in clinical settings. *Journal of Cognitive Psychotherapy, 23*, 270–280.

Carmody, J., Baer, R. A., Lykins, E. B., & Olendzki, N. (2009). An empirical study of the mechanisms of mindfulness in a mindfulness-based stress reduction program. *Journal of Clinical Psychology, 65*, 613–626.

Chan, D., & Woollacott, M. (2007). Effects of level of meditation experience on attentional focus: Is the efficiency of executive or orientation networks improved? *Journal of Alternative and Complementary Medicine, 13*, 651–657.

Chiesa, A., Calati, R., & Serretti, A. (2011). Does mindfulness training improve cognitive abilities? A systematic review of neuropsychological findings. *Clinical Psychology Review, 31*, 449–464.

Craigie, M. A., Rees, C. S, Marsh, A., & Nathan P. (2008). Mindfulness-based cognitive therapy for generalized anxiety disorder: A preliminary evaluation. *Behavioural and Cognitive Psychotherapy, 36*, 553–568.

Delgado, L. C., Guerra, P., Perakakis, P., Vera, M. N., del Paso, G. R., & Vila, J. (2010). Treating chronic worry: Psychological and physiological effects of a training programme based on mindfulness. *Behaviour Research and Therapy, 48*, 873–882.

Evans, S., Ferrando, S., Findler, M., Stowell, C., Smart, C., & Haglin, D. (2008). Mindfulness-based cognitive therapy for generalized anxiety disorder. *Journal of Anxiety Disorders, 22*, 716–721.

Fan, J., McCandliss, B. D., Sommer, T., Raz, A., & Posner, M. I. (2002). Testing the efficiency and independence of attentional networks. *Journal of Cognitive Neuroscience, 14*, 340–347.

Fresco, D., Moore, M. T., van Dulmen, M. H. M., Segal, Z. V., Ma, H. S., Teasdale, J. D., & Williams, J. M. (2007). Initial psychometric properties of the experience questionnaire: Validation of a self-report measure of decentering. *Behaviour Therapy, 38*, 234–246.

Hofmann, S. G., Sawyer, A. T., Witt, A. A., & Oh, D. (2010). The effect of mindfulness-based therapy on anxiety and depression: A meta-analytic review. *Journal of Consulting and Clinical Psychology, 78*, 169–183.

Jensen, C., G. Vangkilde, S., Frokjaer, V., & Hasselbalch, S. G. (2012). Mindfulness training affects attention—Or is it attentional effort? *Journal of Experimental Psychology: General, 141*, 106–123.

Jha, A. P., Krompinger, J., & Baime, M. J. (2007). Mindfulness training modifies subsystems of attention. *Cognitive & Affective Behaviour & Neuroscience, 7*, 109−119.

Kabat-Zinn, J. (1990). *Full catastrophe living: Using the wisdom of your body and mind to face stress, pain, and illness.* New York: Bantam Dell Publishing.

Katsukura, R., Ito, Y., Nedate, M., & Kanetsuki, K. (2009). Mindfulness training ga daigakusei no yokuutu ni oyobosu kouka metaninnchi teki kiduki ni yoru baikai kouka no kenntou [Mindfulness training and depressive tendencies in college students: Mediating effects of metacognitive awareness]. *Japanese Journal of Behavior Therapy, 1*, 41–52.

Kertz, S. J., Bigda-Peyton, J. S., Rosmarin, D. H., & Björgvinsson, T. (2012). The importance of worry across diagnostic presentations: Prevalence, severity and associated symptoms in a partial hospital setting. *Journal of Anxiety Disorders, 26*, 126–133.

Kurihara, A., Hasegawa, A., & Nedate, K. (2010). Development of the Japanese version of the Experiences Questionnaire and examination of its reliability and validity. *The Japanese Journal of Personality, 19*, 174–177.

Linehan, M. M. (1993). *Cognitive-behavioral treatment of borderline personality disorder.* New York: Guilford Press.

Lutz, A., Slagter, H. A., Dunne, J. D., & Davidson, R. J. (2008). Attention regulation and monitoring in meditation. *Trends in Cognitive Science, 12*, 163–169.

Meyer, T. J., Miller, M. L., Metzger, R. L., & Borkovec, T. D. (1990). Development and validation of the Penn State Worry Questionnaire. *Behaviour Research and Therapy, 28*, 487–495.

Mirams, L., Poliakoff, E., Brown, R. J., & Lloyd, D. M. (2012). Brief body-scan meditation practice improves somatosensory perceptual decision making. *Consciousness and Cognition, 22*, 348–359.

Molina, S., & Borkovec, T. D. (1994). The Penn State Worry Questionnaire: Psychometric properties and associated characteristics. In G. C. L. Davey, & F. Tallis (Eds.), *Worrying: Perspectives on theory, assessment and treatment. Wiley series in clinical psychology* (pp. 265–283). Chinchester, England UK: Wiley.

Moore, A., & Malinowski, P. (2009). Meditation, mindfulness and cognitive flexibility. *Consciousness and Cognition, 18*, 176–186.

Purdon, C., & Harrington, J., (2006). Worry in psychological disorders. In Davey, G., Wells, A. (Eds.), *Worry and psychological disorders: Theory, assessment and treatment* (pp. 41–50). Chichester: John Wiley & Sons Ltd.

Rapgay, L., Bystritsky, A., Dafter, R. E., & Spearman. M. (2011). New strategies for combining mindfulness with integrative cognitive behavioral therapy for the treatment of generalized anxiety disorder. *Journal of Rational-Emotive & Cognitive-Behavior Therapy, 29*, 92–119.

Schmertz, S. K., Anderson, P. L., & Robins, D. L. (2009). The relation between self-report mindfulness and performance on tasks of sustained attention. *Journal of Psychopathology, Behaviour & Assessment, 31*, 60–66.

Segal, Z. V., Williams, J. M. G., & Teasdale, J. D. (2002). *Mindfulness-based cognitive therapy for depression: A new approach to preventing relapse.* New York, NY: Guilford Press.

Shapiro, S. L., Carlson, L. E., Astin, J. A., & Freedman, B. (2006). Mechanisms of mindfulness. *Journal of Clinical Psychology, 3*, 378–386.

Starcevic, V., Berle, D., Milicevic, D., Hannan, A., Lamplugh, C., & Eslick, G. (2007). Pathological worry, anxiety disorders and the impact of co-occurrence with depressive and other anxiety disorders. *Journal of Anxiety Disorders, 21*, 1016–1027.

Sugiura, Y., Sato, A., Ito, Y., & Murakami, H. (2012). Development and validation of the Japanese version of the Five Facet Mindfulness Questionnaire. *Mindfulness, 3*, 85–94.

Sugiura, Y., & Tanno, Y. (2000). Kyohaku shojyo no jiko kinyuusiki situmonhyo: Nihongoban Padua Inventory no sinraisei to datousei no kentou [Self-report inventory of obsessive-compulsive symptoms: reliability and validity of the Japanese version of the Padua Inventory]. *Archives of Psychiatric Diagnostics and Clinical Evaluation, 11*, 175–189.

Valentine, E. R., & Sweet, P. L. G. (1999). Meditation and attention: A comparison of the effects of concentrative and mindfulness meditation on sustained attention. *Mental Health, Religion & Culture. 2*, 59–70.

Zeidan, F., Johnson, S. K., Diamond, B. J., David, Z., & Goolkasian, P. (2010). Mindfulness meditation improves cognition: Evidence of brief mental training. *Consciousness and Cognition, 19*, 597–605.

BIOGRAPHICAL SKETCHES

Keisuke Tanaka

Affiliation: Joetsu University of Education

Education: PhD (Hiroshima University)

Address: Joetsu University of Education, Graduate School of Education, 1, Yamayashikimachi, Joetsu City, Niigata Prefecture, 943-0815, Japan

Professional Appointments: Lecturer

Publications from the Last 3 Years:

Tanaka, K., & Sugiura, Y. (2015). Executive function and mindfulness. *Japanese Psychological Review*, 58, 139-152.

Takebayashi, Y., Tanaka, K., Sugiura, Y., & Sugiura, T. (2017). Well-Being and Generalized Anxiety in Japanese Undergraduates: A Prospective Cohort Study. *Journal of Happiness Studies*, 1-21.

Yoshino, A., Okamoto, Y., Doi, M., Horikoshi, M., Oshita, K., Nakamura, R., Otsuru, N., Yoshimura, S., Tanaka, K., Takagaki, K., Jinnin, R., Yamashita, H., Kawamoto, M., Yamawaki, S. (2015). Effectiveness of group cognitive behavioral therapy (GCBT) for somatoform pain disorder patients in Japan: A preliminary non-case-control study. *Psychiatry and Clinical Neurosciences*, 69, 12, 763-772.

Yoshinori Sugiura

Affiliation: Hirosima University

Education: PhD (Univetsity of Tokyo)

Address: Hiroshima University, Graduate School of Integrated Arts and Sciences, 1-7-1, Kagamiyama, Higashi-Hiroshima, 739-8521, Japan

Research and Professional Experience: Fellow of the Japan Society for the Promotion of Science

Professional Appointments: Associate Professor

Honors: Kido Research Prize (2000)

Publications from the Last 3 Years:

Sugiura, T., & Sugiura, Y. (2015). Common factors of meditation, focusing, and cognitive behavioral therapy: longitudinal relation of self-report measures to worry, depressive, and obsessive-compulsive symptoms among nonclinical students. *Mindfulness, 6,* 610-623.

Sugiura, Y. (2017). Metacognitive, emotional, and avoidance predictors of generalized anxiety disorder. *Psychology, 8,* 636-653.

Sugiura, Y., & Sugiura, T. (2015). Emotional intensity reduces later generalized anxiety disorder symptoms when fear of anxiety and negative problem-solving appraisal are low. *Behaviour Research and Therapy, 71,* 27-33.

ABOUT THE AUTHORS

Keisuke Tanaka is Lecturer at Joetsu University of Education. The focus of his work is on cognitive behavior therapy, mindfulness, and repetitive negative thought. He publishes many articles related to these themes.

Yoshinori Sugiura is Associate Professor at Hiroshima University. He was a recipient of Kido Research Prize from Japanese Association for Educational Psychology in 2000. The focus of his work is on cognitive behavior therapy for anxiety disorder, mindfulness, and psychopathy and publishes many articles related to these themes.

In: Meditation
Editor: Lucia Brewer

ISBN: 978-1-53613-223-6
© 2018 Nova Science Publishers, Inc.

Chapter 6

COGNITIVE DECENTERING AND EATING DISORDER SYMPTOMS: THE MEDIATING ROLE OF THINKING ERRORS

Tomoko Sugiura[1] and Yoshinori Sugiura[2,]*
[1]The Japan Society for the Promotion of Science, Tokyo, Japan
[2]Hiroshima University, Hiroshima-Prefecture, Japan

ABSTRACT

The effect of cognitive decentering, skills to be distanced from distressing thinking, on eating disorders symptoms was examined. We focused on the mediating role of thinking errors. Cognitive decentering captures voluntary use of cognitive behavioral therapy- or mindfulness-like techniques in daily life, while thinking errors are the supposed

---

[*] Corresponding Author: Yoshinori Sugiura, Graduate School of Integrated Arts and Sciences, Hiroshima University, 1-7-1, Kagamiyama, Higashi-Hiroshima City, Hiroshima Prefecture, 739-8521, Japan. Contact: ysugiura@hiroshima-u.ac.jp.

vulnerability to eating disorder. A structural equation model of questionnaire data from women's college students ($N = 173$) revealed that cognitive decentering reduced eating disorder tendency by ameliorating thinking errors. This result is consistent with the recent evidence showing the effectiveness of cognitive behavioral therapy or mindfulness-based intervention on eating disorder. In addition, logical analysis of problems enhanced cognitive decentering in structural equation modeling. This is consistent with the findings that standard cognitive-behavioral therapy also enhances decentering. Prospects for future studies are discussed to suggest that, to enhance the effects of cognitive decentering on eating disorder, it would be essential to include educational interventions that convey physiological knowledge of the human body's functions.

Keywords: eating disorders, cognitive decentering, thinking errors, structural equation modeling

INTRODUCTION

This study focuses on psychological factors related to eating disorders symptoms in female college students. According to reviews by Cash and Grant (1996) and McCrea (1991), cognitive behavioral therapy, a kind of psychological therapy codified by Beck (1976), is effective in the psychological treatment of eating disorders. The basic premise of cognitive behavioral therapy is that personal cognition (thought patterns) is closely related to abnormal behavior and that it is precisely the correction of distorted cognition that serves to correct abnormal behavior (Hofmann, Asnaani, Vonk, Sawyer, & Fang, 2012).

Garner and Bemis's (1982) study is representative of cognitive theories of anorexia nervosa. According to their theory, thinking errors regarding the relationship between food intake and changes in body shape and regarding the relationship between body shape and evaluations from others lies behind the fear of eating that characterizes anorexia nervosa. Thinking errors are thought patterns such as *arbitrary inferences*, in which negative conclusions are drawn without evidence, and *overgeneralizations*, in which extensive beliefs are founded on limited experiences. According to cognitive behavioral therapy, thinking errors are cognitive tendencies that are supposed to lie behind various psychological problems (Beck, 1976). Regarding eating disorders, thinking errors such as "Everyone is looking at me because I'm fat (arbitrary inference)" and "Even if I only eat a little, I'll get fat, and my stomach will start to stick out (overgeneralization)" can be observed (Maeda, 2002; McCrea, 1991). In cognitive behavioral therapy, the objective is the mental transformation of cognition. To that end, techniques such as objectively analyzing problems and one's own thinking are used (Freeman, 1989; Freeman, Pretzer, Fleming, & Simon, 1990).

Although the importance of thinking errors has been pointed out, there has been insufficient development of techniques to operationally measure them. The objective of this study is to clarify the relationship between thinking errors and eating disorders symptoms using the scale of thinking errors developed by Tanno, Sakamoto, Ishigaki, Sugiura, & Mori (1998).

The second objective of this research is to examine the influence of cognitive self-control skills (cognitive control) which are used spontaneously in daily life with regard to eating disorders symptoms. Cognitive control refers to controlling one's behavior by adjusting one's way of thinking. According to Bandura's (1977) social learning theory, appropriately adjusting and correcting one's cognitive interpretations of one's surrounding situation leads to adaptive behavior. Today's cognitive behavioral therapy is a refinement of the concept of cognitive control. Prior studies by Slater (1989) and McCarthy and Newcomb (1992) have investigated cognitive control using questionnaires, but this is an indirect method that taps cognitive control by variables expected to be the consequence of it as indicators (e.g., reduced anxiety), not by directly asking about cognitive control. Therefore, it is hard to say that they provide direct measurements. To more directly measure cognitive control, Sugiura and Umaoka (2003), with reference to Freeman's (1989) techniques of cognitive behavioral therapy, created a measure of cognitive control consisting of two subscales: *logical analysis* and *refraining from catastrophic thinking*. The scale measures one's tendency to voluntarily use cognitive skills such as those used in cognitive behavioral therapy in one's daily life. *Logical analysis* measures skills by which one attempts to analyze problems objectively and logically and is thought to represent techniques in classical cognitive behavioral therapy. On the other hand, *refraining from catastrophic thinking* measures skills by which one prevents negative thoughts from developing excessively when they emerge. Refraining from catastrophic thinking can be considered to represent cognitive decentering, a skill to be cultivated in both standard cognitive behavioral therapy and mindfulness-based interventions.

These two subscales show an effect of reducing anxiety and depression (Sugiura & Makioka, 2003). Furthermore, Sugiura and Umaoka (2003) demonstrate a possibility that cognitive control may reduce worries and obsessive thoughts.

Based on the finding that cognitive control has the effect of reducing depression and anxiety (Sugiura & Umaoka, 2003) and on the finding that cognitive behavioral therapy is effective for eating disorders (Cash & Grant, 1996; McCrea, 1991), cognitive control can be expected to have an effect of alleviating eating disorders symptoms. Furthermore, based on the finding that thinking errors play an important role in the formation of eating disorders and the fact that cognitive behavioral therapy is aimed at correcting such distorted cognition, cognitive control can be expected to alleviate eating disorders symptoms by reducing thinking errors.

In this research, we explore empirically what effect cognitive control, being a skill that voluntarily uses techniques used in cognitive behavioral therapy, has in non-clinical groups of female students on the process of *thinking errors* → *eating disorders symptoms* through questionnaire surveys. Even though they are not always at the level of diagnosable eating disorders, tendencies towards eating disorders symptoms are a problem amongst young women. If these processes can be clarified, it should be useful for preventing eating disorders symptoms and excessive diets. Cognitive control is expected to reduce eating disorders symptoms by reducing thinking errors. Of two subscales of cognitive control, Refraining from catastrophic thinking is expected to have stronger direct effect on thinking errors and eating disorders symptoms. This expectation is based on two research findings. First, it is a common skill of both standard CBT and mindfulness-based interventions (Sugiura & Sugiura, 2015). Second, it

Cognitive Decentering and Eating Disorder Symptoms   165

has stronger negative relationship to symptoms (Sugiura, 2014; Sugiura & Sugiura, 2017).

METHOD

Participants and Method

We investigated cognitive control, thinking errors, and eating disorders symptoms in 173 female university students in Tokyo (average age 19.5 years old, *SD* 2.2). The survey was conducted in classrooms in December of 2001. The purpose of the survey was explained to participants before each class (in the humanities). Students were advised that they could refuse to participate. Once participations had given their consent, they were asked to fill out a questionnaire anonymously. The breakdown of participants was as follows: Department of Pedology 16.8%, Department of Food Science 4.6%, Department of Housing Studies 4.0%, Department of Clothing Studies 15.0%, Department of Home Economics 6.4%, Department of Japanese Literature 16.2%, Department of English Literature 25.4%, Department of History 8.7%, Department of Mathematical and Physical Sciences 1.7%, Department of Material and Biological Sciences 1.2%.

Questionnaires

Cognitive Control Scale

Sugiura and Umaoka's (2003) scale was used for evaluating cognitive control. This scale is composed of the subscales of *logical analysis*, which consists of six items such as "I can think of several alternatives about how to think or act" and "I can think of several reasons that may have caused this problem," and *refraining from catastrophic thinking*, which consists of five items such as "I don't develop a negative scenario from a situation" and "Even if the bad consequences of a problem come to mind, I can reassure myself that they are nothing more than my imagination." (Appendix A). Participants were asked to rate each item in reference to when they felt anxious from 1 (I think that I cannot do it at all) to 4 (I think that I can surely do it).

Thinking Errors Scale

To evaluate thinking errors, we adopted Tanno et al.'s (1998) Thinking Errors Scale (TES). Participants were asked to grade 19 items such as "I sometimes draw conclusions that are disadvantageous to myself without evidence" and "If I have trouble with a friend, I feel that my friends dislike me" from 1 (absolutely not applicable) to 5 (very applicable) to the extent that they usually apply to themselves (Appendix B).

Eating Disorders Symptoms Scale

To measure eating disorders symptoms, we chose 26 items from the Eating Attitudes Test created by Garner and Garfinkel (1979) to use in the Eating Attitudes Test-26 (EAT-26) (Garner, Olmsted, Bohr, & Garfinkel, 1982). There is a Japanese version by Mukai, Crago, and Shisslak (1994). This scale consists of three subscales—*diet (restriction of energy intake)*, *binge eating and preoccupation with eating*, and *controlled eating and social concern for weight gain*—but can also be used to compute a total score of eating disorders symptoms. In Garner et al. (1982), *controlled eating and social concern for weight gain* is referred to as *oral control*, but, in this study, we revised the name of this subscale to *controlled eating and social concern for weight gain*, which seems to better represent its contents. The instructions given to participants were as follows: "Please read each sentence, choose the expression that best applies to you, and circle the number in the response field on the right (Options: 1. Never, 2. Rarely, 3. Sometimes, 4. Frequently, 5. Very frequently, 6. All the time)."

Analysis

The data analysis consisted of (a) investigating the average value, standard deviation, and reliability of each measure; (b) investigating zero-order correlations; and (c) structural equation modeling to predict eating disorders symptoms from cognitive control and thinking errors, in that order. Structural equation modeling (also known as covariance structure analysis) is a statistical method that expresses the strength of the associations between variables by path diagrams (models) that use single headed arrows to represent causal effects. This is similar to a multiple regression analysis, but it has the following advantages, which are not seen in multiple regression analyses. (a) The goodness of fit between the model and correlation matrix can be evaluated from the values of indicators such as Goodness of Fit Index (GFI), Adjusted Goodness of Fit Index (AGFI), and A Root Mean Square Error of Approximation (RMSEA). Both GFI and AGFI usually take values from 0 to 1. Scores of .90 or more indicate good fit (Toyoda, 1998). RMSEA (Marsh, Balla, & Hau, 1996) smaller than 0.08 indicates reasonable fit (Browne & Cudeck 1993). (b) We can handle not only associations among manifest variables, but also those of latent variables. Latent variables are factors that influence manifest phenomena from behind those phenomena. In the path diagrams, they are represented by ellipses. Manifest (observable) variables, on the other hand, are represented by squares. By using latent variables, errors can be eliminated from the manifest variables (Toyoda, 1998). Since latent variables can theoretically be interpreted as true values with errors eliminated from manifest variables, using latent variables can make the associations between variables clearer. The calculation of average values, the estimation of reliability, and the correlation analyses were performed with SPSS 9.0 J for Windows, while structural equation modeling was performed with Amos 4.0.

RESULTS

Investigating the Basic Statistics and Reliability of Each Scale

Table 1 shows the mean value and standard deviation of each scale and the reliability of the Cronbach α coefficients estimated from the viewpoint of internal consistency across scale items. The α coefficient of *logical analysis* was 0.609, but all others were above 0.739 Therefore, a mostly satisfactory internal consistency was achieved.

Table 1. Descriptive statistics and internal consistency of study measures (N = 173)

	M	SD	α
Logical Analysis	16.557	2.747	0.609
Refraining from Catastrophic Thinking	11.734	2.825	0.739
Thinking Errors Scale (TES)	45.628	10.344	0.915
Eating Attitudes Test (EAT-26)	55.995	17.645	0.886

Investigating Zero-Order Correlations among Variables

The zero-order correlation coefficient between the variables is shown in Table 2. "Thinking errors" showed a positive correlation with EAT-26 ($r = 0.388$, $p < 0.001$). The subscales of *cognitive control, logical analysis,* and *refraining from catastrophic thinking* showed a negative correlation with *thinking errors* ($r = -0.317$ and $r = -0.553$, $p < .001$, respectively). In the associations between eating disorders symptoms and cognitive control, *refraining from catastrophic thinking* showed a trend for negative correlation ($r = -0.131$, $p < 0.10$) with regard to *eating disorders symptoms*, and the association between *logical analysis* and *eating disorders symptoms* was not significant.

Structural Equation Modeling to Predict Eating Disorders Symptoms by Cognitive Control and Thinking Errors

The results of the correlation analyses above suggested that *thinking errors* may affect *eating disorders symptoms*. Moreover, *cognitive control* showed an effect of reducing *thinking errors*. As such, to investigate how *cognitive control* affects the process of *thinking errors → eating disorders symptoms*, we conducted an investigation using structural equation modeling.

In this study, the model assumed a causal link of *cognitive control → thinking errors → eating disorders symptoms*. With regard to the association between the two subscales of *cognitive control*, objective and logical analyses of the problem will establish a sense of distance with relation to it. Based on the cognitive behavioral therapy idea that this can be a means to ameliorate catastrophic thinking, it is theoretically assumed that the path going from *logical analysis* to *refraining from catastrophic thinking* is appropriate between the two subscales of *cognitive control* (Sugiura & Umaoka, 2003). The direct path from refraining from catastrophic thinking to thinking errors is also consistent with the effect of mindfulness-based interventions on eating disorders (Wanden-Berghe, Sanz-Valero, & Wanden-Berghe, 2010). As such, the model became one of *logical analysis → refraining from catastrophic thinking → thinking errors → eating disorders symptoms*.

Table 2. Zero-order correlations among cognitive control, thinking errors, and eating disorders symptoms ($N = 173$)

	Logical Analysis	Refraining from Catastrophic Thinking	TES	EAT-26
Logical Analysis	1.000	0.368***	−0.317***	−0.077
Refraining from Catastrophic Thinking		1.000	−0.553***	−0.131
Thinking Errors Scale (TES)			1.000	0.388***
Eating Attitudes Test (EAT-26)				1.000

*** $p < .001$.

As mentioned above, *logical analysis, refraining from catastrophic thinking, thinking errors,* and *eating disorders symptoms* were treated as latent variables in the structural equation modeling. For *eating disorders symptoms*, the three subscales of EAT-26 shown in Garner et al. (1982), (*diet [restriction of energy intake]*, *binge eating and preoccupation with eating*, and *controlled eating and social concern for weight gain*), were used as manifest variables.

These is one manifest variable for each of the two subscales of *cognitive control* and *thinking errors*. In other words, one manifest variable (item) corresponds to one latent variable (factor). In such cases, factor analysis is usually impossible, so here we estimate the factor-scores based on the reliability coefficients of each manifest variable as recommended in Toyota, Maeda, and Yanai (1992). For example, from the ellipse of *logical analysis,* arrows are stretched towards the square of the same name, and, at the same time, this square also receives an arrow from the error variable e1. This is because the score of *logical analysis* that is actually observed expresses that it consists of the sum of the latent variable (factor) of the same name and the error. The magnitude of a path from the error e1 to logical analysis is obtained from the reliability coefficient. If e1 and the scores of the manifest variables of logical analysis are known, the latent variables can be estimated from them. The same procedure was followed for *refraining from catastrophic thinking* and *thinking errors*.

The results of the structural equation modeling are shown in Figure 1. As can be seen, a serial association of *cognitive control* (*logical analysis* → *refraining from catastrophic thinking*) → *thinking errors* → *eating disorders symptoms* was obtained. Even if we tried to draw the paths to *thinking errors* or *eating disorders symptoms* from *logical analysis*, there was no significant effect. The GFI, which indicates the goodness of fit between the model and the data, was 0.98, the AGFI was 0.96, and the RMSEA was 0.02, which indicated sufficiently high fitness of the model to the data. In other words, *cognitive control*, especially *refraining from catastrophic thinking*, has been shown to have an effect of reducing *eating disorders symptoms* by reducing *thinking errors*. The coefficient of determination of *eating disorders symptoms* was 0.17, meaning the variance of *eating disorders symptoms* was found to be explained by 17% by variables such as *cognitive control* and *thinking errors*.

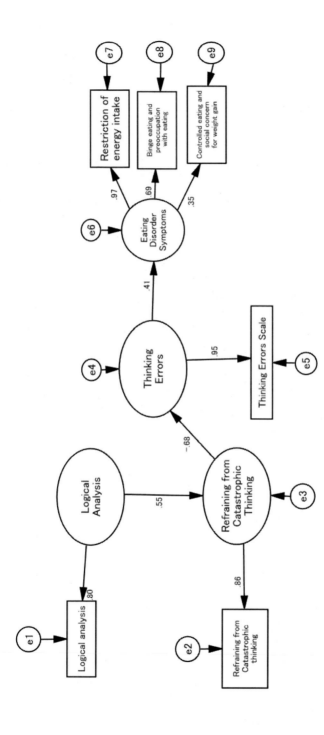

Figure 1. Structural equation model to predict eating disorders symptoms from cognitive control and thinking errors.

$GFI = 0.98$, $AGFI = 0.96$, and $RMSEA = 0.02$. The numerical values of unidirectional arrows are normalized causal coefficients (all being statistically significant at $p < 0.001$). e is the error variable.

DISCUSSION

A positive correlation was found between *thinking errors* and *eating disorders symptoms*, supporting theory of Garner and Bemis's (1982) theory that thinking errors are an important factor in eating disorders symptoms. As mentioned in the introduction section of this paper, with regard to eating disorders, distorted thought patterns (thinking errors) such as excessively linking one's body shape with how one is evaluated by others, and such as associating even slight eating with obesity, can be seen in those with eating disorders.

Furthermore, as a result of the structural equation modeling, which also introduced cognitive control, it was suggested that cognitive control, in particular refraining from catastrophic thinking, may have an effect of reducing eating disorders symptoms by reducing thinking errors. This is consistent with the findings of previous studies that suggest that cognitive behavioral therapy is effective for eating disorders (Cash & Grant, 1996; McCrea, 1991). Logical analysis influenced thinking errors and eating disorders symptoms by promoting refraining from catastrophic thinking. This is consistent with previous findings (Sugiura & Umaoka, 2002; Sugiura, Sugiura & Umaoka, 2003) that logical approaches to one's problems and thoughts can ameliorate negative thinking, via enhanced detachment from negative thinking. We will examine the relation found in detail below.

Refraining from Catastrophic Thinking Reduced Thinking Errors

Refraining from catastrophic thinking measures the skill of alleviating the development of overly negative thinking in stressful situations. Since thinking errors are thought to be characteristic of extreme thought patterns as exemplified by people with various emotional disorders, it is convincing that refraining from catastrophic thinking helps to alleviate this. This result is consistent with recent developments in cognitive behavioral therapy. In

Cognitive Decentering and Eating Disorder Symptoms   173

the original cognitive behavioral therapy based on Beck et al.'s (1979) model, treatment aims to modify negative thought contents. However, Wells and Matthews (1994) focused on the difficulty of changing thought patterns through cognitive behavioral therapy, then presented the necessity of identifying and intervening in the specific thought patterns that are involved in maintaining negative thinking and that prevent change. Such thought patterns are close to the thinking errors that are dealt with in this study. As such, to disrupt such thought patterns, it was first necessary to establish a sense of distance between participants and their thought processes. This method is similar to the skill measured by refraining from catastrophic thinking (*e.g., Even when I do not feel good, I do not think catastrophically; Even if the bad consequences of a problem come to mind, I can reassure myself that they are nothing more than my imagination*). From these facts, it can be said that *refraining from catastrophic thinking* measures important skills that have been brought to light in recent developments in cognitive behavioral therapy.

It is notable that this dimension has also been found to increase with mindfulness-based interventions. Therefore, its effect on eating disorders symptoms via reduced thinking errors may suggest the efficacy of mindfulness, as well. Meditation increased Refraining from Catastrophic Thinking among outpatients with diverse mental disorders (pre-post $d = 1.17$; Katsukura, Ito, Kodama, & Ando, 2008) and analogue samples (pre-follow-up $d = 1.15$; Ito, Ando, & Katsukura, 2009; and pre-post $d = .90$; Tanaka, Sugiura, Shimizu, & Kamimura, 2011). In addition, Katsukura et al. (2008) found that increase in Refraining from Catastrophic Thinking was correlated with symptom reduction ($r = -.87$ to $-.79$). These findings suggest that Refraining from Catastrophic Thinking may also be the working mechanism of mindfulness.

On the other hand, logical analysis is considered to be important as a concrete skill to develop refraining from catastrophic thinking. Cognitive behavioral therapy techniques are considered to promote distance from problems and negative thoughts through encouraging participants to analyze problems objectively and logically and to quantify their problems using standardized assessment techniques. These kinds of typical cognitive behavioral therapy techniques are what are dealt with by logical analysis (*e.g., I can think of several reasons that caused this problem; I can think of several alternatives about how to think or how to act*).

However, the simple correlation between the *cognitive control* subscales and *eating disorders symptoms* was not strong, and, while *refraining from catastrophic thinking* remained a significant trend ($p <$ 0.10), it did not reach the level of statistical significance (Table 2). As such, it is necessary to be cautious when considering the relationship between *cognitive control* and *eating disorders symptoms*. As for why the relationship between *cognitive control* and *eating disorders symptoms* was not so strong, it is conceivable that, with regard to eating disorders, knowledge related to physiological processes such as the relationship between eating behaviors and body shape is having an effect. With regard to eating disorders, for example, cognition such as "When I eat sweets, my stomach will no doubt soon get fat" and "If my weight increases even a little, it will no doubt keep increasing" can be seen (Matsumoto & Sakano, 1998, p. 21). To notice such cognitive errors, knowledge of human digestive functions as well as objective thinking abilities are necessary. Indeed, in the treatment of eating disorders, an educational approach to communicating such knowledge has been adopted (Kiriike, 2000).

Fairburn, Shafran, and Cooper (1999, p. 23), based on reviews of prior research, proposed a model that emphasizes strong control desire as a maintenance mechanism of anorexia nervosa. As seen in the concepts of self-efficacy (e.g., in Bandura, 1995) and the locus of control (Rotter, 1966), having a sense of control over the events around oneself can improve one's self-esteem and mental health in general. People with anorexia nervosa are thought to satisfy their control desire by controlling their dietary behaviors (Fairburn et al., 1999). However, control of one's eating behaviors is likely to lead to a loss of feelings of control. For example, one's weight does not diminish proportionally with the amount of effort expended. Moreover, worsening of one's nutritional status due to dietary restrictions reduces one's cognitive function, causing difficulty with concentration, which, in turn, may lower one's feelings of control. If one lacks objective knowledge about the relationship between eating

Cognitive Decentering and Eating Disorder Symptoms 175

behavior and weight, it would be difficult to notice such a vicious cycle. It is necessary to share scientific knowledge to make those affected aware of this point. The fact that Maruyama, Fukushi, Amari, Umaoka, and Horie (1999) have pointed out that widespread malnutrition caused by weight loss preferences and dietary restraint, and the fact that many female college students are not aware of healthy body weights in many cases, points to a need to educate people about correct eating habits. Based on this point of view, by combining a scientifically accurate transmission of nutritional and physiological knowledge with cognitive treatments such as cognitive control that focus on changing thought patterns, it can be expected that we will be able intervene in eating disorders symptoms and unhealthy diets. Maruyama et al. (1999) also point out that, in order to have the correct eating habits, it is important that participants have a sense of control over their correct eating habits.

Cognitive control has been shown to be effective in alleviating depression and anxiety (Sugiura & Umaoka, 2003), but, to investigate how to better treat problems that are deeply related to physiological and physical domains, it will be necessary in the future to examine the association between cognitive control and panic disorder and hypochondriac symptoms, in which beliefs related to the physiological area have an effect.

REFERENCES

Bandura, A. (1977). *Social Learning Theory*. Englewood Cliff, NJ: Prentice-Hall.

Bandura, A. (1995). Comments on the crusade against the causal efficacy of human thought. *Journal of Behavior Therapy and Experimental Psychiatry, 26,* 179–190.

Beck, A. T. (1976). *Cognitive therapy and emotional disorders*. New York: International Universities Press.

Beck, A. T., Rush, A. J., Shaw, B. F., & Emery, G. (1979). *Cognitive therapy of depression*. New York: Guilford Press.

Browne, M. W., & Cudeck, R. (1993). Alternative ways of assessing model fit. In K. A. Bollen & J. S. Long (Eds.), *Testing structural equation models* (pp. 136–162). Newbury Park, CA: SAGE.

Cash, T. F., & Grant, J. R. (1996). Cognitive-behavioral treatment of body image disturbances. In V. B. Van Hasselt, & M. Hersen (Eds.), *Sourcebook of psychological treatment manuals for adult mental disorders* (pp. 567-614). New York: Plenum Press.

Fairburn, C. G., Shafran, R., & Cooper, Z. (1999). A cognitive behavioural theory of anorexia nervosa. *Behaviour Research and Therapy, 37*, 1–13.

Freeman, A. (1989). *Ninchi ryōhō nyūmon* (Y. Yusa, Trans.). Tokyo: Seiwa Shoten.

Freeman, A., Pretzer, J., Fleming, B., & Simon, K. M. (1990). *Clinical applications of cognitive therapy*. New York: Plenum.

Garner, D., & Bemis, K. (1982). A cognitive behavioural approach to anorexia nervosa. *Cognitive Therapy and Research*, 6, 123–150.

Garner, D. M., & Garfinkel, P. E. (1979). The Eating Attitudes Test: An index of the symptoms of anorexia nervosa. *Psychological Medicine, 9*, 273–279.

Garner, D. M., Olmsted, M. P., Bohr, Y., & Garfinkel, P. E. (1982). The Eating Attitudes Test: Psychometric features and clinical correlates. *Psychological Medicine, 12*, 871–878.

Hofmann, S. G., Asnaani, A., Vonk, I. J., Sawyer, A. T., & Fang, A. (2012). The efficacy of cognitive behavioral therapy: A review of meta-analyses. *Cognitive Therapy and Research, 36*, 427–440.

Ito, Y., Ando, O., & Katsukura, R. (2009). The effect of stress reduction program of Zen meditation on mental health: Cognitive change as active ingredients. *Japanese Journal of Psychosomatic Medicine, 49*, 233–239.

Katsukura, R., Ito, Y., Kodama, K., Ando, O. (2008). The effect of stress reduction of Zen meditation program on outpatients. *Japanese Journal of Psychosomatic Medicine, 48*, 139–147.

Cognitive Decentering and Eating Disorder Symptoms 177

Kiriike, N. (2000). *Sesshoku shōgai: tabenai, taberarenai, tabetara tomaranai* [Eating disorders: Not eating, unable to eat, and difficult stop eating once starting]. *Igakushoin.*

Maeda, M. (2002). Sesshoku shōgai [Eating Disorders]. In Shimoyama, H., & Tanno, Y. (Eds.), *Kōza rinshō shinri gaku 3 ijō shinri gaku [Series in clinical psychology 3, Abnormal psychology]* (pp. 267-282). *Tōkyō daigaku shuppan kai.*

Marsh, H. W., Balla, J. R., & Hau, K. Y. (1996). An evaluation of incremental fit indices: A clarification of mathematical and empirical properties. In G. A. Marcoulides & R. E. Schumacker (Eds.), *Advanced structural equation modeling: Issues and techniques* (pp. 315-353). Mahwah, NJ: Erlbaum.

Maruyama, C., Fukushi, A., Amari, T., Umaoka, K., & Horie, T. (1999). Joshi daigakusei no daietto keiken to eiyō jūsoku ritsu oyobi kenkō teki na shoku kōdō suikō no jiko kōryoku kan to no kankei [The interrelationship among experience of dietary weight-reduction, nutrient sufficiency, and self-efficacy for healthy eating behavior in female university students]. *Shishunkigaku, 17,* 446–452.

Matsumoto, S & Sakano, Y. (1998). Sesshoku shōgai no chiryō ni okeru ninchi teki, kōdō teki sokumen no hyōka [Evaluating cognitions and behaviors in treating eating disorders]. *Seishinka shindangaku, 9,* 489–499.

McCarthy, W. J., & Newcomb, M. D. (1992). Two dimensions of perceived self-efficacy: Cognitive control and behavioral coping ability. In R. Schwarzer (Ed.), *Self-efficacy: Thought control of action* (pp. 39–64). Washington, DC: Hemisphere.

McCrea, C. (1991). Eating disorders. In Dryden, W. & Rentoul, R. (Eds.), *Adult clinical problems: A cognitive behavioural approach.* London: Routledge.

Mukai, T., Crago, M., & Shisslak, C. M. (1994). Eating attitudes and weight preoccupation among female high school students in Japan. *Journal of Child Psychology and Psychiatry, 35,* 77–688.

Rotter, J. B. Generalized expectancies for internal versus external control of reinforcement. *Psychological Monographs, 80,* 1–28, 1996.

Sakano, Y. (1995). *Ninchi kōdō ryōhō* [Cognitive behavioral therapy]. Nippon Hyōronsha.

Slater, M. D. (1989). Social influences and cognitive control as predictors of slf-efficacy and eating behavior. *Cognitive Therapy and Research, 13*, 231–245.

Sugiura, T. (2014). *Cognitive control of emotional distress.* Tokyo, Japan: Kazama Shobo.

Sugiura, T., & Sugiura, Y. (2015). Common factors of meditation, focusing, and cognitive behavioral therapy: longitudinal relation of self-report measures to worry, depressive, and obsessive-compulsive symptoms among nonclinical students. *Mindfulness, 6*, 610-623.

Sugiura, T., & Sugiura, Y. (2017). The effects of cognitive decentering on depression: Multiple cognitive vulnerabilities as mediators. In B. Muireadhach & G. Colin (Eds.) *Mindfulness: Past, Present and Future Perspectives* (pp. 209-231). New York: Nova Science Publishers.

Sugiura, T., Sugiura, Y., & Umaoka, K. (2003). Correlates of cognitive control: Personality traits, meta-cognitions, and coping styles. *Journal of the Graduate School: Home Economics-Human Life Science, 9*, 13–23.

Sugiura, T., & Umaoka, K. (2003). Cognitive control and depression in female university students. *Japanese Journal of Health Psychology, 16*, 31–42.

Tanaka, K., Sugiura, Y., Shimizu, K., & Kamimura, E. (2011). The effect of mindfulness meditation for worry: The examination of mediational variable. *Japanese Journal of Cognitive Therapy, 4*, 46–56.

Tanno, Y., Sakamoto, S., Ishigaki, T., Sugiura. Y., & Mōri, I. (1998). Ykuutsu to suiron no ayamari: Suiron no ayamari shakudo (TES) no sakusei. *Kono hana shinri rinshō jānaru, 4*, 55–60.

Toyoda, T. (1998). *Kyōbunsan kōzō bunseki (Nyūmonhen): Kōzō hōteishiki* [*Introduction to covariance structure analyses: Structural equation modeling*]. Asakura shoten.

Toyoda, T., Maeda, T., Yanai, H. (1992). *Gen-in wo saguru tōkei gaku: kyō bunsan kōzō bunseki nyūmon* [*Statistics to infer causal* relationships: *Introduction to covariance structure analyses*]. Kōdansha.

Wanden-Berghe, R. G., Sanz-Valero, J., & Wanden-Berghe, C. (2010). The application of mindfulness to eating disorders treatment: a systematic review. *Eating disorders, 19*, 34-48.

Wells, A, & Matthews, G. (1994). *Attention and emotion.* Hove: Laurence Erlbaum.

APPENDIX A. ITEMS OF THE COGNITIVE CONTROL SCALE

Logical Analyses

- I can quietly consider the meaning of the problem to myself.
- I can think of several reasons which caused this problem.
- I can think of several alternatives about how to think or how to act.
- I can consider both good and bad aspects of the situation and will be able to search for possible actions.
- I reflect on my habitual ways of conceiving or seeing situations.
- I imagine solving a problem.

Refraining from Catastrophic Thinking

- Even when I do not feel good, I don't think catastrophically.
- Even if the bad consequences of a problem come to mind, I can reassure myself that they are nothing more than my imagination.
- Even in such a situation, I keep bright hope and think that I can change adversity into benefit.
- I don't develop a negative scenario from a situation.
- When I start thinking about the situation seriously, I can stop it for a while.

Note: Rated on a 4-point scale: 1 (I absolutely I cannot), 2 (I perhaps cannot), 3 (I perhaps can), and 4 (I definitely can).

Appendix B. Items of the Thinking Errors Scale (TES)

Arbitrary Inferences

- I sometimes draw negative conclusions about myself without evidence.
- I sometimes come to pessimistic conclusions without basis.
- I sometimes jump to hasty conclusions without basis when people react badly to me.
- I sometimes think that my current situation is worse than before without basis.

Selective Attention

- I become anxious about even trivial things that are negative to me.
- Even when good things happen to me, I tend to ignore them.
- Even if only one bad thing happens, I end up worrying a lot about it.

Overvaluation and Undervaluation

- I think too much about the successes and strengths of others, and tend to overlook the failings and shortcomings of others.
- I think too much about my own failings and shortcomings and undervalue my successes and strengths.

Cognitive Decentering and Eating Disorder Symptoms

181

Overgeneralizations

- When I have trouble with my friends, I end up feeling that they don't like me.
- Even when it is just a small mistake, I feel as if everything is a failure.
- When something bad happens to me, I feel as if it keeps happening over and over.
- Even if just one thing is not good, I feel that it is that way everywhere in the world.
- I find myself drawing arbitrary conclusions about broad areas based on minor events.
- Even when it is just a small success, I feel as if everything is a success.

Individualization

- Even when I know that something has no relation to myself, I can't help but feel as if it does.
- When something bad happens, I can't help but feel as if it's my fault.

Perfectionism and Black-or-White Thinking

- I tend to look at things from extremes, as either being perfect or disastrous.
- I tend to look at things as if they are black and white.

BIOGRAPHICAL SKETCHES

Yoshinori Sugiura

Affiliation: Hirosima University

Education: PhD (Univetsity of Tokyo)

Address: Hiroshima University, Graduate School of Integrated Arts and Sciences, 1-7-1, Kagamiyama, Higashi-Hiroshima, 739-8521, JAPAN

Research and Professional Experience: Fellow of the Japan Society for the Promotion of Science

Professional Appointments: Associate Professor

Honors: Kido Reserach Prize (2000)

Publications from the Last 3 Years:

Sugiura, T., & Sugiura, Y. (2015). Common factors of meditation, focusing, and cognitive behavioral therapy: longitudinal relation of self-report measures to worry, depressive, and obsessive-compulsive symptoms among nonclinical students. *Mindfulness, 6,* 610-623.

Sugiura, Y. (2017). Metacognitive, emotional, and avoidance predictors of generalized anxiety disorder. *Psychology, 8,* 636-653.

Sugiura, Y., & Sugiura, T. (2015). Emotional intensity reduces later generalized anxiety disorder symptoms when fear of anxiety and negative problem-solving appraisal are low. *Behaviour Research and Therapy, 71,* 27-33.

Tomoko Sugiura

Affiliation: Japan Sociaty for the Promotion of Science

Education: PhD (Japan Woman's University)

Professional Appointments: Fellow of the Japan Society for the Promotion of Science

Honors: Naruse Jonzo Memorial Prize (2003)

Publications from the Last 3 Years:

Sugiura, T., & Sugiura, Y. (2015). Common factors of meditation, focusing, and cognitive behavioral therapy: longitudinal relation of self-report measures to worry, depressive, and obsessive-compulsive symptoms among nonclinical students. *Mindfulness, 6*, 610-623.

Sugiura, T., & Sugiura, Y. (2016). Relationships between refraining from catastrophic thinking, repetitive negative thinking, and psychological distress. *Psychological Reports, 119*, 374-394.

Sugiura, Y., & Sugiura, T. (2015). Emotional intensity reduces later generalized anxiety disorder symptoms when fear of anxiety and negative problem-solving appraisal are low. *Behaviour Research and Therapy, 71*, 27-33.

ABOUT THE AUTHORS

Yoshinori Sugiura is Associate Professor at Hiroshima University. He was a recipient of Kido Research Prize from Japanese Association for Educational Psychology in 2000. The focus of his work is on cognitive behavior therapy for anxiety disorder, mindfulness, and psychopathy and publishes many articles related to these themes.

Tomoko Sugiura is Fellow of the Japan Society tor the Promotion of Science. She won Naruse Jollzo Memorial Prize in 2003 from Japan Woman's university. The current research interest includes metacognitive approach to emotional disorders and measurement of cognitive control skills. Her representative book is *Cognitive Control of Emotional Distress* (Tokyo: Kazama Shobo, 2014).

In: Meditation
Editor: Lucia Brewer

ISBN: 978-1-53613-223-6
© 2018 Nova Science Publishers, Inc.

Chapter 7

EXPLORING THE RELATIVE CONTRIBUTIONS OF SELF AND MINDFULNESS DIFFERENTIATION FOR PREDICTING BURNOUT

Thomas V. Frederick, Scott Dunbar, Susan Purrington, Sarah Y. Fisher and Richard Ardito*

California Baptist University – Online and Professional Studies

ABSTRACT

This study seeks to combine three distinct, yet important literatures. First, burnout is a huge concern as workers and employers experience losses and challenges due to its effects. DoS and mindfulness have been identified as important psychological traits for coping with burnout. The results of the present study suggest that both DoS and Mindfulness are negatively correlated with burnout indicating that these traits are important buffers against and resources for coping with emotional

---

* Corresponding Author Email: tfrederick@calbaptist.edu.

exhaustion. However, mindfulness is a better predictor of burnout than DoS in the current study. Implications for future research are provided.

Keywords: differentiation of self, mindfulness, burnout, emotional exhaustion

INTRODUCTION

This study seeks to combine three distinct, yet important literatures. First, burnout is a huge concern as workers and employers experience losses and challenges due to its effects. There are two psychological constructs that have been studied due to their theoretical relevance for coping with stressful experiences. There is a growing literature on the impact mindfulness has on burnout. Finally, there have been several attempts to understand the role of differentiation of self has in preventing or managing burnout.

BURNOUT

The construct of burnout, credited to Freudenberger and Maslach, originated in the 1970's in the human services and healthcare fields. Dubbed the pioneering phase, the 1970's was characterized by a focus on burnout symptoms, mental health, underlying motives and values of the individuals, and the relationship between the individual provider and recipient. Early research found emotional exhaustion was a common response to job overload and depersonalization, or cynicism, was used as a coping mechanism from emotional stress. The next phase of burnout, the empirical phase, emerged in the 1980's and saw research shift from interviews and observation to systematic empirical research. Larger populations were studied through quantitative studies that utilized questionnaires and surveys. It was during this phase of burnout that Maslach and Jackson created the Maslach Burnout Inventory (MBI). Empirical research on the construct of burnout continued into the 1990's, but with expanded populations and longitudinal studies. Research in this phase extended to occupations outside the human services and education fields, and involved statistical tools and methodologies (Maslach, Schaufeli, & Leiter, 2001).

While the majority of burnout studies continue to take place in the healthcare field, the construct of burnout has been applied to a multitude of industries and occupations. Examples include the construction industry, academia: teachers, students, faculty, newspaper editors, and athletes; religion: pastors; sports: referees, administrators, and players (Chandler, 2009; Enhassi, Al, & Arain, 2016; Filak & Reinardy, 2011; Fowler, 2015; Hue & Lau, 2015; İlimdar & Atalay, 2016; Oliveira, Maroco, & Campos, 2016; Saatoğlu & Elif, 2014; Schaufeli, Martinez, Pinto, & Bakker, 2002; Vitali, Bortoli, Bertinato, Robazza, & Schena, 2015; Zucoloto, Al-Haliq, Altahayneh, & Oudat, 2014). Major findings reveal burnout may be caused by work and non-work factors such as a perceived high work load, unfair rewards, poor worker treatment, job role ambiguity, job insecurity, work culture, work-family conflict, work-life balance (Abbott, 2013; Enshassi, Al Swaity, & Arain, 2016; Kokt & Ramarumo, 2015). Individuals with burnout may experience mental and physical consequences including fatigue, headaches, cardiovascular disease, psychological disorders, anxiety, depression, lack of motivation, and loss of memory(Kim, Ji, & Kao, 2011; Sauter, et al., 1999; University of Cambridge, 2011). Organizations are adversely affected by individuals experiencing burnout. Examples include increased employee turnover, potential work-place violence, unpunctuality, increased risk of work-place injury, and decreased customer satisfaction (Maxon, 2011). These adverse effects of burnout pose hard costs such as financial costs, as well as soft costs such as a poor work culture.

DIFFERENTIATION OF SELF

Differentiation of Self (DoS) derives from the theorizing of Murray Bowen (Bowen, 1978; Titleman, 2014; Papero, 1990, 2014). DoS is considered a relational characteristic whereby relational partners are able to (1) take I-positions, i.e., maintain personal value-based preferences and commitments, while (2) maintain interpersonal relationships. That is, DoS entails one's ability to know those beliefs and values which are non-negotiable and maintaining relationships with others, even in the face of extreme pressure to conform or change one's beliefs. To this end, DoS is comprised of two distinct drives. One is the drive for togetherness or relationships while the other is individuality. High levels of DoS consist of balancing these drives.

DoS is also theorized to buffer against anxiety (Bowen, 1978; Titleman, 2014; Papero, 1990, 2014). Individuals experiencing anxiety rely on many different coping strategies. Gilbert (2006) identifies four processes which are used to manage anxiety and stress. These four processes are: (a) triangulation, (b) conflict, (c) distance, and (d) over-functioning/under-functioning reciprocity. When this anxiety or stress occurs, individuals seek to manage this stress by engaging in triangulation. Relational partners may include others, i.e., a child, another person, or even an issue, in order to draw closer to one partner and increasing emotional distance from the conflict. Conflict results due to the inability of individuals to control their relationships to manage anxiety. Conflict arises as each partner tries to manage anxiety through the other which in turn increases the level of anxiety. Individuals increase the amount of emotional distance in the relationship to avoid the subjective experience of anxiety. In some cases, this process will focus anxiety in one of the relational partners who will be unable to function as a result of the symptoms. This will create in the other partner the need to over-function for the symptomatic spouse. As the over-functioning partner maintains focus on the under-functioning spouse, anxiety increases in the relationship which furthers this relationship pattern.

Due to DoS theoretical connections with anxiety and stress, several researchers have utilized it in understanding burnout. There have been two main foci for DoS and burnout. First, DoS and burnout have been studied among Christian clergy (Beebe, 2007; Wasberg, 2013). Beebe (2007) identified the role that DoS plays among role perception, conflict

Exploring the Relative Contributions ...

management, and burnout. In this study, burnout moderates the relationship between DoS and turnover among clergy. Specifically, clergy with higher levels of DoS tend to have lower levels of burnout and turnover. Second, DoS has been identified as an important variable for nurses (Walker, 1997). Walker described the overall positive effect of DoS on burnout for nurses in management positions.

MINDFULNESS

Mindfulness has become an increasingly researched topic. Since its use in mindfulness-based stress reduction (MBSR) in the early 1980s, it has been a focus of both clinical and empirical research. Mindfulness is a process whereby individuals focus on their present moment awareness (Williams, 2008; Quaglia, Warren, Lindsay, Creswell, & Goodman, 2015). In other words, mindfulness is paying attention to one's current experiences – thoughts, feelings, and situations of everyday life. This idea of purposeful attention is associated with an attitude of non-judgmental acceptance of that experience. In other words, mindfulness is nonjudgmental acceptance of one's awareness of thoughts, feelings and experiences.

Several studies have explored the potential benefits of health care professionals using MBSR to address burnout concerns. Medical professionals and premed students reported reduced anxiety, depression and an increase in empathy and spirituality after using MBSR. Nursing students experienced reduced burnout and reported an increase of life satisfaction, after four weeks of using MBSR. Counseling psychology students reported a decline in "negative affect, perceived stress, rumination, and...anxiety" (Irving, Dobkin, & Park, 2009, p. 63). Although various research studies suggested potential benefits of mindfulness with health care professionals, not all research had the same outcome. One study looked at pediatric oncology staff, mostly nurses, who participated in eight weekly sessions of mindfulness education. After completion of the mindfulness based course, almost all the participants reported no change in burnout signs (Moody et. al, 2013). Mindfulness was also identified as a resource against compassion and fatigue among social work interns; the results of this study suggested that mindfulness may be a protective factor for helping professionals (Decker, Brown, Ong, & Stiney-Ziskind, 2015).

RESEARCH QUESTIONS

Based on the literature connecting burnout with mindfulness and differentiation, we explored the interrelationships among these variables. First, we wanted to determine if DoS and mindfulness would be positively correlated. Second, we wanted to determine if DoS and mindfulness would be negatively correlated with burnout as suggested in the cited literature. Third and finally, we wanted to determine the relative contributions of DoS and mindfulness in predicting burnout.

METHODS

To explore the research questions above, participants consisted of students recruited from the online and professional studies division of a private, Christian university in Southern California. This division provides undergraduate and graduate degree programs for non-traditional students. The internal review board for this university approved this project August 2016.

MEASURES

The Haber Level of Differentiation of Self Scale (LDSS) (Haber, 1993) measures participants' levels of differentiation. The LDSS is a 24-item scale which seeks to measure one's ability to maintain one's cognitive functioning and goal directed behavior, especially in times of anxiety and stress. This is a core component of Bowen's Differentiation of Self construct (Bowen, 1978; Popenoe, 2014; Titelman, 2014). The items use a 4-point format ranging from 1 = strongly disagree to 4 = strongly agree. Haber (1993) reports an internal consistency of .90 for this scale; in the present study, the LDSS scale has an internal consistency of .90.

Burnout is operationalized for the present study using the Maslach Burnout Inventory (MBI) (Maslach & Jackson, 1981). As originally defined, "Burnout is a syndrome of emotional exhaustion and cynicism" (Maslach & Jackson, 1981, p. 99) indicating the emotional exhaustion emphasis for this construct. Further, the MBI has four subscales. These scales are (1) emotional exhaustion (EE), (2) depersonalization, (DP) (3) personal accomplishment (PA), and (4) involvement. Of note, the involvement scale is an optional one, so it is not utilized in the present study. According to multiple studies, the emotional exhaustion subscale of the MBI is the core component in measuring burnout (Bianchi, Schonfeld, & Laurent, 2015; Schaufeli & Taris, 2005; Wheeler, Vassar, Worley, & Barnes, 2011). In addition, the emotional exhaustion subscale is the closest subscale to a traditional stress variable (Maslach, Jackson, & Leiter, 1997). As such, the emotional exhaustion subscale is the primary component used to measure burnout in this study based on the relatively low reliabilities obtained for DP (.76) and PA (.81). For the present study, EE scale reliability is .88. The mindfulness construct is measured using the Southampton Mindfulness Questionnaire (SMQ) (Chadwick et al., 2008). The SMQ is a 16-item scale developed to assess the *awareness* of distressing thoughts and feelings in a mindful manner. This scale utilizes a 7-point Likert-type scale. Chadwick et al., reported α for SMQ of .89. For the present study, the reliability of the SMQ is .88.

RESULTS FOR DOS, MINDFULNESS AND BURNOUT

Participants

Table 1 represents a summary of the demographic categories of the sample. Consistent with the student body of the working adult division of the private Christian university, 66.8% of the respondents identify being enrolled in an undergraduate program. The average age of respondents is 29.30 years which is consistent with the sample of working and professional adults in this university division. There are dramatic differences between the amounts of female (70.3%) to male (29.2%) respondents. Participants predominantly identify Caucasian as their ethnicity (43.3%) followed by Hispanic/Latino (29.3%) and African American (11.5%). Over 4 percent of the sample identify as being multiracial (4.8%).

Table 1. Demographic characteristics

Variable[1]	Total %
Age (Years) (M/SD)	29.30 (8.86)
Level of Degree Program	
BA	40.4
BS	26.4
MA	3.4
MS	10.6
MBA	19.2
Gender	
Male	29.2
Female	70.3
Prefer not to say	.5
Ethnicity	
African American	11.5
Asian American	7.2
Arab American	.5
Caucasian	43.3
Hispanic/Latino	29.3
Multiracial	4.8
Native American	.5
Other	2.9

[1] (N= 208).

Exploring the Relative Contributions ... 193

Variable[1]	Total %
Denominational Affiliation	
Baptist	22.1
Catholic	18.8
Church of Christ	1.4
Evangelical	5.8
Lutheran	2.9
Methodist	.5
Non-denominational Christian	31.7
Other	9.1
Pentecostal	5.3
Presbyterian	1.0
Seventh Day Adventist	1.4
Relationship Status	
Married	36.5
Single	56.3
Divorced	4.8
Separated	2.4

Data were analyzed three ways using SPSS version 24. First, sample means and standard deviations were calculated for DoS, mindfulness (SMQ), and Burnout (EE). Second, a correlation coefficient matrix was created to determine the nature of relationships among study variables. Third and finally, hierarchical regression was used to determine the relative contributions of the demographic data, DoS, and mindfulness on burnout.

Table 2 contains the means and standard deviations of the study variables and the correlation coefficient matrix for DoS, mindfulness and burnout. There are two important notes related to the correlations. First, DoS and mindfulness are positively correlated meaning that individuals with higher levels of differentiation tend to have higher levels of state mindfulness. In fact, the amount of variance accounted for among these two variables is 15%. Second, both DoS and Mindfulness are negatively correlated with burnout indicating that higher levels of differentiation and mindfulness are inversely associated with burnout. As indicated in table 2, the study variables are relatively normally distributed as both skewness and kurtosis are between -1 and 1.

Table 2. Means and standard deviations and correlation coefficient matrix for DoS, mindfulness, and burnout

Variables	DoS	Mindfulness	MBI EE
DoS	1.00		
Mindfulness	.39**	-	
MBI EE	-.20**	-.30**	-
Mean (Standard Deviation)	77.28 (9.02)	48.31 (15.18)	18.42 (10.86)
Skewness (Standard Error)	.03 (.17)	.21 (.17)	.67 (.17)
Kurtosis (Standard Error)	-.47 (.34)	-.33 (.34)	-.09 (.34)

Notes: ** = $p \leq .01$. N = 208. DoS – Level of Differentiation of Self Scale; Mindfulness – Southampton Mindfulness Questionnaire, MBI EE – Maslach Burnout Inventory – Emotional Exhaustion.

Table 3 details the results for the regression analysis. It is interesting to note that the demographic variables of age, gender, ethnicity, marital status, and program level do not account for a significant portion of the variance associated with emotional exhaustion as described in Model 1. Based on model 2, Differentiation of Self is a significant predictor of the emotional exhaustion aspects of burnout. Of note for model 2, marital status and program level have larger b score absolute values compared with differentiation. In comparing β weights, however, DoS (β = -.21) has a larger absolute score than either marital status (β = .17) and program level (β = -.05) indicating that DoS is the best single predictor of burnout for model 2. Model 3 indicates that mindfulness is by and far the best single predictor of emotional exhaustion. Including mindfulness in the regression analysis accounts for another 7% of the total variance associated with the study variables. Further, comparing the β weights for DoS (β = -

Exploring the Relative Contributions ... 195

.10), marital status (β = .18) and program level (β = -.07) with mindfulness (β = -.30) demonstrates that it is the best single predictor of burnout for model 3. When discussing regression models, it is also important to include the Cohen's f^2 which is 0.16 in the present study. Cohen (1988) identifies f^2 between .15 and .34 as having a medium effect indicating that the regression presented in this study has a medium effect.

Table 3. Hierarchical regression analyses for variables predicting burnout

Variables	Model 1		Model 2		Model 3	
Block 1	*b*	*SE b*	*b*	*SE b*	*b*	*SE b*
Age	.04	.09	.08	.09	.15	.09
Gender	-1.36	1.66	-.97	1.63	-2.05	1.59
Ethnicity	-.18	.26	-.22	.25	-.21	.24
Marital Status	2.06	.88	2.10	.86	2.25	.83
Program Level	-.31	.42	-.26	.41	-.37	.40
Block 2						
DoS	-	-	-.25	.08	-.11	.09
Block 3						
SMQ	-	-	-	-	-.22	.05
Constant	17.78		35.08		34.84	
Adjusted R^2	.01		.05		.12	
F change	1.44		8.91**		17.22**	

NOTE. ** = $p \leq 0.001$.

DISCUSSION

Based on the results, mindfulness and DoS are important psychological traits that negatively impact burnout or emotional exhaustion. Differentiation of self, in comparison to demographic characteristics, is negatively correlated with burnout. This corresponds to findings like

Haber's (1993) research on DoS and stress. Haber finds an inverse relationship between stress and anxiety and DoS. In other words, individuals with higher levels of differentiation have lower levels of stress and anxiety which correspond with Bowen theory and the results presented in the current study.

More specifically on the relationship between DoS and burnout, the LDSS is designed to measure emotional maturity (Haber, 1993). Haber (1993, p. 166, italics in original) focuses her measure of differentiation along intellectual system function, or "[a]s such, it is defined as the degree to which a person can maintain intellectual system functioning as opposed to being controlled by emotional forces within the relationship system." This equates emotional maturity with one's ability to act in a values-based manner during times of stress and anxiety. In theorizing about the link between DoS and burnout in the present study, it seems likely that DoS allows individuals to maintain their commitments while experiencing emotional exhaustion. In other words, individuals with higher levels of DoS can tolerate emotional exhaustion and identify coping strategies to deal with it. Further, due to the inverse nature of this relationship, it seems possible that individuals have the ability to cope with their stressors before experiencing higher levels of burnout.

Mindfulness, or the ability to attend to one's experience without judging it, allows one to tolerate stress and exhaustion. The SMQ is specifically designed to measure the mindfulness capacity of tolerating and accepting distressing thoughts and experiences (Chadwick et al., 2008). If mindfulness is attending to one's experiences in an open, non-judgmental manner, this ability is a useful skill when coping with burnout and emotional exhaustion. Mindfulness is an important trait for respondents in the present study as it is negatively correlated with burnout indicating those individuals with higher levels of mindfulness have lower levels of emotional exhaustion. Further in the present study, mindfulness outperforms differentiation in accounting for burnout. Based on our findings, mindfulness may play a crucial role in preventing and ameliorating burnout over and above DoS. Theoretically, this finding could be connected to the experiences of burnout and then goal directed behavior. That is, mindfulness allows one to experience emotional exhaustion associated with burnout. As individuals are aware of this experience, they may accept this experience nonjudgmentally. Only after awareness and openness to this experience is one perhaps able to engage in goal directed behavior (DoS). This is a similar finding to Voci, Veneziani, and Metta (2016) in investigating the relationships between mindfulness, organizational commitment, and burnout. Voci et al., document the protective role mindfulness has between organizational commitment and burnout among Italian health care professions. In the Voci et al., study, mindfulness allows one to maintain organizational commitments despite burnout. In considering that mindfulness is the single best predictor of burnout in the present study, it is a crucial aspect for individuals for dealing with stress and emotional exhaustion. This finding corresponds well with the literature on mindfulness and burnout. For example, Taylor and Millear (2016) identify mindfulness is indeed an important personal resource in preventing burnout as well as in dealing with stressful work experiences. Thus, they encourage businesses to include mindfulness resources to prevent burnout and turnover.

LIMITATIONS AND SUGGESTIONS FOR FUTURE RESEARCH

An important consideration for the current study is the student sample it is based on. It would be helpful to include different religious groups as part of future research as mindfulness and DoS have been used in research with Christian populations (e.g., Pieris, 2010; Jankoswki & Sandage, 2012; Jankowski & Vaughn, 2009; Wachholtz & Pargament, 2005, 2008). As this sample of students comes from a religiously affiliated university, it is important to determine the relationships among DoS, mindfulness, and burnout among other religious and spiritual group.

A second aspect of the study is to consider the similarity of DoS and mindfulness. There has been only one empirical article specifically researching the relationships between mindfulness and DoS (Khaddouma, Gordon, & Bolden, 2015) despite the seeming similarities among these constructs. Using the LDSS as the measure of DoS may have operationalized it too similarly to mindfulness. For example, the LDSS items identify one's ability to make purposeful decisions despite one's feelings, experiences, or social pressure. This is similar to how the SMQ operationalizes the cognitive components of mindfulness. It may be important to operationalize DoS in more intrapersonal, emotional terms (Licht & Chabot, 2006) in order to clarify the specific contributions DoS and mindfulness have on burnout as these variables are more individual as opposed to relation in nature.

In conclusion, DoS and mindfulness have been identified as important psychological traits for coping with burnout. The results of the present study suggest that both DoS and Mindfulness are negatively correlated with burnout. However, mindfulness is a better predictor of burnout than DoS in the current study. We recommend including a broader sample and using a DoS measure designed for specifically assessing intrapersonal DoS in future studies.

REFERENCES

Abbott, P. M. (2013, October). Work/Life balance. *Accountancy* SA, 44-45.

Al-Haliq, M., Altahayneh, Z. L., & Oudat, M. (2014). Levels of burnout among sports referees in Jordan. *Journal of Physical Education and Sport*, 14(1), 47-51.

Beebe, R. S. (2007). Predicting burnout, conflict management style, and turnover among clergy. *Journal of Career Assessment*, 15, 257-275. doi: 10.1177/1069072706298157.

Bianchi, R., Schonfeld, I., & Laurent, E. (2015). Is burnout separable from depression in cluster analysis? A longitudinal study. *Social Psychiatry and Psychiatric Epidemiology*, 50(6), 1005-1011. doi:10.1007/s00127-014-0996-8.

Bowen, M. (1978). *Family therapy and clinical practice*. New York: Jason Aronson.

Chadwick, P., Hember, M., Symes, J., Peters, E., Kuipers, E., & Dagnan, D. (2008). Responding mindfully to unpleasant thoughts and images: Reliability and validity of the Southampton mindfulness questionnaire (SMQ). *British Journal of Clinical Psychology*, 47, 451-455. DOI: 10.1348/014466508X314891.

Chandler, D. (2009). Pastoral burnout and the impact of personal spiritual renewal, rest-taking, and support system practices. *Pastoral Psychology*, 58, 273-287. doi:10.1007/s11089-008-0184-4.

Cohen J. E. (1988). *Statistical power analysis for the behavioral sciences.* Hillsdale, NJ: Lawrence Erlbaum Associates, Inc.

Decker, J. T., Brown, J. L. C., Ong, J., & Stiney-Ziskind, C. A. (2015). Mindfulness, compassion fatigue, and compassion satisfaction among social work interns. *Social Work and Christianity*, 42(1), 28-42.

Enshassi, A., Al Swaity, E., & Arain, F. (2016). Investigating common causes of burnout in the construction industry. *International Journal of Construction Project Management*, 8(1), 43-56.

Filak, V., & Reinardy, S. (2011). Editor toast: A study of burnout and job satisfaction among college newspaper editors. *Journalism & Mass Communication Educator,* 66(3), 243-256.

Fowler, S. (2015). Burnout and depression in academia: A look at the discourse of the university. *European Journal for the Philosophy of Communication*, 6(2), 155-167. doi:10.1386/ejpc.6.2.155_1.

Gilbert, R. M. (2006). *The eight concepts of Bowen theory.* Falls Church, VA: Leading Systems Press.

Haber, J. (1993). A construct validity study of a Differentiation of Self Scale. *Scholarly Inquiry for Nursing Practice: An International Journal*, 7, 165-178.

Hall, C. M. (1991). *Bowen family theory and its uses.* New York: Jason Aronson.

Hue, M.-t., & Lau, N.-s. (2015). Promoting well-being and preventing burnout in teacher education: a pilot study of a mindfulness based programme for pre-service teachers in Hong Kong. *Teacher Development*, 3, 381-401. doi:10.1080/13664530.2015.1049748.

İlimdar, Y., & Atalay, G. (2016). Investigation of burnout level of sport faculty students. *Journal of Human Sciences*, 13(3), 5443 - 5448. doi:10.14687/jhs.v13i3.4094.

Irving, J. A., Dobkin, P., & Park, J. (2009) Cultivating mindfulness in health care professionals: A review of empirical studies of mindfulness-based stress reduction (MBSR). *Complementary Therapies in Clinical Practice*, 15, 61-66.

Jankowski, P. J., & Sandage, S. J. (2012). Spiritual dwelling and well-being: The mediating role of differentiation of self in a sample of distressed adults. *Mental Health, Religion, & Culture*, 15, 417-434.

Jankowski, P. J., & Vaughn, M. (2009). Differentiation of self and spirituality: *Empirical explorations. Counseling and Values*, 53, 82-96.

Kerr, M. E., & Bowen, M. (1988). *Family evaluation*. New York: Norton.

Khouddouma, A., Gordon, K. C., & Bolden, J. (2015). Zen and the art of dating: Mindfulness, differentiation of self, and satisfaction in dating relationships. *Couple and Family Psychology: Research and Practice*, 4, 1-13. Doi: 10.1037/cfp0000035.

Kim, H., Ji, J., & Kao, D. (2011, July). Burnout and physical health among social workers: A three-year longitudinal study. *Social Work*, 56(3), 258-268.

Kokt, D., & Ramarumo, R. (2015). *Impact of organisational culture on job stress and burnout in graded accommodation establishments in the Free State province, South Africa.*

Licht, C., & Chabot, D. (2006). The Chabot emotional differentiation scale: A theoretically and psychometrically sound instrument for measuring Bowen's intrapsychic aspect of differentiation. *Journal of Marital and Family Therapy*, 32, 167-180. doi: 10.1111/j.1752-0606.2006.tb01598.x.

Maslach, C. & Jackson, S. (1981). The measure of experienced burnout. *Journal of Occupational Behavior*, 2, 99-113.

Maslach, C., Jackson, S., & Leiter, M. (1997). Maslach burnout inventory. *Evaluating stress: A book of resources, 3*, 191-218.

Moody, K., Kramer, D., Santizo, R., Magro, L., Wyshogrod, D., Ambrosio, J. … Stein, J. (2013). Helping the helpers: Mindfulness training for burnout in pediatric oncology- A pilot program. *Journal of Pediatric Oncology Nursing*, 30(5), 275-284.

Papero, D. V. (1990). *Bowen family systems theory*. Boston: Allyn and Bacon.

Papero, D. V. (2014). Emotion and intellect in Bowen theory. In P. Titelman (Ed.). *Differentiation of self: Bowen family systems perspectives* (pp. 65-81). New York: Routledge.

Pieris, A. (2010). Spirituality as mindfulness: Biblical and Buddhist approaches. *Spiritus*, 10, 38-15. DOI: 10.1353/scs.0.0082.

Qualglia, J. T., Brown, K. W., Lindsay, E. K., Creswell, J. D., & Goodman, R. J. (2015). From conceptualization to operationalization of mindfulness. In K. W. Brown, J. D. Creswell, & R. M. Ryan (Eds.). *Handbook of Mindfulness: Theory, Research, and Practice* (pp.151 - 170). New York: Guilford Press.

Saatoğlu, M., & Elif. (2014). Assessment of burnout levels of sport club administrators. *Nigde University Journal of Physical Education and Sport Sciences, 8*(1), 49-59.

Sauter, S., Murphy, L., Colligan, M., Swanson, N., Hurrell, J. J., Scharf, J. F. ... Tisdale, J. (1999). Stress...at work. *Retrieved from Centers for Disease Control and Prevention*: http://www.cdc.gov/niosh/docs/99-101/.

Schaufeli, W., Martinez, I., Pinto, A., & Bakker, A. (2002). Burnout and engagement in college students. *Journal of Cross-Cultural Psychology*, 33(5), 464-481.

Schaufeli, W., & Taris, T. (2005). The conceptualization and measurement of burnout: Common ground and worlds apart. *Work & Stress, 19*(3), 256-262. doi:10.1080/02678370500385913.

Taylor, N. Z., & Millear, P. M. R. (2016). The contribution of mindfulness to predicting burnout in the workplace. *Personality and Individual Differences*, 89, 123-128. doi: 10.1016/j.paid.2015.10.005.

Titelman, P. (1998). Overview of the Bowen theoretical-therapeutic system. In P. Titelman (Ed.). *Clinical applications of Bowen family systems theory* (pp. 7-49). New York: Haworth Press.

Titelman, P. (2014). The concept of differentiation of self in Bowen theory. In P. Titelman (Ed.). *Differentiation of self: Bowen family systems perspectives* (pp. 3-64). New York: Routledge.

University of Cambridge. (2011, November 29). *Effects of work-related stress.* Retrieved from Human resources policies and procedures: http://www.admin.cam.ac.uk/offices/hr/policy/stress/effects.html.

Vitali, F., Bortoli, L., Bertinato, L., Robazza, C., & Schena, F. (2015). Motivational climate, resilience, and burnout in youth sport. *Sport Sciences for Health*, 11(1), 103-108. doi:10.1007/s11332-014-0214-9.

Voci, A., Veneziani, C. A., & Metta, M. (2016). Affective organizational commitment and dispositional mindfulness as correlates of burnout in health care professionals. *Journal of Workplace Behavioral Health*, 31, 63-70. doi: 10.1080/15555240.2015.1047500.

Wachholtz, A. B., & Pargament, K. I. (2005). Is spirituality a critical ingredient of meditation? Comparing the effects of spiritual meditation, secular meditation, and relaxation on spiritual, psychological, cardiac, and pain outcomes. *Journal of Behavioral Medicine*, 28, 369-384. Doi:10.1007/s10865-005-9008-5.

Wachholtz, A. B., & Pargament, K. I. (2008). Migraines and meditation: Does spirituality matter? *Journal of Behavioral Medicine*, 31, 351-366. Doi: 10.1007/s10865-008-9159.

Walker, P. H. (1997). *An application of Bowen Family Systems Theory: Triangulation, differentiation of self and nurse manager job stress responses.* (Unpublished doctoral dissertation). University of Rochester, NY.

Wasberg, G. D. (2013). *Differentiation of self and leadership effectiveness in Christian clergy: A mixed methods study.* (Unpublished doctoral dissertation). Capella University, USA.

Wheeler, D., Vassar, M., Worley, J., & Barnes, L. (2011). A reliability generalization meta-analysis of coefficient alpha for the Maslach Burnout Inventory. *Educational and Psychological Measurement,* 71(1), 231-244. doi: 10.1177/0013164410391579.

Williams, J. M. G. (2008). Mindfulness, depression, and modes of mind. *Cogntive Therapy Research*, 32, 721-733.

Zucoloto, M., Oliveira, V., Maroco, J., & Campos, J. (2016). School engagement and burnout in a sample of Brazilian students. *Currents in Pharmacy Teaching and Learning*, 8(5), 659-666. doi:10.1016/j.cptl.2016.06.012.

INDEX

A

abuse, 46, 90, 122, 124, 128
access, 70, 86, 95, 98, 99, 103
acting with awareness, 142, 146, 149, 152
adjunctive therapy, 114
adults, viii, x, 38, 109, 110, 111, 112, 113, 120, 127, 129, 192, 200
African, 85, 192
age, xi, 93, 102, 107, 135, 143, 146, 165, 192, 194
alerting, 137, 138, 143, 144, 147, 149, 150, 153
altered states of consciousness, 80, 98
alternative medical practices, 111, 115
alternative therapies, 120, 123
anandamaya kosha, 84
anger, 5, 7, 32, 60
annamaya kosha, 84
anthropologists, 98, 107
anthropology, 80, 82, 108
anxiety, 13, 25, 30, 36, 37, 45, 63, 82, 92, 112, 114, 115, 117, 118, 119, 120, 136, 154, 155, 156, 157, 158, 159, 163, 164, 175, 182, 183, 187, 188, 189, 191, 196

anxiety disorder, 136, 154, 156, 157, 159, 182, 183
Aristotle, 59, 65, 66, 72, 73
asana, 87, 88
assessment, 49, 63, 113, 120, 122, 137, 153, 156, 173
assessment techniques, 49, 173
Assyrian, 85
attention, vi, viii, xi, 12, 21, 23, 25, 26, 27, 46, 48, 49, 50, 58, 60, 61, 64, 73, 76, 87, 96, 102, 105, 115, 135, 136, 137, 138, 139, 140, 141, 142, 143, 144, 147, 148, 149, 150, 151, 152, 155, 156, 157, 179, 180, 189
attention network test (ANT), xi, 136, 137, 143, 144, 146, 147, 149, 150, 151
attentional bias, 117, 124
attentional control, 137, 139, 140, 153
attentional model of mindfulness, 151
attentional selectivity, 151, 152
attitudes, 32, 51, 59, 137, 177
autonomic nervous system, 38
awareness, 4, 12, 18, 19, 21, 23, 27, 28, 52, 54, 58, 59, 61, 62, 71, 73, 81, 84, 87, 91, 92, 117, 141, 142, 146, 149, 152, 155, 189, 191, 197

B

back pain, 22, 119, 126
bad habits, 5, 12, 13
Batchelor, 55, 62, 65, 72
behavior therapy, 136, 158, 159, 182
behavioral medicine, 111, 125
behavioral sciences, 199
behaviors, ix, 2, 39, 40, 114, 124, 130, 174, 177
beneficial effect, viii, 2, 3, 56, 119
benefits, viii, x, 2, 6, 7, 11, 12, 14, 19, 20, 22, 25, 28, 38, 48, 50, 75, 81, 82, 110, 116, 117, 118, 119, 120, 121, 125, 126, 128, 131, 189
bipolar disorder, 82
bliss, 4, 5, 7, 9, 13, 16, 17, 24, 35, 37, 84, 95
Bodhicitta, 7, 9, 36
body image, 119, 176
body mass index (BMI), 4, 9, 19
body shape, 162, 172, 174
borderline personality disorder, 155
brain, 27, 28, 30, 100, 101, 102, 131
breast cancer, 118, 119, 123, 124, 126, 127, 128, 129, 130, 131
breath work, 91, 99, 104
breathing, 9, 13, 23, 24, 25, 28, 29, 32, 65, 84, 87, 97, 116, 117, 140, 141, 151, 152, 153
Buddhism, 6, 7, 39, 53, 61, 65, 66, 67, 71, 72, 74, 75, 78, 85, 87, 89
Buddhist, vii, ix, 1, 39, 40, 43, 44, 45, 46, 49, 52, 55, 56, 60, 65, 66, 67, 68, 69, 70, 71, 73, 74, 75, 126, 201
Buddhist ethics, 44
burnout, vi, viii, xii, 185, 186, 187, 188, 189, 190, 191, 192, 193, 194, 195, 196, 198, 199, 200, 201, 202, 203

C

caduceus, 86
cancer, v, viii, x, 109, 110, 111, 112, 113, 114, 115, 117, 118, 119, 120, 121, 122, 123, 124, 125, 126, 127, 128, 129, 130, 131
cancer care, 126
capitalism, 54, 55, 68, 69, 70, 71
capitalist production, 53
capitalization, ix, 44, 51, 53
Catholicism, 85
chakras, vii, ix, 79, 80, 84
challenges, viii, xii, 49, 54, 91, 185, 186
Chi, v, viii, x, 6, 38, 80, 85, 109, 110, 111, 112, 114, 116, 117, 118, 119, 120, 124, 126, 127, 128, 130, 131, 132, 133
child health, vii, viii, 1, 2, 3, 4, 11, 32, 37
Chinese medicine, 116, 130, 131
Chinese women, vii, viii, 1, 3, 10, 11, 38, 39, 41
Christianity, 52, 199
clairvoyance, 89, 97
clinical assessment, 113, 120
clinical psychology, 156, 177
cognition, 124, 157, 162, 163, 164, 174
cognitive abilities, 154
cognitive behavioral therapy, xi, 156, 158, 159, 161, 162, 163, 164, 169, 172, 173, 176, 178, 181, 182
cognitive control, 38, 143, 152, 163, 164, 165, 167, 168, 169, 170, 171, 172, 174, 175, 178, 179, 183
cognitive decentering, vi, viii, xi, 161, 162, 164, 178
cognitive function, 174, 191
cognitive perspective, 57, 58
cognitive skills, 141, 153, 163
cognitive therapy, 45, 136, 154, 156, 176
commodification, vii, ix, x, 43, 44, 55, 71, 75, 80, 103

Index

commodified, 45, 46, 47, 103

commodity, 45, 54

compassion, 4, 5, 6, 7, 8, 9, 14, 15, 31, 34, 36, 39, 40, 46, 56, 62, 67, 68, 190, 199

complementary and alternative medical therapies, 110

complementary therapies, 39, 40, 120, 121, 131, 200

complications, 5, 11, 15, 34, 36, 83, 152

concentrative meditation (CM), vi, viii, x, 135, 136, 137, 138, 139, 140, 141, 146, 147, 148, 149, 150, 151, 152, 153

consciousness, vii, ix, 52, 58, 61, 79, 80, 81, 83, 95, 98, 99, 101, 104, 152

construct validity, 142, 143, 199

contemplative, 40, 56, 61, 73, 76, 84, 98, 117

coping strategies, 188, 196

cortisol, viii, 2, 10, 11, 117, 119

count their breaths, 141

Crete, 85

criminal justice system, 45

crises, 15, 16, 96, 98

crisis management, 11

crown chakra, vii, ix, 79, 84, 89

cultivation, 5, 6, 15, 17, 31, 32, 35, 36

cultural appropriation, 80

culturally appropriating, 81

culture, ix, 43, 44, 45, 46, 51, 52, 70, 92, 93, 96, 97, 99, 102, 103, 104, 187, 200

D

decentering, vi, viii, xi, 135, 136, 137, 140, 143, 146, 150, 151, 152, 153, 155, 161

decoupling, 118, 125

delusion(s), 36, 57, 58, 59, 66

Department of Health and Human Services, x, 109, 110, 128

dependent, 71, 103, 114

depersonalization, 186, 191

depression, 3, 10, 17, 35, 39, 45, 47, 50, 63, 77, 82, 92, 112, 113, 115, 118, 120, 137, 141, 155, 156, 164, 175, 178, 187, 189, 199, 203

depressive symptoms, 117

describing, xi, 120, 136, 142, 146, 149, 150, 151

dharma, 51, 55, 59, 62, 65, 67, 71, 72, 73

diagnostic statistical manual, 97

differentiation of self, 186, 196, 200, 201, 202

discomfort, 8, 12, 15, 16, 19, 22, 29, 37

disorder, viii, xi, 82, 158, 159, 162, 172, 175, 182

distress, viii, 2, 3, 10, 11, 16, 25, 38, 114, 178, 183

Dumo fire, 85

E

Eastern based meditative intervention (EBMI), vii, viii, 1, 3, 4, 5, 6, 8, 9, 10, 11, 12, 13, 38, 41

eating disorders, xi, 161, 162, 163, 164, 165, 166, 167, 168, 169, 170, 171, 172, 173, 174, 175, 177, 179

education, ix, 11, 38, 39, 40, 41, 43, 44, 45, 46, 48, 55, 56, 57, 58, 59, 60, 61, 63, 64, 65, 66, 68, 72, 73, 74, 75, 76, 77, 107, 111, 120, 125, 132, 133, 135, 157, 158, 181, 182, 187, 190, 198, 200, 201

education philosophy, 44

education policy, 44

Egyptian, 85

elders, 130, 131

emotion, 5, 15, 33, 37, 63, 124, 179

emotional disorder, 136, 172, 175, 183

emotional distress, 178

emotional exhaustion, viii, xii, 186, 191, 194, 196

emotional problems, 136

Index

emotional state, 22, 48

emotional well-being, 64, 118, 119

empathetic joy, 4, 5, 6, 7, 9, 14, 16, 17, 31, 35, 36

empathy, 56, 189

empowerment, 3, 9, 11, 37

enemies, 8, 34, 35, 36, 37

energy, vii, ix, 5, 6, 12, 13, 19, 79, 80, 82, 83, 85, 86, 88, 89, 91, 96, 105, 106, 107, 116, 117, 166, 170

energy body, 80, 83

environmental destruction, 69

environment(s), 3, 6, 9, 19, 24, 26, 27, 37, 53, 67

equanimity, 4, 5, 6, 7, 9, 14, 17, 31, 36, 37, 40, 56, 62, 67

ethical development, 56, 64

ethics, 44, 56, 65

ethnicity, 192, 194

evolution, ix, 44, 47, 73, 79, 80, 83

executive attention, 138, 139, 143, 144, 147, 148, 149, 150, 152

executive function, 63

exercise(s), 4, 6, 9, 12, 13, 18, 19, 21, 22, 23, 25, 26, 28, 29, 31, 116, 119, 126, 128, 130, 131

experiences questionnaire (EQ), 137, 143, 146, 149, 150, 155

exploitation, 51, 55, 70

F

fatigue, 112, 113, 117, 118, 119, 120, 126, 127, 128, 131, 187, 190, 199

fear(s), 18, 27, 30, 51, 61, 99, 100, 101, 113, 118, 159, 162, 182, 183

feelings, 17, 19, 25, 31, 37, 50, 58, 62, 84, 92, 137, 142, 151, 174, 189, 191, 198

fetal development, 8

fetal growth, 3, 37

fetal health, vii, viii, 1, 2, 3, 4, 6, 11, 14, 27, 28, 29, 32, 37, 38

fetus, 3, 6, 8, 9, 13, 14, 16, 17, 18, 23, 24, 27, 28, 29, 31, 34, 35, 36, 37, 38

fitness, 6, 12, 19, 39, 50, 88, 170

five-facet mindfulness questionnaire (FFMQ), 142, 146

flexibility, 22, 50, 52, 88, 117, 152, 156

focused attention (FA), x, 9, 56, 135, 139, 152

focused breathing, 151, 153

food, 19, 70, 81, 100, 162

four immeasurables meditation, viii, 1, 4, 6, 7, 12, 13, 31, 36, 39, 40

G

generalized anxiety disorder (GAD), 136, 151, 154, 156, 159, 182, 183

Gnostics, 86

God, 52, 83, 85, 86, 90, 91, 98

growth, vii, ix, 3, 28, 37, 43, 44, 45, 47, 48, 68, 70, 81

guidance, 66, 82, 99, 103

Guru, ix, 79, 81, 88, 94, 104

H

Hanh, 60, 61, 65, 67, 74

happiness, 5, 7, 8, 16, 18, 33, 35, 36, 81

harmony, 8, 9, 59, 131

Hatha, 87, 88, 91, 93, 103

healing, 18, 22, 33, 85, 92, 97

health, vii, viii, x, 1, 2, 3, 4, 5, 6, 8, 10, 11, 14, 20, 25, 27, 28, 29, 30, 32, 33, 37, 38, 45, 47, 57, 62, 63, 64, 65, 75, 80, 85, 98, 103, 112, 116, 117, 118, 119, 122, 123, 125, 127, 130, 136, 174, 176, 186, 189, 197, 200, 202

holistic health, 3

Holy Spirit, 85

Index

human body, xii, 83, 162
human condition, 50, 66

I

ida, 85, 86
impoverishment, 69, 70, 71
in utero, 2, 3, 6, 8, 9, 37
India, 67, 81, 86, 103, 104, 106
individuals, 5, 52, 82, 86, 96, 98, 99, 102, 104, 136, 140, 152, 153, 186, 187, 188, 189, 194, 196, 197
institutions, 51, 103, 104
instrumentalist, 63, 64
interaction effect, 147, 149
internal consistency, 168, 191
interpersonal relations, 13, 188
intervention, viii, xi, 1, 2, 3, 4, 5, 6, 9, 10, 11, 12, 13, 27, 28, 32, 113, 119, 120, 122, 127, 135, 136, 138, 140, 141, 151, 153, 162
isolation, 92, 101, 139
issues, x, 46, 49, 67, 78, 80, 124

J

joints, 6, 12, 19, 21, 22, 28
Judaic, 85
Judeo-Christian, 86

K

Ki, 85
koshas, 80, 84
kund, 83
Kunda, 83
kundala, 83
Kundalini, v, vii, ix, 79, 80, 82, 83, 84, 85, 86, 88, 89, 90, 91, 94, 95, 96, 97, 98, 99, 101, 102, 103, 104, 105, 106, 107

Kundalini awakening, x, 80, 82, 91, 96, 99, 101, 102
Kundalini yoga, ix, 80, 86

L

levitation, 89
life satisfaction, 189
life-force energy, 84
lifelong learning, 55
limbs of yoga, 87, 93, 103
livelihood, 46, 67
logical analysis, xi, 162, 163, 165, 168, 169, 170, 172, 173
love, 7, 16, 31, 32, 33, 36, 58, 91
loving-kindness, 4, 14, 32, 33, 34, 35, 46, 62, 67

M

manomaya kosha, 84
marketisation, vii, ix, 43
maternal health, vii, viii, 1, 2, 6, 8, 10, 11, 14, 32, 37
maya, 84
McDonaldization, ix, 44, 46, 51, 62, 72, 74, 77
McMindfulness, vii, ix, 43, 44, 45, 46, 47, 52, 53, 55, 62, 63, 71, 75, 76
medical, 15, 110, 111, 114, 115, 116, 117, 119, 120, 121, 128, 131
medicine, 70, 86, 111, 116, 125, 130, 131
meditation, v, vii, viii, ix, x, xi, 1, 2, 3, 4, 5, 6, 7, 9, 10, 11, 12, 13, 14, 15, 16, 17, 18, 19, 20, 21, 22, 23, 25, 27, 28, 29, 30, 32, 33, 34, 35, 36, 37, 38, 39, 40, 41, 45, 50, 51, 55, 61, 77, 79, 80, 81, 82, 84, 87, 88, 89, 91, 93, 94, 95, 96, 99, 101, 102, 103, 104, 106, 107, 109, 110, 111, 115, 116, 117, 118, 120, 121, 123, 124, 125, 126, 131, 132, 133, 135, 136, 137, 139, 140,

141, 150, 151, 152, 153, 154, 156, 157, 159, 173, 176, 178, 181, 182, 202
meditative practices, 8, 44, 54, 116
mental disorder, 173, 176
mental health, 5, 6, 30, 57, 85, 98, 103, 174, 176, 186
millennial, 92, 102
mind-body exercise(s), 4, 6, 12, 18, 21, 22
mindfulness-based cognitive therapy (MBCT), 45, 47, 49, 51, 62, 136, 154, 156
mindfulness-based intervention(s) (MBIs), v, vii, ix, xi, 6, 43, 44, 45, 46, 47, 48, 49, 50, 51, 56, 57, 59, 61, 62, 63, 75, 78, 123, 124, 126, 162, 164, 169, 173, 186, 191, 194
mindfulness-based stress reduction (MBSR), 45, 47, 49, 51, 54, 62, 110, 112, 115, 118, 122, 125, 127, 129, 136, 138, 154, 189, 200
mindsight, 56, 77
misuse, 46, 110, 114, 120, 121, 122, 124
monks, 81, 98
monophasic, 98, 99, 102
moral, ix, 44, 56, 59, 60, 62, 63, 64, 65, 66, 68, 70, 71, 73, 87
moral development, 66
moral education, 65
moral training, 60, 65, 71
motivation, 130, 187
muscles, 6, 12, 17, 19, 21, 22, 24, 28, 29, 31, 84
music, 27, 93, 95, 99, 100, 107

N

n/um, 85
nadis, 80, 83, 85
national pain strategy, x, 109, 110, 121, 127
Native American, 85, 193
near death experiences, 91

negative effects, 95, 119, 136
negative emotions, 13, 18, 33
negative relation, 137, 164
nervous system, 6, 38, 113, 122
neuropathic pain, 113, 128
new age spirituality, x, 80
next generation, 3, 17, 35
noble eightfold, 56
non-attachment, 7, 36, 81, 88, 89, 104
nonjudging, xi, 136, 142, 146, 149, 150
nonreactivity, 142, 149, 150, 152, 153

O

observing, 142, 146, 149, 152, 153
obstacles, 61, 62, 68, 91
occult, 80, 85, 95, 104
open monitoring (OM), 139
orienting, xi, 136, 137, 138, 139, 143, 144, 147, 148, 149, 150, 151
origination, 71
out-of-body-experiences, 97
over-consumption, 69

P

pain, v, viii, x, 16, 17, 18, 22, 29, 35, 45, 47, 50, 97, 109, 110, 111, 112, 113, 114, 115, 117, 118, 119, 120, 121, 122, 123, 124, 125, 126, 127, 128, 129, 130, 131, 132, 155, 158, 202
paranormal, vii, ix, 79, 80, 95, 101
participants, 5, 11, 48, 49, 50, 62, 81, 115, 119, 138, 140, 141, 143, 144, 152, 153, 165, 166, 173, 175, 190
Patanjali, 80, 86, 87, 88, 89, 91, 92, 105, 106
path, 15, 16, 17, 35, 56, 65, 67, 83, 87, 91, 93, 102, 103, 107, 167, 169, 170
pathway(s), 8, 30, 33, 86, 112
peace, 18, 37, 53, 67, 89, 104

Index

Penn State worry questionnaire (PSWQ), 140, 142, 146, 149, 156
perceived self-efficacy, 177
peripheral neuropathy, 113, 122
personality, 2, 80, 92, 155
personality disorder, 155
Peters, 57, 58, 60, 61, 62, 64, 73, 74, 76, 199
phenomenology, 80, 98
physical fitness, 6, 12, 19
physical health, 118, 200
pingala, 85, 86
polyphasic, 98
positive correlation, 168, 172
positive emotion(s), 5, 14, 17, 33
positive languages, 13
positive relationship, vii, viii, 1, 3, 137
prana, 80, 84, 88
pranamaya kosha, 84
pranayama, 80, 84, 87, 88, 103
precognition, 89, 97
pregnancy, vii, viii, 1, 2, 3, 5, 6, 10, 11, 13, 15, 16, 17, 19, 22, 25, 28, 29, 30, 34, 35, 36, 37, 38
prenatal, v, vii, viii, 1, 2, 3, 4, 6, 10, 11, 12, 13, 18, 22, 37, 38, 39, 40, 41
prenatal meditation, vii, viii, 2, 3, 10, 11, 12, 13, 37, 39, 40, 41
prenatal meditation program, 3, 10
prevention, 119, 123, 125
Protestant ethic, 52
psychedelic drugs, 91
psychic, 80, 82, 85, 87, 89, 94, 96, 97, 102
psychoanalysis, 60, 61
psychokinesis, 89
psychological distress, 3, 38, 183
psychological health, 3, 119, 136
psychology, 9, 32, 40, 49, 73, 74, 78, 80, 82, 108, 122, 126, 140, 153, 154, 155, 156, 157, 159, 177, 178, 182, 189, 199, 200, 201
psychopathy, 159, 182

psychotherapy, 13, 65

Q

qi gong, vii, x, 109, 110, 111, 112, 114, 116, 117, 118, 119, 120, 121, 128, 129, 130, 131
quality of life, x, 6, 13, 19, 37, 64, 68, 109, 110, 112, 113, 118, 119, 123, 125, 127, 128, 129
questionnaire, viii, xi, 142, 155, 162, 164, 165, 199

R

Raja Yoga, 87
refraining from catastrophic thinking, 163, 164, 165, 168, 169, 170, 172, 173, 174, 183
regression, 47, 167, 193, 194, 195
regression analysis, 167, 194
relatives, 7, 8, 13, 14, 18, 31, 36, 37
relax, 6, 12, 13, 17, 19, 21, 22, 23, 24, 25, 26, 27, 28, 29, 31, 37, 46, 116, 122, 129, 137, 202
relaxation, 13, 23, 28, 46, 116, 122, 129, 137, 202
religion, 51, 53, 59, 187
religious traditions, 85
resources, viii, xii, 72, 82, 99, 186, 197, 201, 202
response, 22, 68, 70, 110, 116, 122, 152, 166, 186
restructuring, vii, ix, 5, 79, 91
rewards, 95, 104, 187

S

sadhana, 80, 88, 89, 92
sadhu, 88

212 Index

sadness, 33, 61, 113
samadhi, 80, 87
samatha, 151
schizophrenia, 82
selective attention, viii, xi, 136, 138, 152
self-control, 60, 163
self-efficacy, 3, 8, 9, 174, 177
self-esteem, 5, 63, 117, 119, 127, 174
sensation(s), 20, 21, 22, 23, 24, 25, 26, 29,
   97, 100, 115, 141, 142, 151
sense of control, 4, 174, 175
senses, 84, 87, 92, 101
sensitivity, 100, 113, 125
sensory experience, 23, 101
serpent fire, 80, 85, 102
Shakti, 80, 83, 89, 91
shaktipat, 80, 89, 94, 95, 107
shushumna, 84
siddhis, 80, 87, 89, 91, 92
side effects, 110, 115
sleep disturbance, 112, 113, 119
sleep stage, 30
social and political reform, 69
social learning theory, 163
social media, 92, 102
social relationships, 11
social transformation, ix, 44
socially engaged, 67, 70, 71
society, ix, 44, 49, 54, 55, 69, 71, 72, 94, 98
spiritual emergency, x, 80, 96, 97, 99, 102
spiritual practice, 71, 81, 88, 92, 96
spiritual tourism, 80
spirituality, x, 38, 52, 53, 55, 80, 92, 93, 94,
   98, 101, 102, 103, 107, 118, 189, 200,
   201, 202
spontaneous awakenings, 83, 91, 92, 94, 96
stimulus, 93, 112, 139
stream of consciousness, 152
strength training, 22
stress, viii, 2, 3, 5, 13, 22, 36, 37, 38, 39, 51,
   52, 53, 59, 63, 65, 92, 110, 112, 115,
   117, 118, 122, 123, 125, 127, 129, 132,

133, 136, 154, 155, 176, 186, 188, 189,
   191, 196, 200, 201, 202
stress response, 202
structural equation modeling, xi, 162, 167,
   169, 170, 172, 177, 178
structure, 47, 84, 99, 103, 167, 178, 179
substance use disorders, 123
supernatural, 87, 89
symptoms, viii, xi, 19, 37, 85, 92, 97, 99,
   100, 101, 112, 113, 114, 115, 117, 118,
   119, 120, 126, 130, 137, 151, 155, 157,
   159, 161, 162, 163, 164, 165, 166, 167,
   168, 169, 170, 171, 172, 173, 174, 175,
   176, 178, 182, 183, 186, 188
synchronicities, 101
syndrome, 113, 191

T

tai chi, vii, x, 109, 110, 111, 112, 114, 116,
   117, 118, 119, 120, 121, 122, 123, 124,
   125, 126, 127, 128, 130, 131
Taoist, 53, 85
teachers, 48, 55, 63, 91, 92, 94, 103, 104,
   108, 187, 200
techniques, ix, xi, 5, 48, 49, 51, 55, 62, 79,
   81, 82, 86, 104, 115, 137, 139, 153, 161,
   163, 164, 173, 177
telepathy, 89, 97
temperament, ix, 2, 11, 36
the yoga sutras, 87, 89, 91, 106
therapeutic practice, 60, 63
therapy, xi, 45, 57, 110, 112, 114, 120, 124,
   125, 127, 131, 136, 154, 155, 156, 158,
   159, 161, 162, 163, 164, 169, 172, 173,
   175, 176, 178, 181, 182, 199
thinking errors, viii, xi, 161, 162, 163, 164,
   165, 166, 167, 168, 169, 170, 171, 172,
   173

Index 213

thoughts, 5, 12, 19, 21, 24, 50, 57, 62, 101, 115, 136, 137, 141, 142, 151, 164, 172, 173, 189, 191, 196, 199
Tibetan, 85
Tibetan Buddhism, 85
traditions, vii, ix, 36, 43, 44, 54, 56, 60, 66, 81, 85, 91, 96, 115
training, 5, 12, 13, 19, 21, 22, 40, 46, 48, 49, 50, 54, 60, 63, 64, 65, 66, 71, 73, 75, 81, 98, 115, 122, 123, 124, 125, 133, 136, 137, 138, 140, 141, 144, 151, 152, 153, 154, 155, 157, 201
traits, viii, xii, 66, 178, 185, 196, 198
transcendence, x, 80, 83
transcendental consciousness, 83
transformation(s), ix, 36, 44, 62, 64, 65, 70, 83, 85, 96, 105, 163
transpersonal, 80, 82, 97, 98, 99, 102, 105, 108
transpersonal anthropology, 80
transpersonal psychology, 80
treatment, viii, x, 3, 6, 49, 60, 88, 109, 110, 111, 112, 113, 114, 120, 122, 127, 136, 147, 149, 155, 156, 162, 172, 174, 176, 179, 187

U

unhappiness, 33
unique features, 20
universe, 85, 104
Upanishads, 84

V

validation, 72, 127, 156, 157

variables, 139, 142, 145, 150, 153, 163, 167, 168, 170, 190, 193, 194, 195, 198
Vijnanamaya kosha, 84
virtue ethics, 56, 65
vulnerability, xi, 72, 162

W

Weber, 46, 52, 77
well-being, 3, 7, 8, 9, 22, 25, 30, 45, 47, 56, 64, 66, 68, 118, 119, 124, 154, 200
wellness, 18, 116, 117
withdrawal, 87, 92
work ethic, 92
workers, viii, xii, 53, 92, 185, 186, 200
working mechanism, 137, 173
workplace, ix, 43, 45, 51, 52, 72, 81, 202
work-related stress, 202
worry, vi, viii, xi, 36, 135, 136, 140, 142, 146, 150, 151, 152, 153, 154, 155, 156, 157, 159, 178, 182
worrying, 12, 136, 140, 156, 180

Y

yoga, ix, 6, 79, 80, 82, 83, 86, 87, 88, 91, 92, 93, 94, 97, 99, 101, 102, 103, 105, 106, 107, 124
yoga sutras, 80, 87, 91
Yogi Bhajan, ix, 79, 86, 91

Z

Zizek, 52, 54, 78